The AMERICAN HERITAGE *Book of*
NATURAL WONDERS

The AMERICAN HERITAGE *Book of*
NATURAL

By the Editors of
AMERICAN HERITAGE
The Magazine of History

Editor in Charge
ALVIN M. JOSEPHY, JR.

Chapters by
PETER MATTHIESSEN

WILLIAM O. DOUGLAS

JAN DE HARTOG

BRUCE CATTON

PAUL ENGLE

WALLACE STEGNER

GEORGE R. STEWART

HAROLD GILLIAM

Published by
AMERICAN HERITAGE PUBLISHING CO., INC.

Book Trade Distribution by
SIMON AND SCHUSTER, INC.

WONDERS

AMERICAN HERITAGE

The Magazine of History

PUBLISHER

James Parton

EDITORIAL DIRECTOR

Joseph J. Thorndike, Jr.

SENIOR EDITOR

Bruce Catton

EDITOR

Oliver Jensen

EDITOR, BOOK DIVISION

Richard M. Ketchum

Staff for this Book

EDITOR

Alvin M. Josephy, Jr.

ASSISTANT EDITORS

Jane M. Consolino
Joseph L. Gardner
Kenneth W. Leish
Karen Termohlen Meehan

EDITORIAL ASSISTANT

Trudy Piken

COPY EDITOR

Sylvia J. Fried
Assistant: Brenda Savard

ART DIRECTOR

Irwin Glusker

DESIGNER

David A. Van Inwegen
Assistant: Walter L. Bernard

ORIGINAL MAPS

David Greenspan

Front Cover: *The Sirens Were Singing
From the Tops of the Peaks,* by Alfred
Jacob Miller; C. R. Smith Collection.
Title Page: Mount St. Helens, Washing-
ton, with Mount Adams in the back-
ground, photographed by George Hunter.
Introduction Page: On the Machias River,
Maine, photographed by Shaw Mudge.

Cascade in Timpanogos River Canyon, Utah, by H. V. A. von Beckh, 1859

Table of Contents

INTRODUCTION

Foreign visitors to the United States who fly from coast to coast low and slowly enough to be able to observe its great, almost unending changes of terrain, or who drive hour by hour, day after day, up and down and across the nation, viewing its apparently infinite varieties, are often struck with a profound awareness of the strength that America possesses in its people and its land.

There is nothing new about this to most Americans, who for generations have sung proudly of their own vitality and self-confidence, and of the beauties and resources of their country. What is new, perhaps, is their own realization, come at a late hour, that the contributions of their land were not all in the shape of material rewards, but that they had much to do with the forming of the self-confident American and the government and way of life he fashioned for himself.

It might be stylish for a technological generation, with its eye on Mars and the moon, to smile at the obsolescence of Walt Whitman's earthbound *Song of the Open Road* of a century ago:

> *The earth, that is sufficient,*
> *I do not want the constellations any nearer,*
> *I know they are very well where they are,*
> *I know they suffice for those who belong to them.*

But if those words wheeze, the truth they commence to tell is not out of date—or, if it is, alarm bells need to be rung. For the American land, its shores, rocks, heights, valleys, snows, lakes, deserts, trees, and rivers—its obstacles, challenges, lures, and bounties—inspired and recharged the American spirit every foot of the way, from the beginning of colonial days until today, shaping the American character to its innermost fiber with integrity, courage, and belief in self.

Walt Whitman said it also:

> *Now I see the secret of the making of the*
> *best persons,*
> *It is to grow in the open air and to eat*
> *and sleep with the earth.*

In his time, Thomas Jefferson placed reliance on the rural man for the future of the country. One hundred years later, J. Horace McFarland, of the American Civic Association, was moved to say at a White House Conference on Natural Resources in 1908: "It is the love of country that has lighted and that keeps glowing the holy fire of patriotism . . . this love is excited, primarily, by the beauty of the country."

This is not to say that the man who is born in a city and does not leave it fails to match the virtues and achievements of the farmer, rancher, logger, or man of the mountains. But even the urban dweller instinctively searches for a tree of his own in the public park, away from crowding company, and knows what Jefferson and McFarland meant and what Whitman breathed:

Why are there trees I never walk under
but large and melodious thoughts
descend upon me?

Even as the clangor of his life grows more harsh and oppressive, the city man seeks alcoves of nature where he can refresh his soul and re-assert his individuality:

Now I re-examine philosophies and religions,
They may prove well in lecture-rooms, yet
not prove at all under the spacious clouds
and along the landscape and flowing currents.

It is possible that Americans know all this and are dedicated more deeply than they realize to a sacred regard for the outdoors and the works of nature that helped to mold them in the past. If it were not so from love, it would undoubtedly be so from a continuing elemental hunger and need.

But time is slipping. In the building and re-building of the nation, quickened now by the expanding population, the increased appetites of modern industry, commerce, and agriculture, and by the emergency demands of national defense, the land and its inspiring beauty are vanishing bit by bit, so subtly that the speed of the phenom-enon is not easily perceived save by conservation-ists who are beginning to sound the tocsin. A park—always on the other side of town, so it seems—is condemned for a new turnpike. Birds disappear—because a "wasted" marshland has been drained for houses. A dam and its access roads are built—and a whole, rugged wilderness with its uncaged wildlife is no more. Where is the lonesome silence of southern California's Mojave Desert? Where the solemn beauty of the depths of the Colorado's Glen Canyon? Both—and more—have been recently "conquered."

Conquered—or eliminated? At an explosive, nerve-racking period of history, precisely when Americans, as never before, require the spiritual regeneration and renewed faith in themselves and country that the outdoors helped to provide their ancestors, the glories and splendors of the nat-ural land are disappearing the fastest. In 1962, year of the Cuban crisis, vacationing families made a record 88,457,100 visits to the national parks, an 11 per cent increase over the preceding year. The forests and state and local parks felt an equal pressure. Where will adequate, unclaimed space be found—among atomic energy plants, missile stations, real estate developments, power projects, highways, and industrial parks, all still to come—for the even greater millions of Ameri-cans in succeeding years? Future generations will claim this as their country too, but long before their day, park visitors may well be limited ac-cording to available room, and the first come will be the first served.

The nation is moving close to that time. This generation, the last that can preserve an adequate natural inheritance for the future, is awakening to what has been called "the quiet crisis," at-tempting hurriedly to match the outer space pro-gram with one for inner space. But the land that still remains for all the people has become a pit-ifully small part of the whole, and conservation-ists must be Solomons in so planning its future use as to provide for the needs of everyone: lovers of the wilderness, viewers from automobiles, swimmers, hikers, boaters, hunters, fishermen, and, not the least, future Walt Whitmans.

"I hear America singing," he wrote, and this book, in its way, has heard the same song. This is not a guidebook in the usual sense of such a specific work of reference. Nor is it a complete compendium of all the majesty and natural beauty of America. Readers will inevitably find some of their favorite scenic sites omitted, not delib-erately, but because no single volume could en-compass the many personal favorites in all the fifty states. The aim of this book, in essence, is to try to thrill with a summation of the whole, and to show how noble, varied, and beautiful the American land still is. Its dedication is to the reader who, loving the land and respecting it, will find that he can live with it and need not conquer it.

ALVIN M. JOSEPHY, JR.

I

THE

ATLANTIC

COAST

By PETER MATTHIESSEN

> . . . We dwell
> On the half earth, on the open curve of a continent.
> Sea is divided from sea by the day-fall. The dawn
> Rides the low east with us many hours;
> First are the capes, then are the shorelands . . .
>
> Archibald MacLeish ("*American Letter*," 1930)

Listen to the names—Monhegan Light, Matinicus, and Mount Desert; the Isles of Shoals and Gloucester, Norman's Woe; Cape Race and Highland Light and Pollock Rip; Tom Nevers Head and Gay Head, Buzzards Bay; Montauk, the Narrows, Sandy Hook; Barnegat, Brigantine, Cape May, the Delaware and Chesapeake; Chincoteague and Tangier Island; Point Lookout, Ocracoke, Cape Fear; Sea Island, Indian River, Big Pine Key, Marquesas, Dry Tortugas.

The Atlantic coast of the United States, from the fog and granite of the Bay of Fundy to the emerald and coral of the outer Keys, is more striking and varied than any coast of any single country in the world; its one competitor might be Australia's eastern coast—fringed in the north by the Great Barrier Reef—which extends from the jungle tropics of Cape York Peninsula to the bleak latitudes of Bass Strait. But the Australian coast inside the reef is uniform in aspect, as if shaped cataclysmically and all at once—it is a high coast in the main, altered little by the range of climate as it marches southward.

At certain points the Atlantic coast is quite unbeautiful—this is the work of man. He has defiled it, in the way a great monument might be defiled by a child with muddy hands; this mud, until the seas rise, will remain.

Certain stretches of the coast, to date, have still withstood us: a boat sailing down from Canada, from blue Passamaquoddy Bay southwest along the coast of Maine, will follow a shore little altered, viewed from the sea, in the centuries since the voyages of Cartier and Champlain. This is true especially in the far Northeast—"east of Schoodic," as the boatmen say—less because this coast is sparsely populated than because of the nature of the coast itself. Geologically, Maine's coast is "drowned"; seas rising with the waning of the ice age have flooded former plains and river valleys, transforming hills to islands and ridges to island chains. These chains, extending mostly in a north and south direction, stretch like ramparts far out into the sea, with outposts still much farther out—Isle au Haut, Monhegan, Matinicus Rock, where the gaudy puffins dive among the dark sea boulders at the eastern end.

It is not the land which extends far out to sea; it is the sea which has surged far inland. Hence the Maine coast—some two hundred miles as the gannet flies, more than two thousand along its tortuous shore—is broken and obscured by islands and promontories, with few of the beaches and long stretches that mark a more transient shore. The shore itself is granite, not readily eroded—though gradually, in future lifetimes, the grind of the sea, with the river detritus accumulating in the upper bays and estuaries, will fill it in and plane it smooth, until it resembles the high coast of Australia—and everywhere it is forested by evergreens, in dense ranks that crowd down to the tidal ledges. In Maine, man works in and around this wall, and has made small change in it.

Yet he is here in numbers, and he has been here a long time: the settlement at Dochet Island, in 1604, up the St. Croix River from St. Andrews, is among those claimed to be the earliest in the Northeast. And on the seacoast, in the main, he is doing what he has always done—felling timber and building boats and fishing the sea. Maine lobsters are celebrated, and as a fishery they still outrank the young herring, the "sardine": until recently, when poor seasons have forced the seiners to pursue the herring shoals into the open water, the sardine fishery took place largely in the coves. Soft clams and hard are another shoreline commerce, and there are the peat moss and blueberries of the salt farms and the edible kelp, the "Irish moss," of the tide flats. Maine boats, and particularly the lobster hull and Friendship sloop, are justly famous; the building of boats, in sea towns like Jonesport and Bath and Kittery, is a natural adjunct to the coastal trade in fish and tourists. The latter brave cold waters and summer fogs for the wild character of Maine: the heavy seas on the granite ledges, the restless evergreens shrouded in mist, the high islands and still coves, the sea rocks with their sea bird populations, where gannets and guillemots, eider and puffins, beat away across the water. Inshore the plaintive yawp of gulls and the soft thump of lobster boats wander in fogs sweet with the smell of evergreens and kelp; man's serious pollution of Maine's waters is not readily apparent to the summer eye, and chiefly affects the clam diggers.

From Kittery to Cape Ann there are few harbors, and the coastline—and especially the brief New Hampshire coast, eighteen miles long—is undistinguished. Long, low New Hampshire beaches are submerged by a litter of tourist resorts, garish in summer, bleak in winter, the counterparts of many like them that strew the coast south to the Carolinas. In New Hampshire, it is the clump of barren islets known collectively as the Isles of Shoals that forms a part of New England's maritime legend. A British fishing company had a post in the Isles of Shoals before the Pilgrims landed, and a treasure of silver bars left by Edward Teach, the notorious "Blackbeard," was supposedly discovered on Smuttynose Island about 1800. And there is a good harbor: coastal vessels working north or south, seeking a haven, usually avoid New Hampshire's sole port of Portsmouth in favor of these sea rocks.

The New Hampshire coast would be less uniform did not the Merrimack River, riding south from the state's

central plateau, cross the Massachusetts line before turning to the sea. The broad mouth of the Merrimack, a welter
of sand bars off the north end of Plum Island, below New-
buryport, is a striking place: though the Merrimack itself
is grossly polluted, this delta region is an oasis for uncommon birds. In winter bald eagles light upon the ice floes,
and white gulls of the arctic haunt the breakwater; one or
more small gulls wandered from Europe appear on New-
buryport's dying water front almost yearly. The north end
of Plum Island is obscured by a wild rash of summer
shacks—Dun Roamin, Dew Drop Inn, Camp Killcare—
but the rest is a long expanse of beach and dune, beach
rose and pea and plum, that includes part of the Parker
River Wildlife Refuge and overlooks the tidal marshes
of the Ipswich River. In the fall these marshes, with
their serpentine black creeks and solitary hummocks—
islands of rocks and trees that seem to drift on a gold autumn sea of bog grass—are as lovely as any part of the
coastal tidewater, and in winter the black ducks swing
across the creeks and snowy owls squat on far solitary
stacks of salt hay.

The south end of Ipswich Bay, where giant tuna are harpooned, is formed by the peninsula of Cape Ann (formerly
Cape Tragabigzanda, after a Turkish lady of this name
who, like Pocahontas, is said to have saved the dashing life
of Captain Smith), with its seashore art communities and
its port of Gloucester. Gloucester once rivaled Boston as a
fishing port, and the swift Gloucester schooners, flying
northeast to the grounds of cod and halibut on Georges
Bank and the Grand Banks off Newfoundland, were
among the finest vessels ever launched on a boat-building
coast. The Portuguese fishermen of Gloucester were im-
mortalized in Kipling's *Captains Courageous,* and the town
still observes the Old World ceremony of the blessing of
the fleet—casting flowers on an outgoing tide in memory
of lost sailors. In recent years Gloucester has attempted
to restore a fading glory with the manufacture of frozen
"fish sticks," the chief ingredient of which is haddock.

From Cape Ann southeast to the great hook of Cape
Cod lies Massachusetts Bay, with such points as Man-
chester (and the reef of Norman's Woe), Marblehead (a
name almost synonymous with small-boat sailing), and
Salem (famed for whales and witches) ornamenting a
coastline overwhelmed by the surge of Boston. Far out to
the eastward, out of sight of land, lie Race Point and
Provincetown, at Cape Cod's tip, and north of Race Point
perhaps five miles lies the Stellwagen Bank where, in certain summers, coasting craft may still find themselves surrounded by the remnant whales—finback and humpback,
pilot whales and the orca or killer whale, a huge, savage

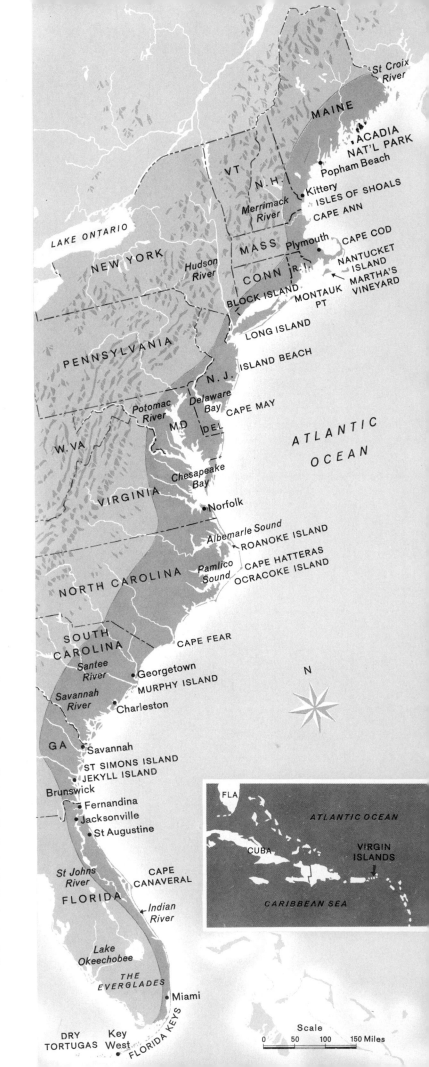

porpoise: the male orca may reach a length of more than thirty feet, with a dorsal fin slicing six feet high out of the water, and the sight of this creature near at hand, in the clear waters out of sight of the scarred, oily coast, reminds one that a vast Atlantic wilderness still exists.

Cape Cod is a peninsula of glacial debris, much of it without bedrock, a land engulfed and shaped unceasingly by wind and waves and tide; the rough waters of Pollock Rip, offshore to the southeast, deflected the *Mayflower,* in 1620, from a destination at the mouth of the Hudson and thus altered the whole history of New England. Cape Cod's gravel and sand is easily undercut and shifted, forming high dune cliffs like those at Highland Light, or the sprawling salt marshes of Nauset and Orleans: from a central point near Nauset Light, the sand washes north to build the mighty dunes at Provincetown, or south to the great sand spit known as Monomoy. The inner loop of Cape Cod Bay, like its southern shore on Nantucket Sound, has less oceanic character, being more protected from the sea; by contrast to the outer beaches, these shores seem mere fringes of the inland cape, with its low scrub oak and pine, its cranberry bogs and sand barrens.

Massachusetts is and has always been a leading state in fisheries and marine commerce, and this is because, in relation to its size, it has one of the longest shorelines of any state in all the nation. In addition to its continental coast and the long perimeter of Cape Cod, it can claim the great sea islands of Nantucket and Martha's Vineyard, as well as the chain of Elizabeth Islands on Buzzards Bay. Though such ports as Salem and New Bedford, with Sag Harbor on Long Island, were its rivals for many years, it is Nantucket and the "Nantucket sleigh ride" that are almost synonymous with the great years of ocean whaling; the relics of that industry, in combination with its wind-misted dunes and ocean moors, still bring the island its chief source of income, a migratory mammal, the summer tourist. Nantucket no longer has a fishery of significance, and the windy ramparts of Tom Nevers Head, looking southeast across Nantucket Shoals, no longer serve as a first landfall for those rough, able ships bound home from the South Pacific and Cape Horn.

By comparison with its sister island, Martha's Vineyard has little history. Both in location and in the character of its scrub woods and low rocky cliffs, it seems scarcely more than a fragment of the Cape Cod mainland, and its natural economy has always been peripheral—small inshore fisheries and marginal farming, all but replaced, in recent decades, by the trade in tourists. But the island is pretty and the red cliffs at Gay Head are magnificent, and the long diadem of salt ponds just inside the great south beach may

yet become a center of a large industry in soft clams and oysters. Martha's Vineyard can claim four excellent small harbors, and one of these, Menemsha, is a port for part of the fleet that pursues the broadbill swordfish in its ocean fields southwest of the small isle of No Mans Land.

The Elizabeth Islands, across Vineyard Sound, are largely controlled by a single family and in consequence have remained wild and very beautiful, with quiet shores and stands of virgin woodland still intact. Only the small island of Cuttyhunk, at the southwest end, is populated. Cuttyhunk, where Bartholomew Gosnold made a brief settlement in 1602, is best known as a base for striped-bass fishermen, who cast in the surf or prowl the rocks in the fast, hardy open craft known as the Cuttyhunk bass boat.

Beyond Cuttyhunk is Buzzards Bay, a shallow, choppy stretch of water—the "hurricane alley" of recent years—that leads southwest from the Cape Cod Canal to the waters of Rhode Island. Rhode Island's short coast, excepting a stretch of salt ponds and barrier beach west of Point Judith, is largely taken up by the islands and wide channels of the Sakonnet River and Narragansett Bay: like Portsmouth, New Hampshire, the bay contains shipyards, commercial harbors, and a naval installation. Rosie's Hole, a deep-water hole just off the beach not far east of Watch Hill, and another hole near Nebraska Shoals, still farther east, are famous grounds for giant tuna of five hundred pounds or more, but the place that contributes most to the state's marine character is Block Island, jutting up like a rude fortress some ten miles out to sea.

The most striking feature of Block Island is its seaward face, a very high, steep cliff of sand and rock that plunges to bouldered beach and submerged ledges; these ledges, extending outward from the shore, form a foul ground that has become one of the best-known marine graveyards on the Atlantic coast. The legend is that, in the early days, the islanders eked out their meager resources by luring ships onto these rocks and looting them: whatever the truth of the matter, the skeletons of broken craft are always visible from the cliff edge, and in the words of the islanders themselves, most of the best appointments of their houses "come by wrack." Much of Block Island, which is largely treeless, is now defaced by gimcrack summer architecture, and only the world of ocean cliffs, of fog and high ponds on the rolling moors, with the muffled rumbling of surf and the ceaseless, soft litanies of bell buoys drifting shoreward on the southwest wind, maintain the island's majesty. Block Island, like so many points along the coast, has been forced to a tourist economy, but its twin harbors still shelter a few local fishermen, in addition to the summer fleet.

The stillness of a misty day on the New England coast was captured by the American artist Martin Heade in this work, The Stranded Boat, *which he painted in 1863, probably in Rhode Island.*

Watch Hill, at the state's marine border with Connecticut and New York, is part of the town of Westerly, where more than one hundred people died in the tidal wave of the 1938 hurricane. Watch Hill lies at the outlet of Fishers Island Sound (Fishers Island itself, though closer by far to both Connecticut and Rhode Island, is part of New York State), a narrow extension of Long Island Sound; the latter, which empties and fills at its eastern end through the swift passage called the Race, is more landlocked than Narragansett Bay, and the large harbors on its Connecticut shore are, by and large, industrial ports without local marine character: the ocean-going vessels for which Connecticut is best known are the Polaris submarines, based at New London. The Connecticut coastline is a network of estuaries and sand spits, with many fine small harbors. One of these is Mystic, with its whale ship and whaling museum. But the salmon are gone from the state's polluted rivers: dull and well protected, studded from end to end with houses, this coast from which the Pequots once sailed in war canoes to do battle with the Montauks of Long Island has lost its oceanic flavor. Since the same is true of the Sound's Long Island shore, it might be said

that the true coastline in this part of the world is formed by the south beach of the great island that stretches from a point within sight of Rhode Island to Gravesend Bay, within sight of New Jersey.

Montauk Point, due to a remarkable diversity of fish in its adjacent waters, is the base for the largest sport fishing fleet north of Florida. Here the Gulf Stream curves inshore, less than fifty miles from land, so that the cod, pollack, whiting, flounder, and other fish native to the cold waters of the North Atlantic are replaced, in summer, by the bluefish, weakfish, striped bass, bonita, mackerel, dolphin, school tuna, and white marlin, most of which are approaching, in Montauk waters, the northern limits of their range. These are but some of the many species that support commercial and sport fisheries alike; a few hardy draggermen work all winter on the fish congregations at the Gully, near the edge of the great Block Island Canyon, some forty miles from shore. Along the sand coast of Long Island's South Fork, the site of shore whaling of past decades (and now and then the whales still pass in spring, rising somberly in the swells among the migrant phalaropes and sooty shearwaters and scoters), crews still take dories

13

through the surf, haul-seining for striped bass, while off-shore the swift bunker boats sweep up and down the coast, pursuing schools of the oily herring called menhaden.

Long Island's south beach, one of the first beaches of the world, is a wide belt of sand and dune that stretches for more than one hundred miles: waxing and waning with each storm, it is the seaward limit of the glacial outwash plain (like Cape Cod, most of Long Island is without bedrock), characterized by offshore bars, barrier islands, and shallow, shifting bays. Exposed to the full sweep of the Atlantic, it has few inlets and no ports worthy of the name: Long Island's main harbors, beyond the environs of New York City, are at Port Jefferson, on the Sound, and Greenport—now a base for the menhaden boats—which lies inside Montauk Point, off Gardiner's Bay (Gardiner's Island, which has remained for three centuries in the Gardiner family, is sequestered and very beautiful; here a small treasure of Captain Kidd's was actually found).

Much of Long Island's interior, like the interior of Cape Cod, is a barren of sandy scrub, though a stretch of its eastern end is layered with rich soil—the famous "Bridgehampton loam" of the potato country—which extends to the base of the dunes. So long as it resists the onslaughts of the developers, this world of green farmland, dune, and ocean pond, with its ghostly gulls in the sea mists of summer, its legions of geese in the blue-gold days of fall, will remain one of the loveliest on all the coast.

Striped bass and shad still brave the fouled currents of New York harbor to ascend the Hudson River; in the old days the river had a large whaling port one hundred two miles upstream, at Hudson. On the south side of New York's Lower Bay lies Sandy Hook, and south of Sandy Hook the New Jersey shore continues that dull reach of mainland coast, foreshortened by civilization, that extends almost without interruption from the Cape Cod Canal to Cape May, on the Delaware Bay.

New Jersey's coast is a long sand beach, protecting low cliffs and broad, flat marshes from the sea. In the center of this coast, sand scoured from the shoal waters of the continental shelf has formed low barrier islands, several miles from shore; these islands close off shallow sounds like Barnegat Bay. Inlets from the sea are few and treacherous—in fact, for boats with drafts of more than a few feet, Manasquan (Brielle) and Absecon (Atlantic City) are the only all-weather inlets north of Cape May.

The dearth of harbors has severely limited New Jersey's marine commerce, and a rampant population has marred a shoreline that even in its virgin state must have been rather monotonous: part of Island Beach, belonging formerly to the Phipps family and now become state park, is the last unspoiled stretch of any dimension on the Jersey coast. The few inlets permit some local sport fishing and the operation of coastal fish traps: shad, mackerel, and bluefish are taken in commercial quantities. These waters can also claim development of an economical and seaworthy small boat, a lapstrake craft now widely known as the Jersey sea skiff. But the striking element of this coast is probably its marshland, vast areas along the sounds and estuaries that man has not yet found it practicable to spoil. These marshes, notably in the Brigantine area near Atlantic City, are a valuable part of the wetlands still available to the waterfowl of the Atlantic flyway.

Cape May, though densely populated, is an important resting place for migratory songbirds—one of the loveliest of warblers is named for it. It overlooks the mouth of Delaware Bay, a wide, windy stretch of water with few settlements and fewer harbors, fringed by a labyrinth of salt marsh. At Delaware Bay the great oyster industry of the central coast begins; here it is based at the ports of Bivalve and Maurice River, on the Jersey shore. But Delaware Bay, with its shallow floor and choppy seas, is probably best known as the meanest stretch of water on all the coast.

On the south side of the bay lies the coast of Delaware, sliding southeast to Cape Henlopen at the mouth. From Cape Henlopen the coast bends southward, on the open ocean, a barrier land of sea beach that continues down along the outer coast of Maryland to Chincoteague Bay, and beyond the bay to Chincoteague Island, in Virginia, then onward to the Chesapeake, at Cape Charles (one tends to forget that the small north corner of Virginia is cut off from the rest of the state by the broad Chesapeake). This dune coast of three states on the seaward front of the great peninsula jutting down between the Delaware and the Chesapeake is perhaps the most remote left in America: until recent years, wild Barbary ponies said to be descended from stock brought by the colonists were common on the outer islands. The reason for the wildness of this region is its inaccessibility: southbound travelers unwilling to depend on the Cape Charles ferry across the Chesapeake's wide ocean mouth (a tunnel-bridge is now under construction) must return far northward to the Chesapeake Bay Bridge before they can proceed south again, and the coast itself affords few havens even for small craft. Thus, boats heading southward from Cape May are obliged to ascend Delaware Bay to the Chesapeake and Delaware Canal, which crosses to the Chesapeake at the narrow base of the peninsula: here they may turn south again.

The mighty Chesapeake, which dominates the coast from a point just south of Pennsylvania to a point in Virginia not far from the Carolina line, has over five thousand miles of shoreline—a varied shoreline, high in the west, low on the peninsula, and piney on the Virginia shore from the Northern Neck to Newport News. The peninsula coast—the so-called Eastern Shore of Maryland—is a complex of small rivers and streams drowned by the sea, forming a network of tidal creeks and estuaries, harbors and sheltered coves. The Eastern Shore is a peaceful, lovely country of farms and dairies and old manor houses, and its shallow waters are renowned for its canvasback duck—in late years, sadly diminished—for its blue crabs and oysters and diamondback terrapin, and for the fleets of fishing smacks—the jaunty, graceful "skipjacks"—that harvest the crabs and shellfish. Striped bass are netted in some quantity—the bass is Maryland's most valuable fish—and Reedville, across the bay on the Virginia shore, is a port for the menhaden fishery. In the middle of the bay is the oyster settlement at Tangier Island, until recent years a picturesque anachronism with neither electricity nor autos.

To the Chesapeake come the great rivers of Virginia—the Potomac, Rappahannock, and the James, with their old currents out of history. And up and down the bay ride ocean freighters, bound north for Baltimore: Baltimore, far from the sea, is one of the great seaports of the country. Near the bay's mouth, at Norfolk and Newport News, the armada of the nation swings on its moorings, in the seaway called Hampton Roads.

At Norfolk begins the Intracoastal Waterway—better known as the Inland Waterway—a system of canals, rivers, and charted sounds providing safe passage for small boats along the thousand miles of coast south to Miami. Below Norfolk one has a choice of two canals, one passing through the pine, black gum, juniper, and cypress woodlands of the Dismal Swamp, the other cutting eastward to Currituck Sound at the head of the long Carolina Banks; Currituck was once one of the foremost shooting regions on the coast and is still a leading wintering ground for the beautiful wild whistling swan. The system of barrier island reefs called the Carolina Banks actually commences in Virginia, not far south of Cape Henry, then veers out toward the southeast as it passes into the Carolinas: Currituck, then Albemarle Sound, brown, windswept, and mean—the southern counterpart of Delaware Bay—Croatan Sound and Roanoke Island, where the Lost Colony disappeared between 1587 and 1591, and finally, the shallow expanse of Pamlico Sound. On the outer fringe of Pamlico Sound, some thirty-five miles from the mainland, lie the great sand bars of Cape Hatteras.

The wilder parts of Hatteras Island, of all the islands on the Banks where man has not seen fit to throw up beach shacks, are truly moving, with some of the same anachronisms—archaic English and wild ponies—that are found in the region of Chincoteague. The narrow spine of grass and sand, with clumps of live oak and other hardy trees fighting for footholds in the hollows, seems lost in a swirl of wind and water: the wind shifts the giant dunes, while the water roars through ragged, transient inlets. Together, the elements surge along the coast, and join in a spume above the beach. Like Monomoy and the south beach of Long Island, Nantucket and Chincoteague, this is a true ocean frontier, with the gull cries and the fluting melancholy of the shore birds like lost voices in the sea mist. The Kill Devil Hills, where the Wright brothers tested their first airplane in 1903, are no more than great dunes patched with low scrub; offshore to the southeast lie the infamous Diamond Shoals, where a collision of cold northern currents with the Gulf Stream, in combination with high winds, has brought about so many shipwrecks—over two thousand in the Hatteras region—that the place is known as the Graveyard of the Atlantic. Once, it is said, the islanders gained a living from the wrecks: the name Nags Head (there is also a Nags Head in New Jersey) may derive from the trick of leading a horse up and down with a lantern swinging from its neck, simulating the light of a boat riding at safe anchor; this technique was also said to have been a favorite among the resourceful natives of Block Island.

The outer banks of Pamlico Sound are a rich fishing ground, where commercial landings of shad and alewives, mullet, even porpoise, have given way to rockfish (the striped bass of the north), croakers, channel bass, drum, bluefish, and other species: the diamondback terrapin once taken in the sounds are much diminished, but oysters, eels, and crabs are plentiful. Since the inlets are transient and dangerous, there are no seaports in all the reach of the Carolina Banks, and marine commerce is confined to fishing. The fisheries, as in so many other areas of the coast, are now declining, due to pollution, overfishing, and other causes, but a few men still set nets throughout the sounds and haul-seine along the ocean beach. Cape Hatteras and its outlying shoals, like Cape Cod, appear to serve as a kind of ecological barrier for marine fishes; from this point southward, the fish populations begin to take on a tropic character.

Southwest from Hatteras, the Banks turn back toward the mainland. On this coast lies Ocracoke Island, where in 1718 the pirate Blackbeard was killed in a furious sea battle, where the steam packet *Home,* in 1837, ran aground with a loss of ninety lives, where a scattering of wild ponies roams the sand hills. The mainland coast itself, across

Pamlico Sound, is quite unspoiled, and that part of it in Dare County, where bear, wild turkey, deer, and alligator rule a forest of sweet gum and pine, is one of the last wild places in the eastern part of the nation.

Where the Banks swing to the mainland lie the twin ports of Beaufort (pronounced Bo-fort; the port of the same name in South Carolina is called Bew-fert) and Morehead City: the latter, like Reedville, Virginia, and Promised Land, Long Island, is a base for the menhaden fishery. Though few have ever heard of the menhaden— it is used in the manufacture of fish meal and glue and fertilizer—the lowly "bunker" (North) or "pogy" (South), a bony relative of the herring, supports the most prosperous of all fisheries on the Atlantic coast.

From Morehead City to Charleston, South Carolina, lie two hundred and fifty miles of salt marsh and narrow sounds, with low dune islands sandwiched between marsh and sea. To this coast flow the Cape Fear River, with its graveyard of rusting Liberty ships, literally hundreds, near the port of Wilmington, and the Pee Dee River, in South Carolina, famous for little but its name; the Pee Dee ends at Georgetown, and this lovely old town, with its magnolia and Spanish moss and boxwood, yellow jasmine and verandas, its oyster-packing plant and its ill-smelling paper mills, serves on this coast as a kind of gateway to the South.

Below Georgetown, at the mouth of the North and South Santee rivers, the "sea island" coast begins, continuing through Georgia into Florida. Unlike the barrier islands farther north, which are flat and narrow, little more than reefs of sand, the sea islands are apt to be forested and relatively wide; they are not continuous, but are interrupted by wide deltas and stretches of open coast. Murphy Island, at the mouth of the South Santee, is typical, with its inland ponds and alligator sloughs, its forest of gum and live oak, pine and yaupon—Murphy Island has a population of wild, wary cattle, some of them very large. As in most of the islands, its inner shore, fronting on the Inland Waterway, is a broad marsh, and because this marsh was diked in former times in an effort to grow rice, and the dikes have been maintained by a nearby shooting club, the marsh water is largely fresh, and supports enormous flocks of wintering waterfowl—blue, snow, and Canada geese and black, mallard, pintail, baldpate, teal, shoveler, gadwall, ruddy, and ring-necked duck—as well as otter and other animals. Bulls Island, farther south, is now a sanctuary of the U.S. Fish and Wildlife Service, supporting wild turkey and deer in numbers; on its inner shore, wide oyster flats attract shore birds in great variety.

The sea islands, which gave their name to a cotton fiber developed in this region, are broken by the mouth of

Charleston Harbor, but begin again almost immediately— Folly Island, Edisto, Hunting Island, and many others down to the Savannah River mouth and Georgia. On the short Georgia coast, the sea islands are large and wide; the seven largest occupy almost the entire coastline. Those in the south part of the state, in the area of Brunswick, are the best known, and especially Sea Island itself (scarcely more than a fragment of adjacent St. Simons Island). Sea Island is the most fashionable resort between Southhampton, Long Island, and Hobe Sound, near Palm Beach.

Across St. Simons Sound lies Jekyll Island, taken over as a shooting place—quail, turkey, duck—by the Morgans and Vanderbilts at the beginning of the century. Jekyll Island, as a private club, died out during World War II, but its great houses still remain, grown up in forest: a state park has been created here, and the island's eight miles or so of beaches are now at the disposal of tourists and the people of the state. Cumberland, the next island to the south, was used formerly by the Carnegies: sea island cotton was grown on Cumberland, and more recently rich mineral deposits have been found.

Off St. Simons Sound, inland from these exotic places, lies Georgia's second port of Brunswick: Brunswick is a commercial harbor, sheltering a menhaden fleet as well as a large shrimp fleet. In recent decades, huge beds of shrimp have been discovered off the coast. The captain who first came upon one of these beds, around 1945, loaded all three of his large shrimpers to the gunwales; having made, it is said, some $125,000 from this single haul, he sold his boats and retired from the sea. Shrimping has now become a major fishery from South Carolina to Florida, and the big, broad-beamed white shrimp boats, high in the bow and rust-streaked, are as characteristic of this coast as the skipjack of the Chesapeake and the lobstermen and draggers of the North.

Above Fernandina, across the Florida line, have flown the flags of Spain, England, Mexico, the Republic of Florida, the Confederate States of America, and the United States. Fernandina is another shrimp port of importance, but its paper mills make Fernandina memorable: the stink of wood pulp—mostly sweet gum and the longleaf and loblolly pines—is the first harbinger of the large harbors of this coast (Georgetown, Charleston, Savannah, Fernandina, Jacksonville). Jacksonville itself lies somewhat inland, upriver on the wide St. Johns; farther upstream the St. Johns becomes one of the wildest and most beautiful of the nation's waterways, and with the Red River, one of two important rivers in the country that flow north. To the east of it, along the coast, the Inland Waterway continues southward to St. Augustine, he "oldest permanent white settlement" (since 1565), with its Castillo de San Marcos and its beach-front honky-tonk, to Marineland, with its inspired dolphins, to Daytona, where the sports cars race, to Cape Canaveral, with its grim, cosmic fireworks. Near Cape Canaveral the barrier islands move offshore, and the canal joins a natural waterway between the islands and the mainland. The Indian River, as this narrow sound is called, extends southward for one hundred fifty miles or more between Ponce de Leon Inlet and Stuart—one sometimes forgets that the great peninsula of Florida, stretching south into the tropics, is nearly four hundred miles in length. From Stuart to Miami the waterway is very pretty, parting a mild landscape of winter estates, palms, and citrus groves to westward, pine and palm islands, marsh and mangrove to the east. It passes the lovely harbor at Eau Gallie, above Stuart, the sports fishing centers at Fort Pierce and St. Lucie Inlet, the St. Lucie Canal to the inland sea of Okeechobee, the millionaire coast of Hobe Sound, Palm Beach, Boca Raton, and finally Fort Lauderdale, which styles itself the "Venice of America." The teeming shore is washed by the blue Gulf Stream, flowing northward within ten miles of the beach: pursuing the sailfish, Spanish mackerel, yellowtail, and wahoo, the charter boats and private craft troll the bright, rough waters of the ocean river, which, at Palm Beach, is in plain sight of the bathers.

Miami is the colossus that belongs to all the world, so vulgar on so grand a scale that it becomes attractive. South of Miami lies Biscayne Bay, and south of the bay the Florida Keys begin: as in the other prevailing wildernesses of Florida—the Kissimmee Prairies and the Everglades—only the outer fringes of the Keys have been despoiled. The majesty of the myriad islets of Florida Bay lies in a vast and dignified monotony, an oppressive yet exhilarating waste of mangrove tangle and pale shallow flats, where barracuda hang suspended in the shadow of the branches, and the white herons, far out among the coasting rays, the conchs, and nurse sharks, seem to stalk on the surface of the water. Some larger keys support pinewoods and the miniature key deer, as well as odd birds strayed north out of the tropics—anhingas, man-o'-war birds, spoonbills, anis, mangrove cuckoos. The American crocodile, which formerly attained lengths of twenty-three feet, finds its last refuge in the inner bay, toward Cape Sable, and the green turtle is still brought in numbers to Key West. In its several heydays Key West has been a haven for explorers, pirates, shipwreckers, rumrunners, shrimpers, spongers, turtlers, the manufacturers of cigars, and Harry Truman; its inhabitants, as cranky and independent as all coastal people north to Maine, are known as conchs, after the tough mollusk of the same name.

Key West lies far out to the southwest, at the end of the arc of islands, but the terminal point of the Atlantic coast is the Dry Tortugas, some seventy miles farther, in the Gulf of Mexico. Though many Americans have never heard of the Dry Tortugas, these islets were discovered by Ponce de León as early as 1513, and remain today the site of Fort Jefferson, erected by edict of President Polk with an eye to controlling the Gulf; Fort Jefferson is said to be the largest fort ever constructed in the United States—it occupies almost the whole of Garden Key—and it is certainly the most useless. Dr. Samuel Mudd, who once ministered to the wounds of John Wilkes Booth, was incarcerated here, but today the Dry Tortugas are largely occupied by colonies of sooty and noddy terns, except in time of storm, when its anchorage gives shelter to commercial fishermen, both American and Cuban. Garden Key with its great dead fort excepted, the Tortugas are too small and remote to have felt the heavy hand of civilization. But long reaches of the Atlantic seaboard have succumbed to exploitation and pollution, oiled waters and the glint of industry. Certain wild coasts are still intact, and at least three—Maine's Acadia National Park, on Mount Desert Island, and the Cape Cod and Cape Hatteras national seashores—may retain at least a whisper of their former voices in years to come. But the whales are gone, the fisheries depleted, and the rude grandeur of the Atlantic coast, the scene of so much heroism and violence, must reside in these strong names, sea names . . .

Eggemoggin Reach and Kennebunkport, Georges Bank, Nantucket Shoals, the Gully, Gravesend Bay, Sandy Hook and Ambrose Lightship, Cape Henlopen and Hampton Roads, Nags Head, Diamond Shoals, and Cape Romain, Key Largo, Loggerhead Key Light . . .

An Atlantic storm pounds against Maine's "Western Coast" at Perkins Cove, an art colony near Ogunquit.

The Stern "Main"

Off the coast of Maine lie hundreds of islands, remnants of mountains pressed down by ice age glaciers and then drowned by melting ice and swirling ocean waters. Past these myriad islands sailed Verrazano and other early explorers, searching for "the main," the fabled mainland of the north that held out hope of gold and riches to rival the treasures of Peru.

But "the main" was a bitter disappointment. The French, English, and Spanish captains who cruised its coast in the sixteenth century found jagged rocks and treacherous reefs, dense fogs and dark forests that promised not gold but unknown dangers. For a hundred years Maine discouraged encroachment with no weapon other than the frown of her cold and forbidding face.

In 1598 John Walker, an English captain, went ashore briefly at Penobscot Bay, and in the next decade Europeans made several attempts at settlement. Maine fought these efforts with ice, fog, and snow: a winter's experience was enough for Frenchmen who camped on Dochet Island in 1604 and for English settlers who tried to establish themselves at Popham in 1607.

In time, as fishermen and fur trappers continued to visit the coast, Maine succumbed. But she did so on her own terms, remaking the settlers in her own image.

She produced a hardy breed of people who could survive her rigors and make the best of her bounties. In addition to fish and furs she gave them granite and limestone to quarry, and timber and harbors, so that Maine ships were seen in ports all over the world. And, ironically, the coast that once terrified explorers became at last a magnet for artists and tourists, who delighted in the rugged, salt-drenched beauty of "the main."

The granitic image of coastal Maine is symbolized by the hardy "salt" above, photographed about 1910, and by the sheer drop of Otter Cliff (right), a 100-foot-high ocean fringe of Acadia National Park. The top of the promontory affords a sweeping view of Frenchman Bay and of Schoodic Point beyond it.

The Face of Acadia

Of all the rugged men of Maine, none were more industrious than the New England Yankees who settled on high-cliffed Mount Desert, largest of Maine's many islands. They cut down acres of forest, using the cleared land for farming and the pine trees for the hulls and spars of ships. They packed fish and ice to the mainland and quarried granite for use in buildings as far west as Omaha. And they collected the small round stones that lay on the island's sea walls and sold them as cobblestones for the streets of America's burgeoning cities.

Samuel de Champlain, the French explorer, came upon Mount Desert in September, 1604. Sailing down the coast from Dochet Island, he saw the island "very high, and notched in places, so that there is the appearance to one at sea, as of seven or eight mountains extending along near each other. The summit of the most of them is destitute of trees, as there are only rocks on them. . . . I named it Isle des Monts Déserts" (Island of Bare Mountains).

In the years after Champlain's explorations Mount Desert was a battleground in the struggle between France and England for domination of North America. In 1613 a party of French Jesuits established a mission on the island after a heavy fog had diverted them from their original mainland destination. The English opposed them, however, and in a surprise raid wiped out the French settlement a few months later.

After that, warships of both nations plied the waters of the region, making life on Mount Desert precarious for potential settlers. The Sieur de Cadillac, who was granted ownership of the island by the governor of French Canada in 1688, lingered there only briefly before moving to safer French territory near Detroit. But the tallest mountain on Mount Desert, the highest peak on the Atlantic coast, is still named Cadillac Mountain (1,532 feet).

Not until 1761, after the French and Indian War was over, did permanent settlers arrive. The first were James Richardson and Abraham Somes, who gave his name to Somes Sound, the fiord that almost bisects the island. Others followed, and Mount Desert grew into a busy, peaceful community, isolated by water from the tumult of the Revolution and the bustle of the rapidly growing nation.

21

ACADIA NATIONAL PARK

ter Harbor

SCHOODIC PENINSULA

Schoodic Head

der Hole

ter
iff

LITTLE
CRANBERRY
ISLAND

N

BAKER
ISLAND

ISLE
AU HAUT

Isle
Au Haut

Jerusalem
Mtn

Long
Pond

N

ATLANTIC
OCEAN

Two hundred forty years after Champlain first sighted it, Mount Desert was discovered a second time. In 1844 Thomas Cole, a leader of the Hudson River school of painting, paid a visit to the island. He was so enchanted by the beauties of Mount Desert that he told his friends about it, and it became a Mecca for artists. The rich and socially prominent followed, and by 1890 the island had become an exclusive resort, with a cluster of elaborate "cottages" at Bar Harbor.

Two of the "summer folk," George Bucknam Dorr and Dr. Charles Eliot, repaid Mount Desert for the lovely summers it gave them by saving the island's beauty at a critical moment. Lumbermen threatened to raze a section of the forest, but Dorr and Eliot enlisted the help of others and purchased the endangered land. From their initial efforts and from a subsequent donation of land by John D. Rockefeller, Jr. emerged Lafayette National Park, which was established in 1919, the first national park east of the Mississippi.

Renamed Acadia in 1929, the park now consists of more than thirty thousand acres, half on Mount Desert and half on spruce-covered Isle au Haut and the mainland's Schoodic Point, famed for its 400-foot headland and magnificent views.

Today's visitor to Mount Desert can look down from the summit of Cadillac Mountain on unspoiled forests, glistening lakes, and island-dotted waters. Along the ocean drives he can marvel at the steep cliffs, at the assortment of sea life in Anemone Cave, and at the spray that jets high into the air as the Atlantic's waves crash into Thunder Hole. He can wander across flower-strewn slopes and walk through cool woods, where he may have a deer for company. He can swim or sail, or simply sit and enjoy the beauty around him, agreeing with those who regard Mount Desert as the gem of the Maine coast.

Home Is the Sailor

Despite its characterization as a "stern and rockbound coast," much of the New England shore is notched with tranquil coves and bays, once snug harbors for barks that roamed the seven seas, and today picturesque shelters for fleets of small sport and commercial craft. FitzHugh Lane, a nineteenth-century American artist, specialized in sentimental paintings of such coastal havens. One of his best-known works is the view below of a hermaphrodite brig off Owl's Head, a point in Penobscot Bay, Maine, which he painted in 1862.

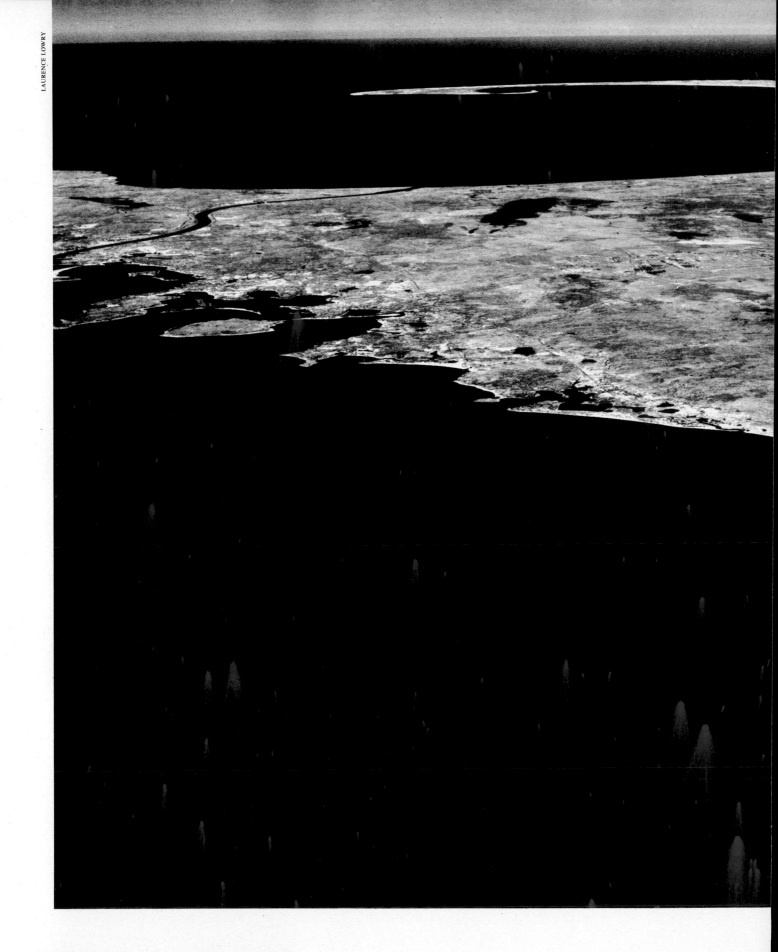

Pilgrims' Landfall

Reaching out toward the Atlantic as if to welcome the Mayflower, *Cape Cod gave the Pilgrims their first glimpse of the New World in 1620. It was at Provincetown, sheltered by the fishhook at the Cape's tip, that they first disembarked and replenished their supplies of food and firewood before sailing on to a permanent settlement. At the left of this spectacular aerial view by Laurence Lowry is the Cape Cod Canal, which was first suggested by the Pilgrims' Myles Standish, but was not begun until 1909.*

27

A Beach to Walk Upon

Henry David Thoreau

Still held on without a break the inland barrens and shrubbery, the desert and the high sand-bank with its even slope, the broad white beach, the breakers, the green water on the bar, and the Atlantic Ocean; and we traversed with delight new reaches of the shore."

To Henry David Thoreau, the great naturalist and author of *Walden,* Cape Cod was a place of peace and solitude as well as a cornucopia of wonders. He made four visits there between 1849 and 1857, wandering on foot across the plains, marshes, and beaches of the glacier-hewn area, and recording his experiences and impressions in a series of magazine articles that eventually became a book, *Cape Cod.*

Thoreau reveled in the waves, "curving green or yellow as if over so many unseen dams, ten or twelve feet high, like a thousand waterfalls"; in the beach grass that "anchored" the sand; and in the great variety of marine life. He walked for hours along the shore, stopping "frequently to empty our shoes of the sand which one took in in climbing or descending the bank," and to watch the sandpipers and other birds "trotting along close to each wave, and waiting for the sea to cast up their breakfast."

Although Thoreau foresaw that Cape Cod would one day become a seaside resort, he was sure that "this shore will never be more attractive than it is now." To him, the Cape was a natural shrine, an unspoiled frontier jutting out into the ocean. "A man may stand there," he wrote, "and put all America behind him."

Treasures to Save

The wind and the tides have always been Cape Cod's enemies, carrying away its sand and eroding its high bluffs. But after the invention of the automobile, which helped bring vacationers by the thousands, man changed the face of the Cape, as Thoreau knew it, with thoughtless misuse and disregard for many of its unique natural features. In 1961 Congress authorized the establishment of the Cape Cod National Seashore, to preserve for future generations much of the still-unspoiled ocean shore, as well as parts of the bay, dunes, marshes, and woodlands.

LEE BOLTIN

NATIONAL PARK SERVICE PHOTO BY M. W. WILLIAMS

Cape Cod's tall, hard-packed dunes, like those at New-comb Hollow in Wellfleet (above), are adventurous play-grounds for children. Nearby, at Chequessett Beach (far left), quiet waters provide opportunities for boating and clamming. At left, common terns frequent Nauset Beach.

LAURENCE LOWRY

Down to the Sea

According to an Indian legend Nantucket Island (seen, opposite, in autumn when the heath lands are splotched with the reds and pinks of huckleberry, blueberry, and sumac) was created by a giant god, Maushope. As he slept on Cape Cod one day, sand filled his moccasins. When he kicked them off angrily, they fell into the sea and became Nantucket and its sister island Martha's Vineyard.

Fourteen miles long, with an average width of three and a half miles, Nantucket grew into a great whaling port, giving its name to the "Nantucket sleigh ride," the whalers' facetious term for the fast, ocean-skimming ride they endured when a harpooned whale hauled them furiously through the foam (as seen in the anonymous primitive above). The whaling era ended in the 1860's, after ships became too large to sail across the sand bar into Nantucket's harbor. But summer visitors eventually discovered the island, and made a popular vacation resort of the sea-oriented land the Indians had once called Canopache, "the Place of Peace."

33

Ramparts
of the Hudson

Rising like the wall of a natural fortress, from 350 to 550 feet above the lower Hudson River, are the massive basalt cliffs of the Palisades, which stretch for some thirty miles along the western shore. Although they appear to be composed of separate columns of lava, they are actually a single mass, pushed up as molten liquid from the earth's interior.

During the Revolution, the Palisades provided American forces with a commanding view of British movements on the river. But although Fort Lee atop the cliffs and Fort Washington across the river in Manhattan had the benefit of high, strategic locations, they were poorly equipped; and in 1776 British vessels were able to sail past them, unmolested save for futile efforts by American fire ships to stop them (below). Fort Washington was captured, and on a cold and rainy night, four thousand British soldiers scaled the Palisades and took Fort Lee.

The Palisades were endangered by quarrymen in the 1800's. But by the efforts of the states of New York and New Jersey and of private individuals, the area was eventually bought for an interstate park which saved the majestic beauty of the cliffs from being pocked with quarries.

To denizens of the bay, like the sou'westered waterman above, the Chesapeake is both a livelihood and a zestful way of life, three centuries old. Their vocabularies are flavored with Chesapeake metaphors, like "poor as gar broth," an allusion to the lack of meat on the gar. The photograph at right, of a portion of the Eastern Shore and the twisting Little Blackwater River, shows why the bay's shoreline, indented by rivers and inlets, would extend for over five thousand miles if straightened out.

Bay of the Mother of God

In 1608 Captain John Smith and a party of men from the Jamestown settlement set out to explore the Chesapeake. Near the mouth of the Rappahannock, one of the forty-eight sizable rivers that pour into the bay, they were delighted to find the waters swarming with fish; all they had to do to catch them, according to their journals, was to dip their skillets into the water and then spear the panned fish with swords. The merriment ended when an irate sting ray wounded Smith, but the tale survives as one of the innumerable fish stories of the Chesapeake.

From Smith's time until today, the great body of water that early Spaniards called "The Bay of the Mother of God" has ranked among the world's most bountiful fishing grounds. In 1961 almost five million pounds of striped bass and more than twenty-four million pounds of hard-shelled crabs were caught in the Maryland half of the bay alone.

Oystermen still harvest Chincoteagues and other fat, flavorsome varieties with hand-operated tongs (below), and old-timers of the bay's waters continue to attest to the veracity of time-worn Chesapeake maxims, such as "If you would catch oysters, sing; if fish, be still."

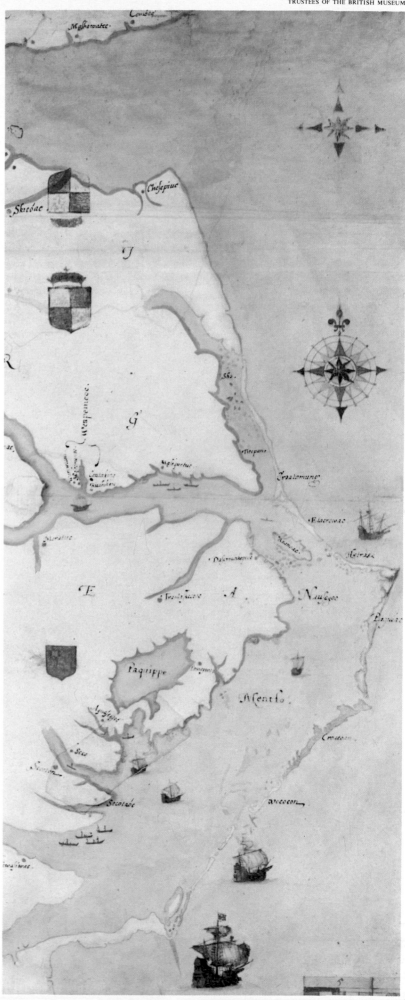

The Atlantic Graveyard

When John White, leader of the "Lost Colony" of Roanoke, drew his map (right) of North Carolina's Outer Banks, around 1585, they were thickly wooded with cedar, pine, and oak. But the permanent settlers who came after 1665 brought axes, fire, and cattle and denuded many parts of the islands, allowing the winds to blow the unanchored sand into huge dunes. Usually the dunes formed around trees, and when the sand shifted again, it exposed gnarled stumps like those shown at left, glistening in the sunlight at Cape Hatteras.

Offshore, the violent meeting of opposite-moving currents built up perilous shoals that extend as much as twenty-five miles out into the Atlantic. Numerous vessels, including the Union's famed ironclad, the *Monitor*, have grounded there and sunk in storms, giving the area its dread name, "The Graveyard of the Atlantic." At the same time, nights of howling gale often benefited the isolated settlers: some earned their living by piloting ships safely around the shoals; others profited by salvaging the wreckage from less fortunate vessels.

Today, forty-five square miles of beach, dunes, and superb fishing grounds, steeped in the lore of the colonists, pirates, and shipwrecks, are preserved as the Cape Hatteras National Seashore.

Isles of Grass

"So:
Affable live-oak, leaning low,—
. . . Bending your beauty aside, with
a step I stand
On the firm-packed sand,
Free
By a world of marsh that borders
a world of sea."

In "The Marshes of Glynn," the
young, nineteenth-century Georgia
poet, Sidney Lanier, celebrated the
hauntingly unreal world of swamp
and cypress, water lily and Spanish
moss that lies between the mainland and the coastal islands of the
southeastern states.

On those heavily wooded sea islands, grow longleaf pine and
magnolias, palms, myrtle, and
moss-draped live oaks, some of
which provided shade for Indians
and Spaniards, for pirates, and for
the slaves of great ante bellum rice,
indigo, and cotton plantations.
This remarkably beautiful photograph of the Georgia sea marshes
is by the late Edward Weston.

40

"Wattoola Great Savannah Crane" (Florida Sand-hill Crane)

"Rice Bird" (Bobolink), Speckled Snake, and Frog

"Great Black Bream" (Copper-nosed Bream)

Bartram by C. W. Peale

"Caron Crow" (Black Vulture)

42

The Southeast of William Bartram

Do you know *Bartram's Travels?* This is of the Seventies (1770) or so; treats of *Florida* chiefly, has a wondrous kind of floundering eloquence in it . . . All American libraries ought to provide themselves with that kind of book; and keep them as a kind of *biblical* article."

So wrote Thomas Carlyle to Ralph Waldo Emerson in 1851 of an unusual volume that had been published in America sixty years before. It was by William Bartram, a Philadelphia naturalist, who had traveled widely through the Carolinas, Georgia, Florida, and Alabama from 1773 to 1777, sketching the birds and animals of the region, and collecting so many plant specimens that the Indians called him "The Flower Hunter." His journals contained detailed scientific descriptions of flora and fauna, but they also pictured an exotic world of alligators and snakes, of curious fish and long-legged birds. It was a fascinating guidebook to a remote area, and can be as rewarding to the modern armchair traveler as it was to Carlyle.

Two sketches of that "terrable monster," the "Alegator of St. Johns"

Keys and Reefs

Photographed from an altitude of eight thousand feet, the tropical waters of the Florida Keys weave patterns of color and movement past coral and limestone islands and over barely submerged sand bars and reefs. These hidden reefs made the Keys a perilous region for Spanish treasure galleons, and a rewarding hunting ground for the Calusa Indians who preyed upon their wrecks.

Ponce de León, the first white man to see the Keys, called them the "Islands of the Martyrs," because their twisted shapes reminded him of men writhing in agony. Today, the low islands are havens for naturalists and botanists, while reefs, teeming with tropical fish, draw underwater explorers, and the ocean and Florida Bay provide some of the best fishing anywhere in the world.

A photographer swims among an unconcerned school of silvery spadefish.

Virgin Islands

The jewel of the Caribbean archipelago, discovered by Columbus during his second voyage (1493), is St. John, above, one of the three American Virgin Islands. Its few roads, navigable only by jeep, are steep and rutted, but the bumpy ride across the island is worth the effort. St. John's slopes, denuded in the eighteenth century by Danish sugar planters, are now covered with lush second-growth vegetation and colored with flowering hibiscus, bougainvillaea,

and flamboyant. From the top of Bordeaux Mountain, 1,277 feet high, the views of the bay, beaches, long-fingered peninsulas, and island-studded sea are dazzling. And the clear waters of Trunk and Hawksnest bays tempt swimmers to submerge again and again to watch schools of darting fish and inspect the multicolored reefs of living coral. Purchased from Denmark in 1917, St. John has been since 1956 the nucleus of a national park of unique tropical beauty.

47

II

THE
EASTERN
FORESTS

By WILLIAM O. DOUGLAS

"The tempered light of the woods is like a perpetual morning, and is stimulating and heroic. . . . The incommunicable trees begin to persuade us to live with them, and quit our life of solemn trifles."

Ralph Waldo Emerson (*Nature*, 1844)

The Appalachians extend from Alabama to Newfoundland. In appearance they are a wild tumble of mountains with cirquelike valleys, knifelike saddles, soft, rounded ridges, and flattened crowns. A person who crosses them from east to west reaches one pass only to find other ridges rising in ranks against the horizon as far as the eye can see.

The ridges are thick with trees that leave few lookouts. Yet even where a granite or quartzite ledge offers a view, it is seldom possible to see the entire east-west sweep of the ranges from any single point.

Throughout their length the Appalachians are usually tinged with mist, so that from afar they seem indistinct, remote, and mysterious. Their hardwood forests stand bare of leaves in wintertime, revealing majestic boles and limbs in infinite patterns. Silver freezes often transform the ridges, making each tree seem as fragile as glass.

These deciduous trees that are gay with color in the fall are tinged with the red of maples and the light green of poplars, birch, and beech in the spring. Rhododendron, azaleas, and mountain laurel grow as far north as Massachusetts; dogwood and redbud, as far north as New York. From there on northward, the shadbush and wild cherries are the main flowering shrubs.

A "creek" in New York becomes a "branch" in Vermont, a "run" in Virginia, and a "prong" in Tennessee. A "gap" in Kentucky becomes a "notch" in New Hampshire and a "clove" in the Catskills. Yet the various parts of the Appalachians have much in common. From Mount Katahdin in Maine to Mount Oglethorpe in Georgia, they offered in the early days a continuous supply of white pine and the equally famous eastern hemlock. Their ridges, now as then, are capped with eastern hemlock and red spruce, but in the north with black or red spruce and birch. Now, as then, their slopes and coves produce hardwoods. From Maine to Georgia these forests were heavily and often recklessly cut during the last century. Yet in this temperate zone, rainfall, temperatures, and soil conditions encourage the rapid renewal of hardwoods.

The white-tailed Virginia deer, the black bear, and the raccoon are found the length and breadth of the Appalachians. The ruffed grouse, a nonmigratory game bird, makes claim to every area. Wild turkeys, which relish last year's cherry pits and the nodules on the roots of squirrel corn, are now as far north as the Berkshires in Massachusetts. The porcupine does not get farther south than Pennsylvania. Rattlesnakes become less numerous as one goes north from Mount Everett, a pine-covered knob in the southern Berkshires. In the Alleghenies of Pennsylvania some hunt them, either with a rifle or with a noose at the end of a fishing rod. The copperhead snake does not reach New England. Only Maine is free of poisonous snakes.

The eastern brook trout is native to all the streams in the range. Bass flourish in the Poconos and in sections of the Connecticut, Potomac, and Shenandoah rivers, as do muskellunge and walleyed pike in parts of the Allegheny.

The various ranges of the Appalachians have different geological histories. The glaciers left their imprint on the northern area, but did not go south of Philadelphia. Thus, the southern ranges, despite their wonders, have no lakes to speak of except man-made ones, while those from the Poconos on north abound with them.

Mount Katahdin in north-central Maine, the highest point in that state (5,267 feet), marks the start of the Appalachian Trail, which ends on Springer Mountain in Georgia. Thoreau described the hundreds of lakes seen from the top of Katahdin as a thousand fragments of a broken mirror. Some are mere blue dots, some are wide expanses, the largest being Moosehead to the southwest. To the southeast is the blue ribbon of the Penobscot River. Far to the southwest is the long barrier mass of the White Mountains in New Hampshire.

Katahdin stands somewhat in isolation. It is part of a long tableland that falls away abruptly from one thousand feet to two thousand feet on all sides. The escarpments are walls of glacial cirques or basins. Trails ascend Katahdin from the southwest, north, and northwest.

Katahdin's crest is shaped like a fishhook, the point being Pamola, named after an Indian god who had the head of a moose, the arms and chest of a man, and the feet and wings of the eagle. The highest point on Katahdin's crest is Baxter Peak. Between Baxter and Pamola is the famous Knife Edge, a narrow ridge over a mile long with a dropoff of about fifteen hundred feet. When the fog moves in, one crawls the Knife Edge lest he fall into the abyss. Thoreau called Katahdin "a cloud factory." Cold air is sucked down the head wall into a warmer belt where it condenses. Then it is quickly swept upward.

The mountain's drainage is both north and south, all of its waters eventually reaching the Atlantic. The line of drainage is not a divide but an inconspicuous height of land north of Moosehead Lake and south of Chamberlain Lake. Northward-bound waters flow into the St. John River, which for part of its length is the boundary between the United States and Canada. Its main tributary is the Allagash, which for about two thirds of its one hundred miles flows through a chain of lakes. These waters ran north until man intervened. During the last century water was needed to run logs in the East Fork of the Penobscot, which rises north of Katahdin and flows to the

An aerial view shows the Alleghenies in Pennsylvania as parallel rows of heavily wooded ridges.

east of it. So the Telos Cut was made, which drew north-bound waters from Lake Chamberlain and sent them south. Dams were also built on the lakes in the Allagash chain to regulate the flow of the north-bound waters, which were used for running logs. The lakes in the Allagash chain bear some permanent scars, for the raising of their water level killed many trees.

Traces of old tote roads, used in the early lumbering operations, can still be found along the Allagash. Allagash means "hemlock bark," which was extensively used for the tanning of leather. Today there are only a few hemlock or white pine the length of the Allagash. Elms dot its islands and banks. White ash, rock maple, white birch, alder, and willow are other water-edge trees. Higher up grow the white maple and the beech. These hardwoods have occasional streaks of tamarack and black spruce. The balm of Gilead tree stands in isolated splendor.

The moose, which once almost disappeared, is on its way back and feeds in the bogans of the Allagash. The banks are lined with sweet gale, sand cherry, viburnum, and the bearded short-husk grass. Gravel bars show the American water willow. Some sections have a fragrant

sweet grass, called sacred grass in the Greek because it was strewn before churches in Europe on saints' days. This is land both of the ruffed grouse and the spruce grouse. Beaver, muskrat, otter, and mink possess the waters; the common loon is on every lake. Each lake also has togue (lake trout); and the squaretail trout flourishes in the shallower waters.

The central core of Katahdin (embracing nearly two hundred thousand acres and shaped in a rectangular fashion) is in Baxter State Park. Roads reach the park, but automobiles and airplanes are barred within its borders. Its trails, north and south, penetrate about twenty miles of wilderness. Its lakes and streams may be fished. But no hunting is allowed; nor may trees be cut. The result is a wooded alcove that is unique in New England.

The climax forest of Maine is white pine, Norway pine, hemlock, and black spruce. In flat areas the black spruce once grew so thick that a person on foot had difficulty in getting his bearings. White pine (which caused Maine to be known as the Pine Tree State) once grew in great groves or stands, sometimes running like "veins" through the primeval forests. Those old forests have been cut. Baxter

State Park is cutover land, which means that it is largely composed of hardwoods. But Maine has great regenerative power, and now that Baxter Park is locked up for perpetuity, the ancient forests will in time be re-created.

Four camps on the edges of the park can be reached by car. There are others deep in a wilderness whose trails are largely maintained by moose and deer. Pogy Pond, Weed, Wassataquoick, and Russell lakes produce squaretail trout. The trails are soggy, at many places being overflowed by water from beaver dams. Paper-bark birch is on display. Here and there is a sturdy beech or a maple. Pencil cedar is dwarfed and the larch, with branches to the ground, is a small tree. Aspen, mountain ash, and hazelnut bushes are common. Chokecherries, shadbush, and pin cherries brighten the woods in the spring. Pussy willows are numerous; the rhodora grows in thick stands; the painted trillium stands in glory above drab floor litter on its way to conversion into humus.

These woods have little grass. Ferns, ground pine, raspberries, wild strawberries, currants, and blueberries are in abundance. Mushrooms, including the delicious boletus, the coral, and the icicle, flourish. One of the best dishes of all is fiddlehead ferns. The choice fern is the ostrich. Like others, its shoots, as they come out of the ground, are curled. These small nibbins are boiled and served with butter. The red fruit of the partridgeberry last from one fall to the next summer. Bog kalmia only inches high has a rose-purple bloom. Here are mountain cranberries, Labrador tea, alpine azalea, and the pitcher plant.

The whisky-jack usually appears around a camp. The pileated woodpecker makes the woods ring with his hammerlike blows. Whip-poor-wills sing lustily at dusk and just before dawn. In the spring the male woodcock performs a sacred mating ritual—soaring to the sky until he is nearly out of sight and then returning to earth in a spiraling flight as he sings his plaintive song—chicharee, chicharee, chicharee.

The segment of the Appalachians known as the White Mountains lies mostly in New Hampshire, though its eastern edge is in Maine. The bulk of these ranges—nearly seven hundred thousand acres—is in a national forest of the same name. They run across the state in a northeast-southwest direction. They have forty-six peaks four thousand feet or higher, if only those peaks that rise three hundred feet or more above a ridge connecting with a neighbor peak are counted. Several ranges, some fifty miles or so in width, make up this mountain complex, which is dominated by the treeless summits of the famous Presidential Range, Mount Washington (6,288 feet) being the highest. These bald summits—white with snow in win-

ter and shining bright in summer—were seen from the Atlantic Ocean in the early days and called "white hills."

The White Mountains, once remote, are now within a day's drive for forty million people. They are heavily used both in summer and winter, skiing extending sometimes into June. A cog railroad runs up the west side of Washington, an auto road up the east side. This is ideal hiking country and the Appalachian Mountain Club with local headquarters at Pinkham Notch maintains in the summer months seven huts where food and lodging are available. The area has over eighty lakes, most of which have fish, and seventeen hundred miles of trails, many too steep for horses. Some of the huts are on or near lakes; others are on wind-blown, barren peaks where campers must pack in their fuel. The tops of the Presidential Range are treacherous even in summer, when winds reach eighty to one hundred fifty miles an hour and the temperature quickly drops from a comfortable sixty-five degrees to near freezing or lower. Hikers, lightly clad, have died of exposure. A weather observatory on Mount Washington, anchored by cables, once recorded a wind of two hundred thirty-four miles an hour.

The hardwood forests of beech, birch, and maples—sprinkled with red spruce and balsam fir—are usually under thirty-five hundred feet. The next thousand-foot zone has head-high birch and mountain ash. Above forty-five hundred feet is the Alpine zone, where prostrate black spruce, balsam fir, birch, mountain ash, and willow grow. These wind-blown tops have arctic plants—cotton grass, Lapland rosebay (*Rhododendron lapponicum*), low-bush blueberries, mountain cranberries, bog bilberries, the pinkish-white arctic diapensia, bog kalmia, to mention only a few. These ridge soils are low in nitrogen and have such low summer temperatures that chemicals are not easily converted into protoplasm. Arctic conditions are duplicated and arctic plant life flourishes.

The Presidential Range is shaped like a "Y," with Washington the right prong, Madison, Adams, and Jefferson on the left one, and Monroe on the stem. Glaciers coming down from the northwest reached high on the Presidential Range, carving out bowl-shaped basins and deep, round-bottomed valleys with semicircular, precipitous head walls. Of these, Tuckerman Ravine is perhaps the most famous. Some of the cirques are filled with granite debris as large as bungalows. The ridges show rounded knobs, known as sheepbacks, which were shaped by glaciers. Perched boulders of quartzites and slates were brought by the glaciers from distant places.

The Presidential Range, like the lesser ranges of the White Mountains, is granite; and the rocks are moss-

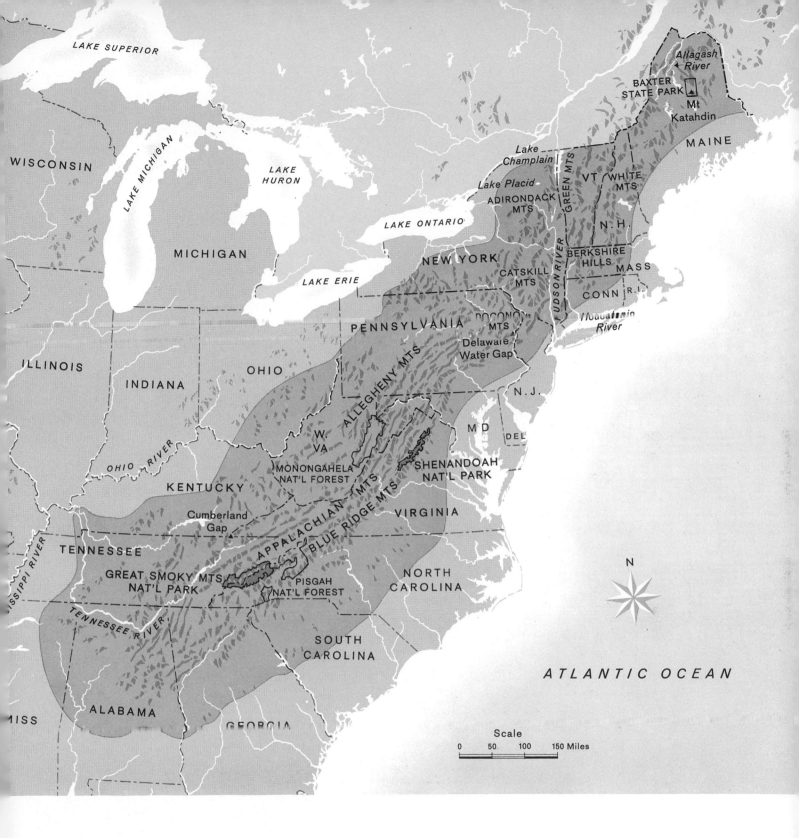

covered in the hardwood zone and decorated with various colored lichens higher up. In wet spots sphagnum moss, once used for surgical dressings, grows thick, and out of it may come many delicate flowers. The Virginia deer prospers here. The fisher roams these hills looking for porcupine, squirrels, chipmunks, and grouse. The beaver, once almost extinct, has returned. The higher one climbs, the more he hears the purple finch, New Hampshire's state bird and the white-throated sparrow, singing as plain as can be, "Old Sam Peabody, Peabody, Peabody."

The Green Mountains, a spur of the Appalachians, run the entire length of Vermont, and the trail that follows their crests from the state of Massachusetts to the Canadian border is over two hundred fifty miles long.

53

These mountains of Ethan Allen are mostly granite, though some valleys have marble and slate and Mount Mansfield (4,393 feet), the highest point in the range, is composed of gneisses, schists, and quartzites. Stowe, one of Vermont's popular skiing resorts, is on its eastern slopes. This mountain—known to the Abnaki Indians as the "Mountain with a Head like a Moose"—is about two miles long and covered with low balsam fir and open rocks. Its profile is visible from the Adirondacks on the west and the White Mountains on the east, and reading from south to north it shows the head and neck, not of a moose, but of a prostrate man—Forehead, Nose, Lips, Chin, and Adam's Apple. The Chin is the highest point, which leads Vermonters to say, "Thank God Vermont carries its Chin higher than its Nose."

The southern peaks are soft and round. The grandeur of the Green Mountains piles up as one hikes north along the backbone of the ridge. The northern peaks offer viewpoints that show the length of Lake Champlain to the west, the Adirondacks beyond it, and to the east the White Mountains. From Bromley Mountain (3,260 feet) in the south, the White Mountains of New Hampshire and Maine, the Berkshires of Massachusetts, and the Taconics of New York are in view on a clear day.

There is little grass on the slopes or ridges except where fire, wind, or other accidents have produced clearings. Oxalis and bunchberries, ground pine and ferns, blueberries, raspberries, and currants, hobblebush, striped maple, and chokecherries are common ground cover. Browse is plentiful and deer are on the increase. The snowshoe rabbit (varying hare) is good hunting. While a cottontail when pursued takes quickly to its hole, a snowshoe rabbit "will run a mile."

Of the many lakes in the Green Mountains, some are far from view, being tucked away in basins below peaks, like Haystack Lake, which is just below the top of Haystack Mountain (3,462 feet). The trails leading to these lakes are often like staircases, the roots of birch trees offering friendly handholds on bright days and treacherous footing in wet weather. Most of the lakes are quiet alcoves that are removed from the noise of the modern world and protected by steep trails from the nefarious motorized scooter, the "tote gote."

Federal law puts a premium on logging even though Vermont's economy has shifted more and more in recent times to recreation. Twenty-five per cent of the gross receipts from sales of timber on national forest lands go to the local unit where the timber is cut. Some of Vermont's townships now count on this income for as much as ninety per cent of their revenues.

While the Green Mountains of Vermont are mostly granite, the Berkshires of Massachusetts and Connecticut (which together with a neighboring range in New York are sometimes referred to as the Taconics) are predominantly quartzite and limestone. This area, which was once a sea bed, shows limestone now turned on edge and greatly weathered. Limestone caves accommodate two species of bats. The whitish quartzite outcroppings are often spectacular, Monument Mountain, near Great Barrington, Massachusetts, being an example.

Mount Greylock (3,505 feet), which stands not far from the Vermont line, is the highest point in the Berkshires. A winding road brings many travelers there. Skiers have two startling runs off its slopes. The road has deprived Greylock of much of its charm, but not its claim to distinction. Two birds, rarely seen elsewhere, summer here— Bicknell's thrush and the mourning warbler.

White ash in the Berkshires, growing in open places, has a broad crown and wide-spreading branches whose foliage is mostly on the outside. The result is that one who lies under the tree has a feeling of open sky above him. The beech, as well as the sugar maple and silver maple, are never more stately than here. An afternoon's hike will produce a hemlock of noble proportions. Ravines and ridges are filled with stands of white birch as diverse and as oddly arranged as a community of people.

The Berkshires are mostly low-lying hills with easy trails. They are so accessible that city residents in western Massachusetts often take their lunch hour in a glade or by a lake. Among the many lakes and ponds, the largest is Twin Lakes, now highly developed as a resort area. Many of the ponds are swampy and the delight of biologists and ornithologists. The view from a ridge or through a forest is reminiscent of the English Lake Country.

Apart from the Housatonic, there are no rivers of any size in this part of the Appalachians. But many minor ones offer good trout fishing in the spring. The Housatonic is polluted and its waters are too dangerous for drinking. Both largemouth and smallmouth bass are found there. Sunfish and pickerel seem to flourish; and in some stretches the rainbow trout lies in wait at the foot of riffles. The Appalachian Trail follows the Housatonic for some miles. Limestone cliffs, luxuriant with ferns, stately elm and silver maple, white birch and balsam fir, line this broad purling river. This is the place for soliloquies hours on end. One who is patient can see the walking fern walk.

The Adirondacks, in north-central New York, contain about two and one-fourth million acres of public-owned land. On a map the area seems much larger because of the private in-holdings. Some of them are maintained as sanctuaries; some are regularly cut. New York buys up these in-holdings whenever possible and puts them under the protection of its constitution, which provides that they "shall be forever kept as wild forest lands" and that none of their timber will be "sold, removed, or destroyed." The cutting of one tree on public land brings a twenty-five-dollar fine to the offender.

Of the public land only five per cent is in the primitive condition of a virgin forest. Fire and blowdown have taken a heavy toll of the primitive stands of spruce, balsam fir, and birch. One hurricane in the 1950's blew down the conifers in rows, piling them in furrows and making cross-country travel difficult.

The Adirondacks are mostly granite, being an extension of the Canadian shield. But there are occasional traces of limestone on some high points—remnants of an earlier range that some estimate to be one billion years old.

The highest peak is Mount Marcy (5,344 feet) and the next highest, Algonquin Peak (5,112 feet). There are forty-six peaks four thousand feet or higher—the same number that are found in the White Mountains. Algonquin Peak marks a divide between drainages. Water on the south side runs to the Hudson, water on the north side, to Lake Champlain and the St. Lawrence River. Near Avalanche Lake—where white cedar grows eighteen inches in diameter and where stands of red spruce are two hundred fifty or more years old—there is a precise divide where a tiny stream pours off a cliff, part of it going north and part south.

Adirondack means "bark eater," a term of derision used by the Iroquois to describe the Algonquians. Boundary Mountain to the west of Algonquin Peak marked the territories of those two tribes, the Iroquois having been on the south.

The Adirondacks contain four main ridges that run mostly east and west. The slopes are thick with trees and undergrowth, except where outcroppings of granite form streaks. Pin cherry, which comes in after a fire, and the green alder, with sticky leaves, are common. Hazelnut bushes are found in some valleys. Striped maple and mountain ash, Labrador tea, and many types of berries flourish. When the red raspberry is in bloom, its fragrance fills the trails. Ground pine, running pine, and the fir club moss grow thick. Acres of oxalis fill some shaded areas. Bunchberry lines some trails; and high on the upper parts of the ridges the clintonia lily is found.

The Adirondacks, like the White Mountains, have arctic bald areas, numbering about eight in all. One is atop Algonquin. These bald areas grow arctic-type flora. Cotton grass is found there; the delicate arctic diapensia flourishes; sandwort forms a mat; a sweet grass, kin to

that on the Allagash, can be found in the tough sod. A dwarf spruce, a dwarf birch, and a dwarf willow grow on these balds. Lapland rosebay, a bilberry, a crowberry, a pale azalea, combine with other dwarfed plants to form a coarse, thick turf.

The Adirondacks have about two hundred lakes over ten acres in size. The Santanoni, the southwestern range, overlooks a vast lake area. The longest direct one-way canoe trip across it is about one hundred three miles.

The lakes in large part lie in wilderness areas where ancient white pines sing in the wind and white-bark birch brightens the forests. The shores are usually crowded with trees or lined with black swamp muck. But ocassionally wide stretches of sand are found and more often tiny beaches at the back of a bay where blue jays stand guard. These days high-powered motorboats fill these sanctuaries with such a roar that a movement is under way to reserve some waters for canoes alone. Viburnum crowds to the water's edge. Shadbush occupies these shores. Alder is commonly found here and also the sheep laurel and chokeberry. The red berry alder is abundant. The twisted-stalk (whose stem pierces the leaf) grows here. The pitcher plant is found in swampy places. But perhaps the most typical plant of this lake country is the sweet gale, whose leaves are aromatic and sometimes cured and brewed into tea.

Canoeists usually make their journeys long after the flowering shrubs have passed their bloom. They never see the witch hazel, which blooms from January to March, its clusters of yellow flowers brightening a cold, bleak land.

The Catskills, first explored by the Dutch, have a name corrupted from *kaats*, meaning "wildcat," and *kill*, meaning "creek." They lie about ten miles west of the Hudson River and near tidewater, their rounded ridges rising over four thousand feet. They are mostly sedimentary rocks—shales, sandstones, conglomerates, and limestones—that were once a sea bottom and were later lifted as a vast plateau that was then carved into valleys and peaks by erosion and stream action. This, the geologists say, explains why the ridges are of uniform height. Then came the glaciers grinding and gouging, leveling some ridges and making others knife-edge, using long arms of ice to produce clefts in the mountains. Once hemlock possessed the Catskills. Its bark was stripped for tanning, the trees left standing. Some of those old hemlock stumps still stand. In the lower reaches oak and jack pine, yellow and white birch, striped maple and white pine, predominate. The eastern edge is an escarpment that rises five hundred feet or more above the valley. Along this escarpment (which has broad limestone ledges for lookouts), blueberries and

This 1800 scene of New Jersey's Falls of the Passaic, a popular place for outings until a power plant at last claimed the site in 1912, was painted by the architect and engineer Benjamin Latrobe, who designed some of the features of the Capitol and White House in Washington.

mountain laurel grow thick. The Hudson is a meandering blue streak to the east and beyond it are the hulk of Mount Greylock and the Berkshires. This escarpment is a place for basking in the sun and daydreaming.

The Catskills play an important part in New York City's water supply. Schoharie Creek once flowed north but, by reason of an eighteen-mile tunnel, it now sends billions of gallons of water south into the Ashokan Reservoir. The Schoharie is a good trout stream. So is the Esopus, which also feeds the Ashokan Reservoir. The streams are lined with willow, cottonwood, and maple. Many contain trout, including the upper reaches of the Delaware and a branch of the Susquehanna.

Slide Mountain (4,204 feet), the highest point in the Catskills, was a favorite haunt of John Burroughs, and today a plaque in his memory marks a cave in a sandstone cliff close to the top where he often slept. Some of James Fenimore Cooper's tales were laid in the Catskills. This was the home of Rip Van Winkle and the locale of many stories by Washington Irving. Today several scenic views have been defiled by vulgar signs advertising the legend of Old Rip, and the Catskills are in many respects more the pride of the motorist than of the hiker or camper. There is no valley unpierced by roads. The canyons are often so narrow that from the trails one can hear the roar of traffic most of the way to the top. Moreover, jeep roads run to fire towers on many peaks; and one who takes a long, circuitous trail to the top often finds that from another side a road comes perilously close to the sacred precincts. The proximity of the range to large centers of population has caused these invasions by the machine. But one who seeks solitude can find it in a few glades and on a few ridges. The distant views of range after range, valley after valley, clove after clove, are as charming now as they were in Washington Irving's day. A great horned owl is worth a night under the stars, and a bed of oxalis or a single cinquefoil is reward enough for a hike to Slide Mountain.

The Poconos of northeastern Pennsylvania are in part a wooded upland lying between eleven hundred feet and two thousand feet, dotted with lakes (many of glacial origin), and abundant with game. The watershed between the Delaware and the Lehigh rivers is an escarpment crossing the Poconos in a northeast-southwest direction and dividing it into two parts: the plateau that makes up the main Poconos with their extensive lake system, and the rolling foothills to the east and south. The southern limit is Kittatiny, a range that runs east into New Jersey. This is the one through which the Delaware River cut its way, forming the Delaware Water Gap. Mount Tammany (1,625 feet) on the New Jersey side of the Gap was named for Tamanend, a chief of the Delaware Indians. Mount Minsi (1,480 feet), named for a tribe of the Delawares, is on the opposite side. Hardwoods are numerous in the Kittatiny, oak predominating. But there are table-mountain pine, spruce, hemlock, white pine, and red cedar, too.

West and south of the Delaware Gap is Wind Gap, which, like several other gaps in the Poconos, was formed by "pirating." That is to say, a stream pouring through it only partially wore it down. Valley streams running parallel to the Kittatiny cut faster into the terrain than did the water flowing across the range through Wind Gap. And so in time the former tapped the latter.

The Kittatiny Range (which the Appalachian Trail follows) and other hills south and east of the escarpment offer excellent hiking. But in this part of the Poconos, as well as in the lake region, there are few places that roads do not reach. Bruce Lake, a newly created state preserve of twenty-three hundred acres, is indeed the only wilderness area. Jeep trails to ridges are common; and here, as in Maryland and Virginia to the south, the ranges are so laced with roads that it is difficult ever to get more than a few miles from a highway.

The Poconos have noble specimens of hemlock, Pennsylvania's state tree. Mountain laurel, the state flower, is a bright mantle on many slopes. Rhododendron grows twenty feet high. Dogwood, as well as purple and white azaleas, is abundant. The basswood reaches southern proportions—one hundred five feet high and twenty feet in circumference. Hickories have grand designs and the tulip tree is patrician. Red maple, black gum, and ironwood, which loggers call "weeds," show magnificent specimens. Even the sassafras reaches the dimensions of a modest tree. Persimmon trees are found at lower elevations. All the birches show off—black, yellow, red, gray, and paper birch. The red birch is river birch, whose feet are usually in wet land and whose reddish-brown bark peels off in papery layers. In swampy places balsam fir, larch, and spruce sometimes form communities. Many species of oak are found in and around the Poconos, the most spectacular being the northern red.

The low, dark-leaved, sweet-scented fern and the dwarf sumac, with webbed leaflets, fill many woods. The Poconos produce a host of berries, it being estimated that about two hundred fifty square miles are covered by huckleberries. Wild grape is as big and as stout as heavy rope. Wild ginger is found on rocky slopes. The marsh marigold brightens swampy places.

Trout and bass cruise the rivers; bass, pickerel, catfish, and muskellunge, the lakes. One of the best trout streams is Kitchen Creek, which during its course has nearly one hundred separate waterfalls, ranging from a few feet in height to over one hundred feet. When logging eliminated the conifers, the hardwoods and understory trees took over. This increase in browse has caused Pennsylvania's deer population to equal or exceed that of any state. Loons are normally found in the Poconos only during migratory seasons. Most birds are protected; but there is an open season year-round on crows, blue jays, starlings, kingfishers, English sparrows, sharp-shinned hawks, Cooper's hawk, goshawk, snowy owl, and great horned owl.

The motorboat and the automobile fill most of the Poconos with a roar. Yet those who seek the solitude of lake shores and swamps will hear the whip-poor-will just before dark and before dawn; and on higher slopes the hermit thrush will sing its haunting melody at dusk.

The Alleghenies and Cumberland, the western flank of the Appalachians, are low-lying hills. They usually show sharp ridges, isolated peaks, and rounded knobs in as wide a variety as the main Appalachians. But where the glaciers plowed the range, as they did in northwest Pennsylvania, the ridges are flat-topped. The Great Valley, which is a trough between them and the Blue Ridge to the east, is rich in limestone and dotted with meadows.

The Alleghenies have no poison ivy or poison oak. Poison sumac, however, grows in swampy places, the plant whose juice turns black on drying. The sourwood tree, which grows to majestic proportions in the southern Appalachians, is here an understory tree. The elderberry flourishes at the lower elevations. Witch hazel, the well-known shrub of New England, becomes almost a tree as it moves south. Wherever it grows, it is known as a "water stick," whose forked stem points downward when it is over a vein of water. In the Alleghenies it shows its long narrow yellow petals in the wintertime. At least six species of oak grow at the lower elevations of these mountains and the Virginia pine is their companion. The beech, along with the yellow birch, marches as far south as West Virginia. Hickories—both pignut and shaggy-bark—dot the lowlands; and a few black walnuts and black locust are found on a day's hike. Western Pennsylvania has the finest stands of black cherry in the nation. But the Cumberland Mountains—the southernmost reaches of the Alleghenies—have few hardwoods save oak and hickory.

The top geological layer is sandstone. In the northern reaches of the range the sandstone is thin. But where it is thick, coal is found. Since the coal is close to the surface, strip mining has been used. Their spoil banks produce acids that kill life in the creeks and destroy all vegetation. On the average, two acres of every square mile of this region consist of strip pits.

Each area of the Alleghenies on close inspection reveals surprises. West Virginia has twenty different kinds of violets, over twenty species of blackberries, and eight species of dogwood. While red spruce is usually associated with high altitudes, in the Monongahela National Forest in West Virginia one cove has a virgin stand of trees over one hundred feet high and nearly three feet in diameter. In the Cumberland National Forest shortleaf pine grows almost as well as it does in the southern coastal areas. Both in West Virginia and Pennsylvania isolated stands of the balsam fir can be found in a few low swampy places. In West Virginia above thirty-five hundred feet one finds over fifty flowers usually associated with the arctic. One is a purple orchid known as *Listera cordata*.

The rivers of the Alleghenies once ran north to the St. Lawrence. But the glaciers diverted the flow with the result that most now drain to the west. Some, though draining the Alleghenies, have cut their way through the Blue Ridge to the east and flow into the Atlantic. These include the Potomac, James, and Roanoke.

Wind and water have produced in the sandstone layer of the Alleghenies spectacular rock arches. There are ten in or near the Cumberland National Forest in Kentucky. A natural bridge near Slade, Kentucky, and another near Luray, Virginia, are unique. Parts of the Alleghenies—particularly the Cumberland area of Kentucky—show rimrock of sandstone that is unique, with exposed rims five hundred feet high.

Kentucky's great Mammoth Cave, once mined for saltpeter and now a national park, is one of numerous caves in the Alleghenies. While some are found in the sandstone layer and an occasional one in the shale, most caves are in the limestone where that rock has outcropped. They were created by carbon dioxide combining with water to produce carbonic acid, which over thousands of years dissolved the underlying limestone to form passages that average from five to ten feet high and from two to four feet wide. Some have heights up to one hundred feet and widths up to twenty feet and at times are seven thousand feet long, being made up from a maze of tunnels. They often have several rooms and stalactites and stalagmites and delicately carved columns and friezes.

The Appalachians of Georgia, North Carolina, Virginia, and Tennessee are in many respects the most unique. The lower slopes have pitch pine and Virginia pine and occasionally the five-needle white pine. The two-needle table-mountain pine—whose limbs are so elastic they can be tied into knots but not broken by hand—usually possesses wind-blown ridges. These lower pine-oak forests have red maple and black gum. Sassafras, one of the

earliest to show buds in spring, grows there. So does the shagbark hickory—for whose toughness Andrew Jackson was named "Old Hickory." Flowering dogwood is common; the flame azalea—with both red and yellow flowers from the same root—brightens the woods in April. Laurel grows twenty feet high and shows pinkish-white. The sourwood tree (especially in both Carolina and Tennessee) sends bees into a frenzy in June, and its lemon-colored honey, which in point of time comes after poplar honey and basswood honey, is the choicest of all.

The places of greatest wonder are the coves, above the pine-oak forests, where the hardwoods grow. They do not make up into a continuous belt but are scattered throughout the twenty-five-hundred to four-thousand-foot zone.

Eastern hemlock is commonly found among the hardwoods, especially on northern slopes. This tree with flat needles that are silver underneath loves shade and takes hold where other trees are thick and the humus is rich. It will tower to great heights, its trunk being free of branches for sixty feet or more. Its broad spread covers lesser trees and creates a shade that is almost free of any streak of sunshine.

Some coves have groves of silver bells—the tree that is usually called peawood and that to many is the monarch of the hardwoods. This tree, whose flowers are silver bells two inches long, has reached one hundred feet in height and four feet in diameter in the Smokies of Tennessee.

The wild black cherry in a hardwood cove may reach one hundred feet to the sky. Some hardwood coves have sugar maples as stately as any in New England. The sweet buckeye has dark-brown seeds with a scar like a deer's eye. They are considered to be lucky pieces if rubbed by the thumb to a bright polish.

A search will disclose a white ash that has lived for three hundred years and grown one hundred seventy-five feet high and produced a trunk five feet through. It shows bronze and mauve in the fall.

The tulip tree, known locally as the "popple," has reached a height of one hundred seventy-five feet and a diameter of seven feet. The white oak and the northern red oak are cove hardwoods. The slightly aromatic yellow birch is scattered throughout these coves. The cherry birch, which has a mahogany-red bark similar to the black cherry, gives off a distinct wintergreen odor. In the old days wintergreen was indeed obtained from it; and some used to tap it, much in the manner of sugar maple, mix its sap with corn, and produce in time the famous "birch beer" of the mountains.

A catalogue of the understory trees and shrubs would exceed two hundred varieties. At least three dozen are browse for deer, including the strawberry bush, button-bush, beauty-berry, dogwood, sweet spice, and greenbrier, apart from some already mentioned. Mosses, lichens, and ferns are thick. The leaf-fall averages about two tons per acre per year. The humus is thick, the earthworms abundant, the mice, shrews, and moles active.

The trees in a cove of hardwoods are so high and their branches so interlocked that they keep out the sun's heat, though they let through some streaks of light. The over-all effect is of a cathedral pervaded by a soft emerald light.

These coves are prolific lumber producers. They can be cut and yet bear few scars from the cutting. Young trees come in fast and the moisture is so great that the slashings are absorbed by the earth in a few years.

The coves that are contained in national parks are locked up for all time. Some coves in national forests and in state parks are protected by regulations against cutting. These are known as wilderness or scenic areas; and they are increasing in number, though each is small in acreage and over-all they comprise only a small percentage of the southern Appalachians.

Chestnuts flourished in the coves until the Asian blight arrived. The roots are still alive and send up shoots that may reach fifteen feet or more before the blight kills them. Ancient chestnut trees stand like ghosts, but are still cut for lumber and often for fuel. In some areas the chestnut made up the climax forest. Wherever it grew its departure was a great loss. With its passing the scarlet oak and hickory often took over; and since they are not merchantable timber, efforts are being made to introduce the white pine. White pine is indeed traditionally mixed with oak, red maple, and yellow poplar. On the lower ridges of the Blue Ridge where the soil is moist, the high rainfall of Virginia and North Carolina favors their growth. These white pine–hardwood ridges, however, are usually in the two-thousand-foot zone, considerably lower than the spruce-fir forests of the ridges

It is above five thousand feet that the spruce-fir forests once thrived, though they are less common today. The spruce is red spruce, with four-cornered needles. The fir is southern balsam, whose needles lie flat. Their fragrance permeates a camp. These spruce-fir forests are dark, the boughs interlocking overhead and cutting out most of the direct sunshine. In this dark, damp shade, oyster mushrooms form tiny shelves on down logs; ferns and mosses are thick; lichens hang like beards from the balsam fir. The spruce-fir zone has some yellow birch and mountain ash with the high-bush blueberry and the huckleberry in open places. The white or great rhododendron is usually found under thirty-eight hundred feet; but it may appear in an open field near a spruce-fir forest. The dwarf or Carolina rhododendron is more common to the high country, as is the laurel, sometimes known as the calico bush or mountain ivy. On some high open slopes in the Smokies it forms long swaths and in July its urn-shaped pinkish-white flowers brighten an entire mountainside. These long swaths of laurel are known as laurel "slicks" by local people and "heath balds" by the botanists. Heath balds customarily have not only laurel but three other members of the heath family—rhododendron, blueberry, and minniebush. The Smokies are famous for a different kind of bald—large open fields on the ridges. They were there when the white settlers arrived near the beginning of the nineteenth century, and were used for grazing.

The Virginia deer find shelter in the open slopes below the ridges, which have been possessed by rhododendron and laurel, by blueberries and mountain ash. Here too are chimney swifts and warblers. The gray fox and bobcat are seldom seen, but their footprints are common. Bears follow the berries to the top. The barred owl is a nocturnal companion. The winter wren, the red-breasted nuthatch, robins, and the vireo accompany the summer hiker. Ruffed grouse go out with a roar at the trail's side.

Some areas are noted for salamanders, and they are apt to be in the trails during a spring or summer rain. There are dozens of species of snails; and there are caterpillars that give off an almond odor.

The streams of the southern Appalachians are gems. They are clear and cold. They pour musically over dark ledges. The bottoms are black, the water is shaded; there are dozens of pools in a one-mile stretch. One fishes with a short line and walks like a bear if he follows the bank.

Our other mountains have their own peculiar distinction and grandeur. But none is so rich and diverse in botanical wonders as the Appalachians. No other welcomes both the spring and the fall with such joyous colors.

The Maine Wilds

Not so far from the cities and suburbs that mottle the coast from Washington to Boston are some of the deepest woods still left to the East —an unbuilt region almost as wild looking in parts as it was in 1775 when Benedict Arnold and some 1,100 Americans struggled through it to reach Canada and attack Quebec. The deer and moose still drink

deeply from the lakes, and the loudest sound is still the cry of the loon across the water at night. Climbing Katahdin, or canoeing across a salmon-filled lake or down the white-water Allagash River, over Devil's Elbow and Twin Brook rapids, visitors find a oneness with nature that the Indian and French-speaking guides take for granted.

61

White Mountain Outings

Emerald Pool—favorite of artists

That there was a district in New England containing mountain scenery superior to much that is yearly crowded by tourists in Europe, that this is to be reached with ease by railways and stagecoaches, and that it is dotted with huge hotels, almost as thickly as they lie in Switzerland, I had no idea. Much of this scenery, I say, is superior to the famed and classic lands of Europe." So wrote the English novelist Anthony Trollope of New Hampshire's White Mountains in 1861.

Trollope was one of a stream of celebrated visitors, European as well as American, who discovered New England's Switzerland in the 1850's and 1860's. Great, rambling, white-framed hotels, with columned porticoes and balconies that looked out on the mountains and notches, catered to vacationers like Mrs. Abraham Lincoln, Cornelius Vanderbilt, and P. T. Barnum. The always-inventive showman one summer amused guests at the Profile House (seen in one of the vintage stereopticon slides at the right) by dressing the hotel employees as animals and staging a circus. But Barnum, as usual, was gilding a lily: the White Mountains, offering a genteel return to nature, needed no supporting acts. For diversion, one could tramp up Mount Washington, scramble down Tuckerman Ravine, enjoy the solitude of a clear, cool lake, or simply sit and breathe the pure mountain air.

Writers and artists, too, were inspired. John Greenleaf Whittier and William Dean Howells both spent summers there. But it was Nathaniel Hawthorne, above all others, who made famous for generations of Americans what he called "those old crystal hills." Even today, his Old Man of the Mountains, brooding above the cliffs and woods of Franconia Notch, is to many people *the* continuing symbol of the White Mountains.

A stop at Halfway House on Mount Washington

Profile House at Franconia Notch

Bustled boaters at Echo Lake

The Glen House and the Presidential peaks

The lawns at Crawford House

The Old Man of the Mountains

Tuckerman Ravine's Snow Arch

Posing at Flume Brook

The Presidential Range

In 1642 an intrepid New Englander named Darby Field made his way inland to the White Mountains and scaled the "white hill" (Mount Washington). Ever since then the range has lured hikers braced for adventure and breath-taking views. The scenery from the ridges is outstanding, but so are the bald summits themselves. The upper portion of Mount Washington, with sixty-three species of arctic plants, is a true outpost of the Far North. Winters are severe, and even in summer sharp changes in weather pose hazards for hikers. But the heights reward with "a sense of the sublime," though some fear the spoiling effect of plans for future "development," including ski tows, night floodlighting, and more trams like the ninety-four-year-old cog railway, seen below chugging up the slope of Mount Washington.

A winter atop Mount Washington, site of a weather station, can rival the harshness of the polar regions.

Route of Empire

The jeweled waters of Lake Champlain, hemmed by Vermont's Green Mountains and New York's Adirondacks, have often echoed with the sound of musket and cannon fire. As a principal link in the easiest route between the St. Lawrence River and lower New York State, the lake has known the canoes of Indian war parties and the warships and transports of British, French, and American forces.

Samuel de Champlain first explored its "handsome islands" and "very fine woods and meadows" in 1609, and at the same time helped the Hurons by using guns against their Iroquois enemies. For two hundred years after that the lake was a battleground. Through colonial wars, the Revolution, and the War of 1812, men fought for possession of the water highway. Only after 1815 did the wooded shores know a lasting peace.

Sir Joshua Reynolds' painting of Lord Jeffery Amherst

The wilderness site of Fort Ticonderoga, commanding the southern end of Lake Champlain, is seen at the left in a water color made during one of the bastion's historic moments. On his way to help seize Canada during the French and Indian War in 1759, Major General Jeffery Amherst invested the fort, which the French finally blew up and abandoned on July 26. The view (complete with an Indian and a porcupine) was painted by Thomas Davies, a British officer, and shows Amherst's positions.

Ticonderoga, which its French builders in 1756 named Fort Carillon (for the bell-like sound of a nearby falls), had a varied and colorful history. But no event connected with the redoubt had greater drama than that of May 10, 1775, when Ethan Allen and his Green Mountain Boys appeared at the fort at dawn and "in the name of the great Jehovah, and the Continental Congress," forced its surrender without a fight.

67

Winslow Homer in the Adirondacks

Life was beautiful, rugged, and often lonely in the great woods of the Adirondacks. From 1870 until shortly before his death in 1910, the American artist Winslow Homer spent many summers working and fishing in this northern New York wilderness. "He did not go in much for expensive or elaborate tackle, but he usually caught the biggest fish," said one of his companions. Part of Homer's legacy—paintings of this magnificent country, which still provides grandeur and solitude—is shown on these pages.

OLD FRIENDS, *water color, 1894*

INDIAN VILLAGE, ADIRONDACKS, *water color, 1894*

ADIRONDACK LAKE, *oil, 1870*

SONJA BULLATY

Appalachian Autumn

As summer recedes and the days of the year grow colder, a wave of color sweeps down the 2000-mile-long range of eastern forests, bringing a glory to the countryside that makes one almost willing to accept the approach of winter. The hardwoods of northern New England reach their peak of brilliance about the end of September; by mid-October the paintbrush has begun to make its mark in the Middle Atlantic States, and until well into November trees are ablaze all the way down the Appalachians to Georgia. A glorious sight wherever viewed, fall in the East is a wondrous drama.

York State Romantics

The "lonely glens" of New York's woodlands, evoking a sense of melancholy and a return to the past, were popular settings for works by nineteenth-century romantic artists and writers. Regions like the Finger Lakes and the Catskills inspired Cooper and Irving, as well as a school of Hudson River painters. The brooding Last of the Mohicans (above) by Thomas Cole typified their imaginative works.

The Virginia Naturalist

W̲hat a field have we at our doors . . . !" Thomas Jefferson once wrote to a friend in Paris. Eagerly interested in every aspect of his country's wildlife, Jefferson sent the French naturalist the Comte de Buffon, the bones and skin of a moose and the horns of an elk and a deer, as examples of "species not existing in Europe."

Among Jefferson's many interests, his delight in the world of nature ranked high. In his *Notes on the State of Virginia,* published in 1784, he described many of his state's natural beauties, such as the fifty-foot-high "cascade," Dark Hollow Falls (right), which is now a part of Shenandoah National Park. But the "most sublime of nature's works," he wrote, was a natural bridge that rises two hundred fifteen feet over Cedar Creek, some twenty-five miles from Lynchburg, and which is shown behind him in the painting at left, done by Caleb Boyle about 1800. Jefferson said the view from below was "delightful. . . . So beautiful an arch, so elevated, so light, and springing as it were up to heaven!"

Today the beauty of the arch that so thrilled Jefferson is difficult to detect; colored lights, an antique automobile collection, and other tourist attractions have tarnished the sublime.

ROBERT B. HOLLAND

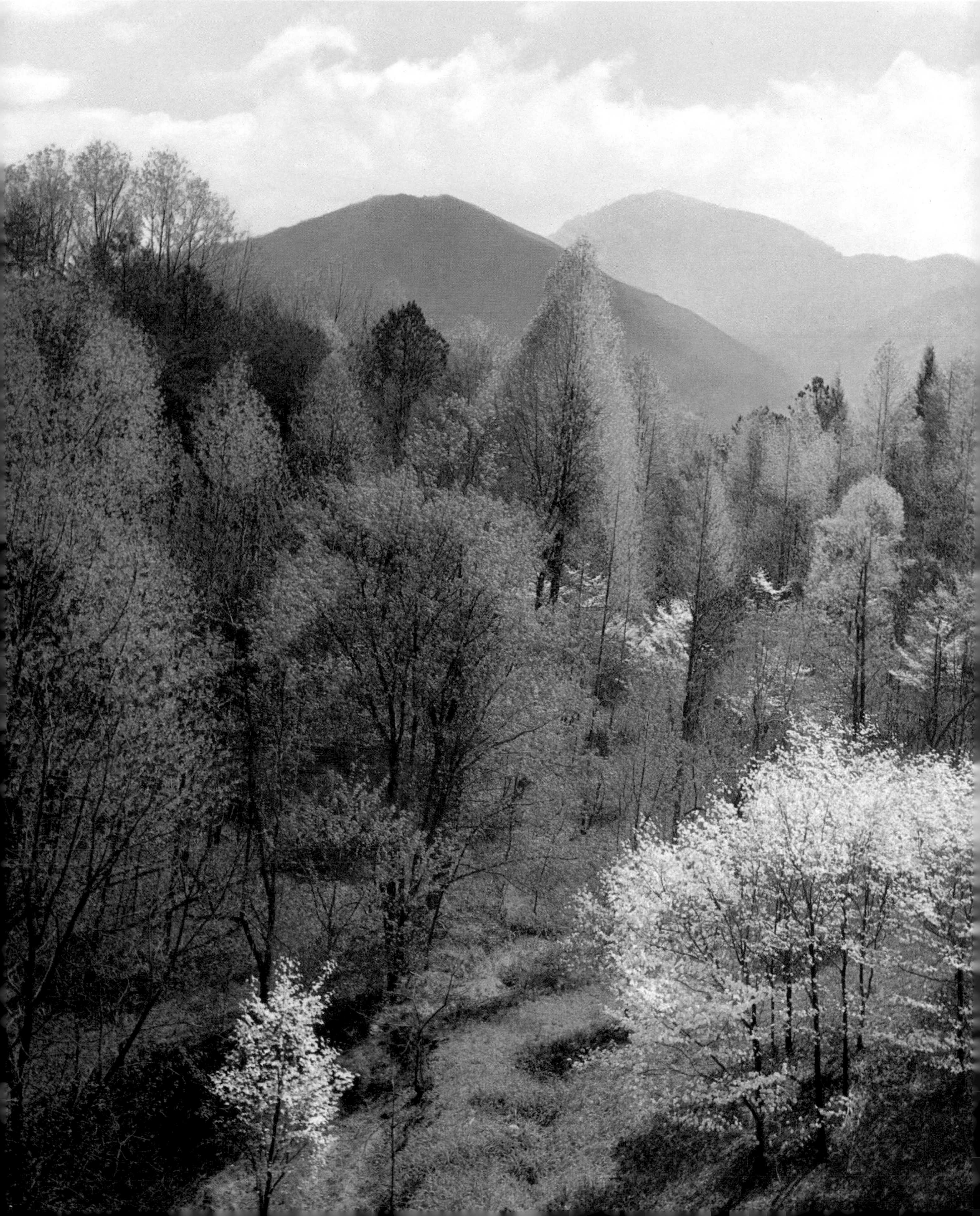

Cherokee Highlands

Rising beyond these flowering spring dogwoods are the Great Smoky Mountains, highest in the Appalachian chain. The first white men to invade this "massive and high citadel" were traders who came over the ridges from the coast to barter with the Cherokee Indians. It was the Cherokees who gave the region its name, calling the bluish haze that hovers in the valleys the "Great Smoke." For many years the Indians lived in harmony with their mountain home: rivers were sacred paths to the afterlife; Thunder was a friendly, if rambunctious, man who roamed the hills in summer; animals were people too (the Uncle Remus stories stem from Cherokee country).

During the westward migration of the early nineteenth century, white settlers poured over the southern Appalachians in search of new homes, and the expansion led to President Jackson's Indian Removal bill of 1830. Eight years later the Cherokees were forced to leave their homeland and embark on a "trail of tears" to Oklahoma—though a small number of them managed to remain behind, hidden in the mountains, where their descendants still dwell.

Relatively few whites ever settled in the Smokies, and the region lost little of its original beauty. In 1926 the Great Smoky Mountains National Park was created. Today the former home of the Cherokees, still an unspoiled mountain area of magnificent hardwood forests, flowering shrubs, and superb views, is one of the nation's most popular parks.

GREAT SMOKY MOUNTAINS
NATIONAL PARK

KNOXVILLE

RT U.S. 441

Sevierville

*LITTLE
PIGEON RIVER*

RT U.S. 411

RT U.S. 411

RT U.S. 441

Wildwood

GATLINBURG

PARK
HEADQUARTERS

Cove
Mtn

SUGARLAN
VISITOR CEN

RT 73

Maryville

Elkmont

Townsend

Tremont

CHILHOWEE MTN

LITTLE   RIVER

Cerulean
Knob

*FOOTHILLS
← PARKWAY*

Look
Rock

Hatcher –
Mtn

CADES COVE

*CADES
COVE*

Gregory
Bald

Happy
Valley

Parson
Bald –

Mt
Lanier –

Parson
High Top

Dalton
Gap

*Abrams
Creek*

Bunker –
Hill

*Panther
Creek*

Deals Gap

RT U.S 129

TENNESSEE

*LITTLE
TENNESSEE
RIVER*

*NORTH
CAROLIN*

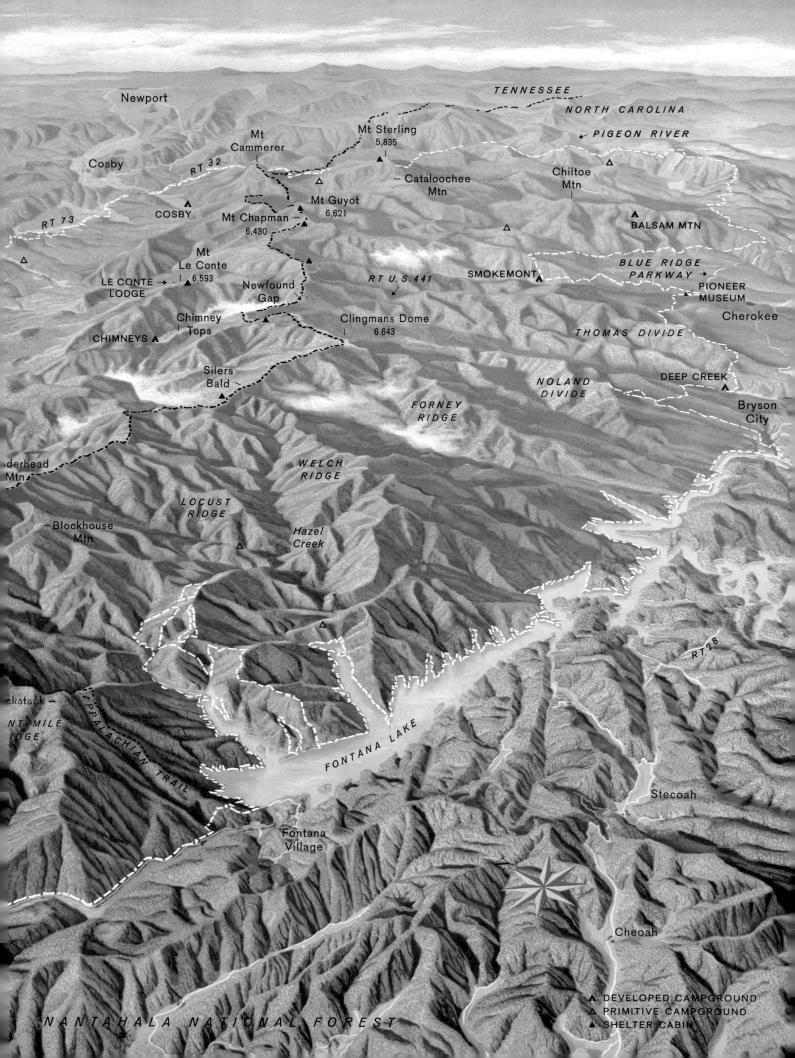

Newport

TENNESSEE

NORTH CAROLINA

PIGEON RIVER

Cosby

Mt Sterling
5,835

Mt Cammerer

RT 32

Chiltoe
Mtn

Cataloochee
Mtn

COSBY

RT 73

Mt Guyot
6,621

BALSAM MTN

Mt Chapman
6,430

RT 77

Mt
Le Conte
6,593

LE CONTE
LODGE

RT U.S. 441

SMOKEMONT

BLUE RIDGE
PARKWAY →

PIONEER
MUSEUM

Newfound
Gap

Cherokee

Chimney
Tops

Clingmans Dome
6,643

THOMAS DIVIDE

CHIMNEYS

NOLAND
DIVIDE

DEEP CREEK

Silers
Bald

FORNEY
RIDGE

Bryson
City

derhead
Mtn

WELCH
RIDGE

LOCUST
RIDGE

Blockhouse
Mtn

Hazel
Creek

RT 28

ckstack

APPALACHIAN TRAIL

NTYMILE
IDGE

Stecoah

FONTANA LAKE

Fontana
Village

Cheoah

NANTAHALA NATIONAL FOREST

▲ DEVELOPED CAMPGROUND
△ PRIMITIVE CAMPGROUND
| SHELTER CABIN

Botanists' Paradise

William Bartram, the naturalist who toured the Southeast, also visited the Great Smokies, and in 1778 he wrote a vivid account of the flora of the mountains. Ever since then, the region has been regarded as one of the world's richest botanical gardens.

Counting mosses, ferns, and fungi (like the mushrooms at right), there are nearly four thousand varieties of plant life—including, from valleys to peaks, almost every wild flower known in the United States. At the left is the flame azalea, which in May and June, Bartram noted, blooms "in such incredible profusion [on] the hill sides, that suddenly . . . we are alarmed with the apprehension of the hill being set on fire." But the Smokies are beautiful in winter too. Then the "smoke" clings to the evergreen forest on the peaks; and ice, taking the place of the colors of spring, rimes the branches of the bare trees on the slopes, creating miracles of delicate design (upper right).

Over the Mountains

We start early and turn out of the wagon Road to go across the mountains. . . . Come to a turable mountain that tired us all almost to death to git over it and we lodge this night . . . under a granite mountain and Roast a fine fat turkey for our suppers . . ." The diary of William Calk, who in 1775 followed Daniel Boone's "Trace" to central Kentucky, described the experiences of many pioneers who went through gaps in the Appalachians to find freedom in the wilderness. Some stayed in the mountains, cleared corn patches and raised cabins "kivered with bark"—and their descendants lived there for generations in isolation. The 1901 photograph at the right shows a venerable homestead tucked in the wooded foothills of the southern Appalachians.

Daniel Boone, after Chester Harding's 1819 portrait

— And Now There Are None

When the Scottish ornithologist Alexander Wilson first encountered a flock of passenger pigeons in 1810, he thought the "loud rushing roar, succeeded by instant darkness," was a tornado. Later he carefully estimated a flock he saw in Kentucky, and came up with the figure of 2,230,272,000 pigeons! Once upon a time the forests of the East were blanketed with immense flocks of these communal birds. But what God wrought, man could destroy. Shooting, poling, even netting the birds, were popular sports. (The netting technique gave rise to the term stool pigeon, a blinded bird whose cries brought the flocks to earth.) By various methods of slaughter, including scatter-shooting and working with decoys from blinds, as seen in the prints at right, Americans by 1914 had achieved the impossible: a species of bird that at its peak numbered some five billion in the United States, had been reduced to zero.

Gifford Pinchot

Birthplace of Forestry

Today the Pisgah National Forest in North Carolina is a delight to the lover of deep woods. Looking Glass Rock (right)— so-named because in wet weather it glistens like a great mirror— offers from its bare height a majestic view of wooded valleys and peaks. But before the advent in 1891 of pioneer American forester Gifford Pinchot, the area was in desperate condition. Many trees were diseased, and farmers had burned great patches for pasture. Pinchot, just returned from training in Europe, began his career here. Employing selective cutting and other new methods, he brought back the yellow poplar and other species that were nearly gone. His techniques rebuilt Pisgah and have served ever since as a model for American forestry.

III

THE SOUTHERN LOWLANDS

By JAN DE HARTOG

Graceful soarers of the Everglades—pink-plumaged
roseate spoonbills—find sanctuary in the matted
tangles of mangrove trees that fringe Florida Bay.

Their very name casts a spell. Say it, slowly, eyes closed: "Everglades." Instantly there will be an image, evoked as at the touch of a magic wand, of . . . what? A cluster of palms, mirrored in the crystalline surface of a lake? Ancient oak trees, with shrouds of Spanish moss gently swaying in the wind? A maze of small waterways, bordered by tall reeds? The dark caverns of a primeval cypress swamp?

The secret of the Everglades, as far as man will ever be able to fathom it, is that they seem to adapt their image to each individual's expectation of what he is about to see. It is a land of nothing, a dream world, where a wanderer who loses his way along the highroad of time and reality, will find himself confronted with a world-large mirror, shrouded in mist, haunted by ghostly birds silently winging upside down among the ghosts of fish in the cloudless depth of a Spirit Lake.

The early Spanish conquistadors were the first men of our era to record their impressions of this world that is nothing, the way a mirror is nothing. The objective picture of reality showed a plain of sawgrass, reaching from the lake in the north to the ten thousand islands in the south, a vast marsh, sparsely dotted with small hammocks of palm, oak, and palmetto shrub, a featureless land underneath a pale-green sky, where faceless clouds in endless pageant slowly sailed from horizon to horizon—a land of utter indifference toward the homunculus gazing at the emptiness of its enigma, with the sun hot on the steel of his armor, and his sweat-soaked horse stirring restlessly beneath him, and no sound to disturb the silence of eternity but the creaking of his saddle and the swish of his horse's tail, swatting the hornets swarming from the swamp. No picture of the mentality of those early Spanish explorers, however conscientiously reconstructed from the facts of history, can convey as true and haunting an image of their souls as their description of the Everglades. The chroniclers of those first expeditions describe a wilderness peopled with giants, haunted by monsters, a landscape of craggy rocks and thundering cataracts, of forests teeming with parrots and birds of paradise, and of a lake, so mysterious in its hazy, luminous stillness that they gave it the name "Laguna del Espiritu Santo"—Lake of the Holy Ghost. But the rocks, the waterfalls, the opulent foliage of imaginary trees, studded with the multicolored blossoms of roosting cockatoos, the sea serpents in the Lake of the Holy Ghost, whose surreptitious splashings and soul-chilling sighs the chroniclers recorded having heard at dead of night as they lay awake, wide-eyed in the wilderness, gazing at the stars —this whole fantastic world of spirits and monsters, faith and superstition, dreams of love and acts of cruelty, was

but the reflection of the soul of the conquistador himself, discerned, as in a glass darkly, when, on his quest for the Unicorn and the gold of the Incas, he reached the Everglades, Sea of Grass, mirror of man's soul.

Each generation that followed sent its representatives, and all of them came back with a different image, a different truth. As recently as ninety years ago, an expedition penetrating the Everglades from the north after crossing the great lake now called Lake Okeechobee, reported rocks and waterfalls, impenetrable forests and ghostly swamps peopled with beasts that were nowhere else to be found. Yet the incorruptible eye of objectivity would have recorded the same image, unchanged after a mere three centuries: a plain of grass, a pale-green sky, and silence.

The mirror that fleetingly reflected the images of the passing generations of man bears a few scratches, made by those who refused to acquiesce in the spell of evanescence the world-large looking glass threw over them. Go-getting Yankees, rugged individualists, tried to carve canals into the heart of the great loneliness: straight ditches, now overgrown with weeds and choked with hyacinths, which peter out after a few miles in the endlessness of eternity. Apart from those ditches there may be found here and there, utterly lost in the solitude of the great swamp, a caved-in roof, a rusty windmill, the skeleton of a dredger, foundered in the sea of grass. They are initials, meaningless now, etched in the glass by forgotten men in a defiant effort to wrench some immortality from the impersonal mirror reflecting their fading faces.

The mirror has not changed. The Everglades are still the same as when the first explorer set eyes on them. Yet, during this twentieth century, man with the aid of a newly acquired technology has managed to make some inroads into the great solitude. In 1923 the first party of surveyors crossed the Everglades from Fort Myers to Miami, a hazardous trek through terra incognita which was hailed in the newspapers of both coasts as a major achievement. Five years later the road they had prospected was opened.

Route 41, the Tamiami Trail, represents a triumph of man's ingenuity, doggedness, and undaunted optimism in the face of incredible odds. First, a canal had to be dredged through the swamp in order to reach the bedrock on which the road could rest. Then teams of bullocks dragged primitive sleighs laden with rocks to the head of the road. Many of them foundered, sank in the mud, vanished in quicksands; men waded up to their necks in poisonous marsh and gnat-infested ponds. When finally the road was completed, it had cost many human lives. Few of the bored, the anxious, the hurried, and the exuberant who rush or trundle along the dead-straight highway in their cars, give

a thought to those men and their triumph. Where once the first conquistador reined in his horse, to stop and gaze at the boundless plain at the edge of the world, now families stop to picnic; where once the chroniclers of that first expedition saw monsters, forests, chasms, and waterfalls, a red and silver billboard reads: "Hi, y'all! Stop at Snorty's Barbecue Pit, and Eat Like Helen B. Happy!"

But two steps away from the shoulders of the road everything is unchanged from what it was at the dawn of time. The mirror that reflected the souls of Spaniard, Frenchman, Briton, Yankee, and Seminole still throws its spell over anyone who wanders guilelessly into the great loneliness. He will lose his way among the clouds in the grass, the fish in the sky, the ghostly birds winging upside down below the surface of a Spirit Lake. The Everglades, like a legendary region out of the sagas of mankind, play havoc with the senses. No one who is not an experienced explorer, or a marshlander by birth, should venture into them without a guide; and no guide will enter the glades without informing someone at his point of departure where he intends to go and when he intends to return.

But this ancient world of legend and mirage, still as remote from reality as Erewhon, is slowly shrinking. The drive by swamp-buggy from, say, Clewiston to the frontier of the Everglades, is gradually getting longer. When I first went there with my guide, five years ago, it took us ten minutes to reach the end of the road and head out,

rolling, splashing, and pitching, into the infinity of the sea of grass; now it takes half an hour. Tomato fields, nurseries, rice fields, have encroached upon the great loneliness. The drive to the frontier will get longer and longer every day; the Everglades are bound to fall, but not under the onslaught of draglines, bulldozers, dredgers, and gigantic levelers, for that kind of attack the great swamp has defeated before. They will, like the other territories that went before, be conquered in the end by the unsung tenderness of anonymous young families, settling precariously on the edge of the wilderness, outposts of humanity in the fear-ridden world of the Pleistocene age. You can see them now: small, flimsy houses at the far end of car tracks, erected tentatively on the banks of creeks and sloughs. Young mothers hang out their laundry in the wind that has caressed three hundred miles of lonely grass before caressing their hair; children lie on their stomachs on homemade docks, peering over the edge to stare at their reflections in a mirror of water that has reflected nothing but clouds since the third day of creation. The next time you come, the car tracks have vanished and you see the children walk down a newly asphalted road, from the world of dreams and childhood now annexed by civilization toward a little shelter at the crossroads, brightly painted landmark in what yesterday was nothing: a new stop for the school bus, true conqueror of the frontier.

Lake Okeechobee, which inspired the first Spaniards to

christen it with the awesome Name of the Holy Ghost, has so far remained unchanged, despite the new levees on its southern shore. It is unlike any other lake I know: of an infinite misty stillness, its hazy horizon a luminous white, its motionless surface mirroring the majesty of mountainous clouds. Few boats cross it; a fisherman or two, a solitary yacht suspended for a few hours above the horizon like a mirage. Only once a year man challenges the Spirit of the lake by charging at it in fifteen hundred outboards: the Kissimmee Boatacade, snarling from north to south at top speed with an ear-splitting roar that makes whole colonies of roosting egrets and sand-hill cranes take off in clouds of terror. Within minutes after their triumphant passage the lake again lies undisturbed in its hazy hue of white and silver, ruffled only occasionally by the fury of a line squall, or the swirling dervish of a water spout, and, once in a man's lifetime, transformed into a cauldron of destruction by a hurricane. Those who have seen a hurricane pass across Lake Okeechobee tell tales of unimaginable horror, in which water turns into sky and sky into earth and the whole of Creation seems to disintegrate in a cosmic catastrophe. Maybe that is the secret of the mysterious awe Lake Okeechobee inspires: no generation of men is allowed to forget that, once upon their lifetime, this shimmering sheet of silver is sucked bodily into the sky, to come thundering down in a colossal avalanche of solid water, as if—so one survivor described it, after the 1928 hurricane that killed some two thousand people—the moon came crashing into the earth.

Compared to the Everglades and the lake, the rest of Florida seems a garden of harmless, Arcadian beauty. North of Lake Okeechobee, the gentle, bucolic Kissimmee Plain dresses itself in gold every summer, as the black-eyed Susans cover its fertile ground with a solid cloak of yellow flowers as far as the eye can reach. Farther north, beyond a string of little lakes bearing reassuring names like "Lake Placid," "Lake Josephine," and "Lake June in Winter," lies, among the orange groves, the first of the Florida state parks of the interior: Highlands Hammock. Centuries-old live oak trees, garlanded with orchids and air plants, little ponds dressed with ferns, reeds, water lilies, hyacinths—no wonder this is the home of Florida's chief botanist, Miss Carol Beck, a woman of encyclopedic knowledge, impressive determination, and a secret understanding with the alligators that abound in her magic garden and all of whom she knows by name, on condition they are more than three days old. For then they start to join their elders in a greedy scramble toward the edge of pond or swamp as soon as they hear the sound of Miss Beck's jeep approach in the distance; those who are on

time are rewarded, incongruously, with a marshmallow; latecomers are reprimanded sternly and forgo their treat. Miss Beck's alligators, rushing toward her in delighted droves made up of all ages and sizes, fill the astounded spectator with an elusive elation, as if he were granted a glimpse of that Utopian world where the lion and the lamb shall lie together and a child shall lead them.

The heart of Florida, which is the region around the Ocala National Forest, is a woodland of romantic lushness and intimate beauty. It abounds in winding creeks, secret ponds, and hidden springs of such clarity that the water itself becomes invisible and the surrounding trees and their reflections are intertwined in a single image of surrealist beauty. It is a spot of such delicate and intimate loveliness that there can be no doubt as to its history: this must have been a trysting place of countless young couples down the ages of man. Until recently a steamboat from Jacksonville made regular trips up the St. Johns River to Welaka, and from there up the Oklawaha River to Silver Springs. It was a popular trip with honeymoon couples, as popular as it must have been with the Calusa Indians and their mysterious predecessors, whose stone ornaments and arrowheads are still found on the banks of Florida's many rivers.

These rivers all seem alike at first, winding their way, through mangrove marsh and cypress swamp, past oak bluffs and hammocks grown with cabbage palm, into the forest. Yet they each have a personality of their own. In order to perceive this, you must take your time; the ideal way of seeing them is by canoe, letting yourself drift downstream, in silence.

One that seems to sum up their haunting beauty, within a few miles of its course, is the Withlacoochee. Its approaches, coming from the Gulf of Mexico, are tortuous. The entrance channel winds its way among shoals, rocks, and spoil banks; a multitude of spidery black and red markers enhances its mazelike aspect. At last it straightens out and leads along the shore of a narrow island toward the river's mouth. The moment you have passed this island a bay opens up in front of you, the like of which you have never seen, except in your imagination as a child when you first read about the foreign splendor of faraway shores. The water is of a light, translucent blue, shading to green around the dazzling white of the beaches of a score of little islands, each in its own shell of mother-of-pearl. The islands, dotted with tall palms sharply outlined against the sky, are each the perfect image of a romantic, uninhabited island, waiting for its Robinson Crusoe, aged twelve.

As your boat slowly rounds the first bend of the river proper, you will see, on your right, the ghost town of

Port Inglis, a bustling harbor mysteriously deserted, almost vanished by now among the reeds and the mangroves of the marshland. To the left, the old road from Yankeetown ends in the water; two dolphins are the remnants of what was once a ferry dock. Close to the point lies a small houseboat tied up among the trees and on it, a lonely man bewitched by the Withlacoochee.

For this is a truly bewitching river. The moment you round the next bend, you will fall under its spell. Suddenly, the marshland vanishes, and the river seems to be bordered by deserted parks. There are lawns run wild, orchards turned back to jungle, tree-lined drives overgrown with weeds. Magnificent old cypress trees, their massive trunks gray and white like weathered marble, stand in isolated majesty on the river's edge, their branches draped with Spanish moss; and beyond them lie the neglected lawns, the parklike squares of oak trees that will make you look for the ruins of old plantation houses, which are not there. For this is primeval country, where nature in a playful quirk fashioned deserted parks and gardens full of the nostalgic memory of men, long before the first man was born. Your boat, slowly gliding, rounds the next bend, and again the landscape changes. Now there is a forest, dense, luxuriant, of towering trees choked with vines and creepers, aflame with the fiery flowers of air plant and orchid. From its thicket, teeming with chirping, chortling, invisible life, a kingfisher flashes down to the water in a breath-taking lunge and streaks back into the jungle, silver and blue; and you realize that this is not just a boat trip on a river, but a journey through time, back to the days when the earth was young and yearning for the fulfillment of immortal longings. Then, suddenly: a dock of moss-grown pilings, the dark presence of a house hidden among the trees, and you are in the seventeenth century. It is an inn, called "Isaac Walton Lodge," and its name is appropriately chosen. For over this river, over all the rivers, lakes, and ponds of this romantic land, hovers the presence of the Compleat Angler. It is the land where a father's most eagerly awaited words are, "All right, son, let's go fishing."

Toward the north, Florida changes: a slow, almost imperceptible transition from the abundance of the tropical garden humming with life, to the melancholy salt marshes of the Mississippi delta. St. Marks Wildlife Refuge, a lonely marshland on the north shore of Apalachee Bay, is blessed with the best of the two worlds. It has the immensity of the marshes without their melancholy, for it still harbors the teeming vitality of tropical Florida in an incredible abundance of young birds and small wild animals. To drive at dusk along the lonely road from St.

Marks to the lighthouse becomes a driver's nightmare, for soon the road is swarming with hopping, waddling, crawling, and toddling young life. In early summer, the lighthouse road seems to turn into the Daytona Beach for all the animal adolescents of the refuge: young herons, egrets, and terns scurry indignantly ahead of the crawling car, then their noisy band is joined by little rats and rabbits, a crowd of youths jeering, with the arrogant innocence of adolescence, at man. They are not afraid of him yet, they have not yet become mortal enemies preying upon each other; if you want to have stirred within you the distant memory of man's state before the Fall, go to St. Marks in July, drive to the lighthouse at dusk, and have your car stopped by the unruly crowd of youth in Paradise.

A few miles west of St. Marks Wildlife Refuge lies the first outpost of the Mississippi delta. It is a small, uninhabited island south of Carabelle called Dog Island, the first of a row strung out along the coast of western Florida, Alabama, and Mississippi, the last being Cat Island south of Gulfport. The lonely islands lie far from the shore, well off the beaconed shipping route known as the Intracoastal Waterway; they have about them an atmosphere of such remoteness that it makes no difference whether they are ten miles away from the nearest mainland, or a thousand. Dog Island is little more than a row of sand dunes lost in solitude, but, to its rare visitors, it offers a magnificent beach of dazzling white sand to the south, and to the north two crescent-shaped little bays, perfect anchorages for small vessels, as the water is deep right up to the beach. To drop anchor there, to watch the sunset and see the evening star rise above the dunes, a scout sent by the moon, gives the lonely boatman a rare sense of serenity, security, and peace. He is not alone; for these islands are the favorite breeding grounds of millions of sea birds, whose faraway screeching and gackering blend into a melodious, sustained harmony that sweetens the silence of sunset and evening star.

All these islands, seemingly so much alike, are different in character. Horn Island, for instance, farther to the west, is wooded and has hidden little ponds of exquisite beauty. It would be accessible to almost any size vessel, as a tidal channel of over twenty-feet depth runs the length of the island within a stone's throw of its northern shore; yet only a few shrimpers occasionally drop anchor in its lee. These islands have about them a deep and intense loneliness, undisturbed for centuries; they seem to have played no part in the wild and varied history of the mainland, a mere ten miles away.

There are few places in the southern lowlands where

man's history forces itself so strongly on your consciousness. Whether the great romantic era of gentility that ended with the Civil War was legend or reality, its atmosphere of nostalgia and graceful decay pervades the Mississippi plain like a perfume. This atmosphere is not limited to the magnificent gardens in Mobile, the great old houses along the Mississippi Valley, or to the Natchez Trace. It is everywhere, unobtrusive but persistent; it is impossible to talk about the beauty of this land in a purely aesthetic sense. For each forest, each field, each highway, each lane, is steeped in the nostalgia of the beauty that was Dixie. Unlike the great prairie of the Middle West, or the history-encrusted hills and rivers of New England, there is no feeling here of momentous migrations, marching armies, massive movements. Here history is written in small, isolated entries, in the first person singular: millions of individual memories, strewn about the countryside like autumn leaves. Slaves and masters, daughters and lovers, gamblers, carpetbaggers—their ghosts haunt each hamlet, grove, and field of cotton, but their melancholy is light, diffuse, as if every man and woman who ever lived here were haunting a private plot of land. You can drive, hike, or ride through these southern lowlands, from Georgia to Texas, and each will see his own Dixie, but no one can reach the Sabine River without having sensed to some degree the irreplaceable uniqueness of the individual.

It is a land of clannish families, most markedly so along the bayous of Louisiana. This intricate maze of creeks, streamlets, sloughs, and canals in the Mississippi delta has been the home, since before the Revolution, of the Acadians, exiles from French Canada, banished by the British in one of those brutal and callous migrations imposed by man upon his brother throughout history. No ethnic group can be more American than they, as every family is composed of sons and daughters of the Revolution; yet they speak French, and a French entirely their own. Their dialect varies not only by region, but by family, for there is no human community where the rights of the family are more rigorously defended. If individualism is the American citizen's most precious characteristic, then the Acadians personify the American ideal, because in every homestead on the banks of the myriad bayous of Louisiana that ideal is expressed in a different French.

What is the outward aspect of this amphibious land? First, coming from the sea, there are the outlying islands, thousands of them, all alike: low, marshy, inhabited only by birds, with occasionally, as in a Japanese painting, a lonely fisherman standing in his pirogue, or a team of trawlers steaming home at full speed, the yellow and vermilion plumes of their nets fluttering gaily from their masts. Beyond the islands there are the salt marshes: a belt, varying from fifteen to a hundred miles wide, of melancholy mud flats, sparsely grown with grass and reeds, saturated with salt, not quite water, not quite land, inhabited by a few taciturn men to whom this lonely landscape with its towering skies is the only place where their souls feel at home: a trapper, an oyster fisherman, a solitary shrimper whose low, old-fashioned boat is trailed by thousands of wheeling, screeching, swooping birds that make his solitude noisier than Canal Street in New Orleans.

Beyond the salt marshes, there are the cypress swamps, in some places preceded by a borderland of tree cemeteries: weird, ghostly places, where even in broad daylight the color camera will record nothing but black and white. The black trunks stand in motionless water, their reflections as stark as their silhouettes: disembodied trees, floating homeless between sea and sky. Beyond these cypress cemeteries lies a lush, semitropical water garden of incredible abundance. The fresh-water zone of the Mississippi delta has a fecund, generous soil, and the Acadians have, over the centuries, turned most of the primeval swamp into arable land yielding two crops a year, sometimes three. They are all smallholders; the big landowners and their palatial homes did not penetrate far into what had been the domain of the small "entrepreneur" since the middle of the eighteenth century. There are only a few plantation houses on the bayous, their white-pillared porches half-hidden by oak trees, heavy with Spanish moss. The homes of the Acadians are modest, rows upon endless rows of them along the banks of the big bayous like Teche, Barataria, and Lafourche, which is called "the longest village street in the world." Roving merchants drive their trucks along the crown of the levees, constantly ringing a bell to attract the attention of the housewives, silent only when they pass a graveyard. There are many graveyards along the bayous, for many have gone before. You can count them, as you listen to the gay tinkling of the merchant's bell, approaching in the distance; you can count the silences.

An unforgettable way of seeing this country is to drive slowly along the levee of Bayou Lafourche after dark on All Saints' Day. On almost all the graves in the many cemeteries along the water's edge, candles are placed; the tombstones seem to drift in the darkness like ghostly pirogues in the flickering light. As you pass the hundreds upon hundreds of small islands of light, among which the living move indistinctly like shadows, you will realize that this is the night when all those who loved this land and gave it their life, find a short resurrection in the memory of their kin. All Saints' Day, among the Acadians—all the Acadians—will give you a new understanding of the old word: fatherland.

And then, suddenly, the traveler on his way west finds himself in another world, another era in the history of man. One moment, there still are the cows placidly grazing at the water's edge, the next the horizon widens into a boundless plain underneath a vast empty sky, and there, along a dirt track, trailing a cloud of dust, bounces the first car with, in its back window, the notice "Built in Texas by Texans."

It is a landscape reminiscent of the Everglades, but it has none of its loneliness, nor of its prehistoric associations. This is the Texas prairie, as barren as the moon, a land so desolate that you will take some time to realize what the secret ingredient in its atmosphere is that causes your incongruous exhilaration: the exhilaration that a lonely man has experienced since time immemorial when, after roaming forlornly through desert or prairie, he realizes that he is at last approaching a settlement of fellow men. No one can really feel alone in the Texas prairie or the salt marshes along the coast, for wherever you go, you will smell the unmistakable scent of man triumphant: oil.

Long before the first derricks emerge from the horizon, you will, at night, see the distant glow of the oil field flames. Then the pumps will start appearing along the roadside and on the banks of the canal: small, black, nodding like patient mechanical mules, they slowly pump the liquid gold out of the barren prairie. This is Texas, and wherever you go, whatever you do, you will never be able to forget where you are. Texas does not belong to the past, it does not belong to the future, it belongs to us, now. You, I, she, and he, all of us make this land hum like a beehive with joy of living and activity. Put your finger on the road map, anywhere you like in the interior that only yesterday was a hostile prairie haunted by buzzards, buffalo, dust storms, and twisters, and you will find names that tell the story. Towns called Holland, Florence, Paris, and Dublin; villages called Energy, Satin, Butter, and Desdemona; settlements called Broom, Noodle, and Necessity. There are many state parks and national forests worth a visit, but somehow they seem less captivating here than they would elsewhere. For the vitality of man, the glory of life, the excitement of the here and now, permeate this land like the smell of its oil wells and fill you with a sense of purpose and self-confidence.

It is a land of crazy contrasts: ramshackle shrimp markets stand in a forest of oil derricks, and both are selling the same commodity: fish, either fresh or three million years old. The Houston Ship Channel, forty miles inland, is lined with the greatest concentration of refineries, factories, and huge industrial plants in the world, whereas on the banks of Brazos River, only a few miles to the west, which has one of the most imposing natural harbors on the continent, there is nothing. It seems, here, as if man did not give himself the time to look around before he settled. He just came, and conquered; the Texas motto might be "Veni, vici," without the "vidi."

But out of the prairie, which ever since the mastodons roamed its boundless immensity had known no conquerors, only parasites, rose the triumphant settlements, with names like clarion calls: Snook, Rita, and Rosebud; Fairy, Blanket, and Dad's Corner; Lydia, Betsy, and Saint Jo. The weary voyager, who has made his way from the waste of the Everglades, where no man ever left a name, along rivers called Withlacoochee and Oklawaha, across bayous called Terre au Boeuf and Pointe au Chien, lakes called Palourde and Misère, will laugh, incredulously but with a sense of immense liberation, when, after all these shades of mood and twilight, this journey over hills of mourning and through the delta of the dead, he arrives at the towns of Bells, Bangs, and Babyhead. Texas seems at that moment to personify our most precious gift: the present, in all its fullness, craziness, coarseness, tenderness, and boundless hope.

Then, as your finger moves farther south, following the road, along the Gulf coast toward Mexico, it will stop as it reaches a notice printed on the map saying, "No gasoline available between Raymondville and Riviera."

No gasoline available?

That phrase, in Texas, means that the dusty car, built in Texas by Texans, has reached the outermost boundary of today, and stands facing that great, virgin prairie: tomorrow.

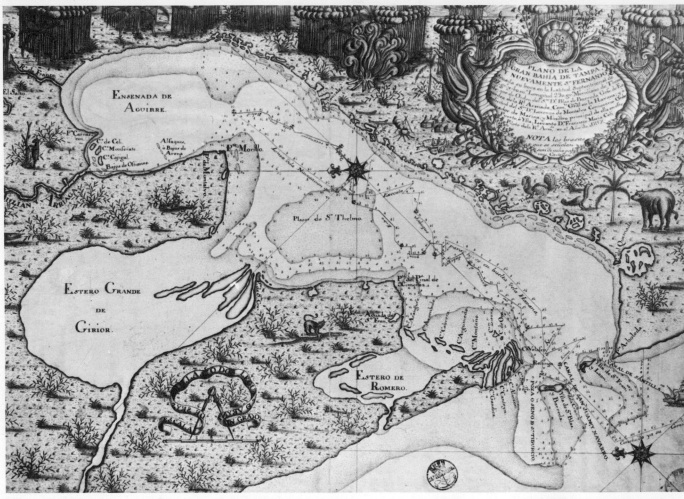

De Soto's ill-fated expedition began at Tampa Bay on Florida's west coast, depicted here in an eighteenth-century Spanish map.

Mirage in the Swamps

To the Indians of the Southeast, the low-lying land was rich and bountiful. The forests and hammocks were filled with deer, bears, and turkeys, and the rivers and coastal waters teemed with fish. Berries and grapes grew in profusion, and the warm soil was fertile for corn, melons, and other crops. To Ponce de León, Hernando de Soto, and other Spanish conquistadors of the sixteenth century this Garden of Eden turned into a miry death trap. In clanking armor the invaders roamed the country, searching for gold, pearls, and fountains of youth. Driven onward by rumors, they floundered in bogs and swamps that were filled with snakes and alligators. Fevers struck them, and the Indians, whom they alienated by their cruelty, attacked them from canebrakes and tangles of thick woods and vines. In their greed, the plenty of the country evaded them, and the trails of their desperate wanderings were marked by their corpses. Escape from this land of mirage, according to Cabeza de Vaca, a member of the Narváez expedition of 1528, was possible "only through death, which from its coming in such a place was to us all the more terrible."

Hernando de Soto

The Great Okefenokee

The Indians called it Owaquaphenoga, the "trembling earth," because the marshy ground quaked when a man strode across it. The phenomenon, it is now known, occurs because the island bogs are only tenuously anchored to the bottom by plant matter; but Okefenokee Swamp, stretching for some six hundred sixty square miles across southern Georgia and into the northern part of Florida, is still a realm of awe and mystery.

The bellows of alligators and the screeches and calls of brilliantly plumaged birds, including the noble white egret (below), break the silence of stands of cypress and tupelo trees, of fresh-water "prairies," and of a labyrinth of islands of dense vegetation called "houses." Now a national wildlife refuge, Okefenokee is a haven for deer, bears, and otters. And it is here that the beautiful Suwannee River, celebrated by Stephen Foster (who never saw it), begins its meandering journey to the Gulf of Mexico.

The Seminoles' Florida

A native hut on the banks of the St. Johns River

Seth Eastman, an officer in the United States Army for over thirty years, is remembered not for his long military career, but for the vivid drawings and paintings he made of scenes in frontier areas in which he served. His views of Florida, where he spent a year in 1840–41, are more romantic than most of his work: it seems obvious that Eastman, a native of Maine, was enchanted by the semitropical beauty of the southern peninsula.

The reason for his tour of duty there was the Second Seminole War (1835–42), a tragic attempt by the government to force the removal of the Seminoles to Oklahoma. The bitter struggle was marked by disease, treachery, and swamp warfare, and it cost the government more than forty million dollars and two thousand lives to round up all but a few hundred of the Indians. But from that harsh period in American history came these lovely water colors of Florida as the Seminoles knew it.

A deserted Seminole village, once the home of the famed chief Sam Jones, is seen in the water color above. The scene is thought to be near Lake Okeechobee. On the opposite page, tents of the First Infantry, Seth Eastman's unit, are pitched underneath live oaks at Sarasota.

Grassy Waters

The Everglades, the great sea of grass that fills the shallow saucer of southern Florida, is the result of aeons of geological activity and change. Time and again, surging ocean waters rose to cover the foundation rocks of the peninsula. Each retreat of the sea left a layer of sediment, which returning waters flattened and enlarged. Eventually the limestone deposits were molded into a low basin, sloping slightly toward the south and west and rimmed with ridges that held out the sea that had formed it.

Heavy rains, as well as overflow from Lake Okeechobee, filled the basin; and marl soil and peat kept the water from draining into the underlayer of porous limestone. And so the waters of the Everglades, now growing with vegetation, some of which was carried north from the West Indies by winds, currents, and birds, had no choice but to flow slowly, a silent river in the grass, escaping through channels in the ridges to the sea.

Today, the Everglades form the major portion of a national park of more than twenty-one hundred square miles. Its heart is the open glades, mile upon mile of Jamaica sawgrass, fresh-water sloughs, and marshes, dotted with dense hammocks of broadleaved tropical trees, and islands of pine, bay, and magnolia. Along the coastal fringes, islands of thick mangroves form a maze of waterways. (as photographed, left, from four thousand feet).

Winter, the dry season, when alligators, otters, herons, and roseate spoonbills congregate around the muddy sloughs, provides the best opportunities to view the abundant wildlife. But the rainy summer months are when the Glades truly deserve their Seminole name—"Pa-hay-o-kee," or grassy waters.

103

TEN THOUSAND ISLANDS

Everglades

TAMIAMI TRAIL

← TO KEY W

EDGE OF MANGROVES

Duck Rock

CHATHAM RIVER

GULF OF MEXICO

LOSTMANS RIVER

Big Lostmans Bay

BROAD RIVER

PONCE DE LEON BAY

SHARK RIVER

WHITEWATER BAY

Mah Har

Pau Po

N W Cape

Mangrove Trail

Middle Cape

Lake Ingraham

CAPE SABLE

Bear Lake

Cool Bay

WEST LAKE

East Cape

FLAMINGO AREA

JOE KEMP KEY

OYSTER KEYS

SANDY KEY

FLORIDA BAY

N

▲ CAMPGROUND
△ PICNIC GROUND
■ ENTRANCE STATION

David Greenspan

RT U.S 41

LOOP ROAD

TAMIAMI CANAL

TO MIAMI →

SEVEN MILE ROAD

RT 27

OPEN EVERGLADES

EDGE OF PINELAND

LONG PINE KEY

Homestead

Pa-hay-okee Overlook

Pineland Trail

PARK HEADQUARTERS

Florida City

ROYAL PALM AREA

Gumbo-Limbo → Trail

Anhinga Wildlife Trail

RT U.S.1

bert Lake ookery

EAGLE KEY

NEST KEYS

BLACKWATER SOUND

Key Largo

COWPENS

Tavernier

EVERGLADES

NATIONAL PARK

FLORIDA KEYS

U.S. 1

White-headed Eagle FALCO LEUCOCEPHALUS. Linn. *Male. Yellow Cat fish.*

The Legacy of Audubon

In October, 1820, John James Audubon, then thirty-five years old, left his wife and children in Cincinnati and, driven by a great and ambitious goal, followed the route of migrating birds down the Ohio River and the flyway of the Mississippi Valley. Supporting himself by painting signs and portraits, and by teaching French and fencing, he pursued a formidable task that he had set for himself: to create a complete set of paintings of the birds of America. In the next twenty-five years he traveled tirelessly from Florida to the western plains, adding new species to his collection. When he died in 1851, his huge store of bird portraits constituted a lasting treasure for all Americans.

Audubon, shown above in a portrait by his two sons, painted some birds that have since become extinct, as well as others that are now in danger of disappearing. The roseate spoonbill (below) and the egret were almost wiped out by plume-hunters. The bald eagle (left) has had to struggle for its existence against hunters, nest-destroyers, and the careless use of modern insecticides. Despite protective legislation, the proud emblem of the United States is now rarely seen outside Florida refuges and Alaska.

The white sand bluffs of Santa Rosa Island were once home to Seminole Indians, who are seen drying fish in this early-nineteenth-century painting by George Catlin.

The Gulf Shore

From northern Florida to the Mississippi delta, the blue waters of the Gulf of Mexico wash against lush coastal flatlands, and the warm Gulf air takes on the scent of magnolia and oleander. Bays, inlets, and lagoons indent a shoreline often protected by long, flat outer bars of sand, like Florida's Santa Rosa Island (right).

To the first conquistadors, the Gulf shore was merely a setting-off point for explorations to the interior. But when their inland wanderings proved unrewarding, the conquerors attempted settlements on the coast itself. Under Tristan de Luna, the Spanish tried to establish the first permanent colony in the present-day United States at Pensacola in 1559, but abandoned it two years later after a storm destroyed their ships.

Today the sparkling waters along the Gulf shore are a sportsman's paradise. Swimming (sometimes in company with a school of porpoises), water skiing, sailing, and fishing for kingfish, tarpon, sailfish, and other species of deepwater game fish draw thousands of visitors to the area each year.

Land of Evangeline

"Over their heads the towering and tenebrous
  boughs of the cypress
Met in a dusky arch, and trailing mosses in
  mid-air
Waved like banners that hang on the walls of
  ancient cathedrals."

*Generations of American school boys have known
the poignant hexameter narrative of Evangeline,
who found her way to the bayous of Louisiana after
the British had evicted her from her Nova Scotia
home in 1755. Inspired by Henry Wadsworth
Longfellow's poem, the nineteenth-century artist
Joseph Meeker painted this moody scene of the
famous heroine and her companions resting in a
bayou setting during their travels.*

*The beauty of the bayous was small comfort to
Evangeline, who continued to search for her lost
love, Gabriel. But to four thousand other exiled
Acadians from French Canada, Louisiana was
a benign new land. The rich waterways provided
easy fishing, and the fertility of the soil moved
Longfellow to write that the grass grew "more
in a single night than a whole Canadian summer."*

*Here the Cajuns (a corruption of Acadians)
reared large families in the old ways of life:
Mass on Sunday, hard work during the week, and
joyful dances called* fais dodos *on Saturday night.*

110

The Mississippi, carrying waters from thirty-one states, winds past New Orleans as it approaches the Gulf.

"Miserable," said Mrs. Trollope of Balize, a settlement of river pilots near the Mississippi's mouth, shown in a painting of the 1820's.

The Waters of a Continent

In 1827 Mrs. Frances Trollope, a British visitor who was later to write *Domestic Manners of the Americans,* a tart commentary on United States life that infuriated many Americans, entered the United States via New Orleans. She was, from the start, unimpressed, finding the vast, fertile delta of the lower Mississippi River "utterly desolate," with "no objects more interesting than mud banks, monstrous bulrushes, and now and then a huge crocodile luxuriating in the slime." But as her ship continued up the stream to New Orleans, she could not maintain her indifference to the New World's powerful river, which drained so great a part of the continent. As she watched the huge, rain-swollen Father of Waters, which made small and puny by comparison the rivers she had known in England and Europe, Mrs. Trollope wondered if the torrent, "so mighty, and so unsubdued . . . would some day take the matter into her own hands again, and if so, farewell to New Orleans."

113

The Pakenham Oaks, photographed by Edward Weston, were planted in 1762, but later named for the British commander.

Governor Claiborne of Louisiana, Jean Lafitte, and Andrew Jackson are shown together in this old woodcut.

Old Oaks and Old Hickory

The spongy country of the lower Mississippi River southeast of New Orleans will always evoke the memory of one of the proudest and most lopsided victories in American history. There, on January 8, 1815, on the plain of Chalmette, between an impassable cypress swamp and the banks of the Mississippi, a motley army of some 5,000 Kentucky and Tennessee frontiersmen, free Negroes, Indians, and Barataria pirates, who came out of the bayous and their Gulf hiding places under Jean Lafitte to help "Old Hickory" Andrew Jackson, hurled back a force of 10,000 British veterans under Sir Edward Pakenham. From their entrenchments, the Americans raked the British ranks, causing more than 2,000 enemy casualties, and having only 8 of their own men killed and 13 wounded. Among the victims was General Pakenham, who is memorialized by the stately avenue of oak trees (left), under which it was erroneously believed that he had died.

115

The Aransas National Wildlife Refuge, on Black-jack Peninsula north of Padre Island, is a haven for endangered species like the whooping crane, seen above in a painting by Audubon. Fewer than 40 of the five-feet-tall, red-crowned cranes exist today. At right is Audubon's portrait of the armadillo, another Aransas resident.

The Texas Coast

Steeped in the lore of cannibalistic Indians, shipwrecked white men, buried pirate treasure, and great hurricanes, the Gulf Coast of Texas is today a busy empire of cattle ranches and petrochemical plants—the latter making use of the abundant local natural resources. But some of its stretches, including 117-mile-long Padre Island (above), part of which was set aside as a national seashore in 1962, are almost unchanged since Spaniards first sighted the region in 1519. Padre's flat, sandy expanse, broken by marshes, clumps of morning-glories and subtropical vegetation, and vine-covered dunes up to 40 feet high, is a habitat of pelicans, egrets, and other waterfowl.

The Era
of Spindletop

Finding a scum the sea casts up . . . they payed the bottoms of their vessels with it."

There is a passing note of interest in this entry in the journals of the De Soto expedition, for the survivors of that futile Spanish search for gold had caulked their ships in 1543 with Texas's black gold.

Pools of the thick, heavy-smelling substance were common along the Texas coast. Indians bathed in them to help cure skin ailments, and settlers built health spas around them. A few wells were drilled, but Texans were more interested in water than in oil; not until the beginning of the twentieth century was the great value of the underground treasure realized.

The modern petroleum age was born in 1901 at Beaumont, a sleepy Gulf town. On a seemingly worthless knoll called Spindletop, where tic-ridden hogs found relief by rolling in the oily dirt, a group of visionary men sank a well. With a great roar, a torrent of oil gushed high into the air at a rate of three thousand barrels an hour, drenching everything in the neighborhood, including the ecstatic drillers whose fortune had come in.

Thousands of derricks now dot the landscape. The greatest natural wonder of Texas supplies the industry of the country, providing a touch of humor in the memory of the man who hollered when Spindletop's fountain of oil poured its black cascade over his land, "The damn stuff's ruined my farm!"

IV

THE
GREAT LAKES

By BRUCE CATTON

*"Oh Aunt! what can I say that shall give you the least inkling
of that wonderful sight! We were silenced, awed by the scene.
Alfred, poor fellow! squeezed my hand . . . I returned the pressure; such scenes are so overpowering . . . As for Alfred's friend
Plenderleath, he would do nothing but suck the end of his cane,
and ejaculate 'By Gad!' at intervals."*
("A Trip to Niagara Falls," Harper's Weekly, *October 2, 1858)*

The linked seas which make up the system of the Great Lakes sprawl in a haphazard fashion for more than a thousand miles, from the St. Lawrence all the way to Minnesota, and in their odd arrangement there may be a hint that the North American continent is still under construction.

These lakes contain (it has been estimated) about half of all the fresh water on earth, and yet their drainage basin is incredibly small. It amounts to little more than the lakes themselves, the hills and slopes along their shores, and the peninsulas of Michigan and Ontario. No great rivers flow into them anywhere. The whole waterway lies on a slanting plateau, and if the rim of the plateau should sag just a little in one place or another the lakes would have a new outlet and our geography would be very different.

The lakes, in short, are new. They were shaped and largely created by the great ice sheet of the last glacial era, and that era ended only a few thousand years ago. Within comparatively recent times the lakes were much smaller and lower than they are now, and not long before that they were much larger and higher; and indeed the plateau that holds them is a good deal higher than it was when the ice sheet first melted. Either this part of the world was finished no more than a few dozen centuries ago or the job is still going on.

Yet along with this newness there goes a touch of extreme age. When the ice sheet came down from the north centuries ago it acted like an enormous bulldozer, shearing mountains down and scraping the soil off a good part of Canada, leaving bare the rock formation known as the Canadian shield; and along the north shore of Lake Superior, in the Arrowhead country of Minnesota, and in a part of the Upper Peninsula of Michigan this rock is exposed. It dates back almost to the beginning of geologic time; parts of the earth's original crust are visible here, bits of the building blocks that were laid down early in the world's bright morning. Here is where the earth's ribs show through.

With the mighty St. Lawrence River, which reaches tidewater at Montreal, and with its short connecting rivers and straits, the Great Lakes system forms an immense waterway that leads straight to the heart of the continent. Around it was built the solid core of America's industrial strength. The waterway not only led Europeans to the center of the continent when European settlement was first beginning, but it made possible the exploitation and development of the earth's resources in a way paralleled nowhere else. Incalculably rich deposits or iron ore, coal, and limestone lie along this waterway.

On them was built the world's greatest steel industry, and on that in turn was erected the vast productive mechanism that has made America the strongest and richest nation on earth. Pittsburgh and Gary, Detroit and Chicago, and all that these cities mean, the industrial sinews of the world's most highly industrialized state—all owe their existence to the Great Lakes.

Yet if this waterway runs straight into the heartland it also lies on the outer edge of everything. It is bordered by mines and factories and electric power installations whose resources are almost beyond comprehension, and yet it skirts the edges of primeval wilderness. Even while it plunges into the center of things it forms a jumping-off-place into sheer emptiness. If it has on one side the age of steel, gasoline, and electronics, it has the old Stone Age on the other side.

Draw a line from the foot of Lake Ontario to the head of Lake Superior, the better part of a thousand miles. Then slide that line straight north, over the top of the world and then on into Asia. Once you get past the north shore of Lake Superior your moving line will touch neither cities nor farmlands: just a tangle of forest, with muskeg and barren lands and the arctic seas beyond, a continental expanse thinly speckled with mining camps and trading posts, with fishing and hunting lodges here and there and, in recent years, military installations and observation stations. Things may liven up a bit after the line gets down into Siberia, but until then the world is quiet.

It is also slightly haunted. It is quite characteristic of this setup that some of these remote mining camps are there because the rocks yield uranium, and that the fearsome tensions of the modern world have put soldiers and airmen and the masters of incomprehensible technologies down in lands which until a decade ago were considered too bleak even for the Indians. The northern Lake Superior coastline is a region of fantastic mirages, where nothing on the horizon is really what it seems to be, and where the invisible veins of minerals under the sea and in the surrounding hills can set compass needles all awry and put good navigators on the reefs. The Great Lakes area is a twilight zone between yesterday and tomorrow, and it occasionally leads one to reflect that today is brief and that its works may be somewhat insubstantial.

The Great Lakes have been called the American Mediterranean, which sounds like hifalutin nonsense and probably is, although this waterway does lead to the future as well as to the past and something magnificent may lie ahead of us; after all, it was the belief that this would be so which led a good many of our ancestors to this part of the country. In any case, the mere fact that these lakes

are where they are has had a profound influence on American history, and that influence was felt right from the beginning. Dates in the Great Lakes country go back farther than you might suppose, and many of them were recorded by men who traveled into the heart of America under the impression that they were going to China.

Jacques Cartier entered the St. Lawrence estuary in 1535 and sailed up to the site of present-day Montreal, where the Indians somehow managed to make him understand that there were great seas off to the westward. Since North America then was looked upon largely as an inconvenient obstacle on the way to the Orient, it was assumed that the Indians were talking about the Pacific; the fabled Northwest Passage, which *must* exist because men needed it so badly, doubtless lay just a little way upstream. When Samuel de Champlain founded Quebec in 1608 he conceived of it as a way station on the route to the Indies. In 1615 he got up to Georgian Bay, an immense and beautiful extension of Lake Huron, all starred with green islands in a blue seascape that seems to run westward to whatever promised land the observer may be thinking about—the lofty clouds that are forever forming and breaking apart over the Great Lakes provide some of the most spectacular sunsets imaginable. Champlain found Georgian Bay impressive, but learned to his regret that the water was fresh and so was not a part of the Pacific.

Be it noted that Champlain did not then know that Lake Huron was part of the St. Lawrence system. The French had come up to Lake Huron by way of the Ottawa River, portaging over a low height of land to Lake Nipissing and following that lake's outlet to Georgian Bay, missing Lake Ontario and Lake Erie entirely. They had aroused the enmity of the terrible Iroquois Indians, who ruled the southern shore of Lake Ontario, and it was much safer to go roundabout. (In any case, for men who had to carry their canoes and cargoes around any obstruction in the waterway, Niagara Falls offered quite a barrier.) So it was logical enough to think that this inland sea might lead to the Pacific Ocean, and presently an expedition went west to find out if this was the way to China.

This expedition was led by Jean Nicolet, who had learned from the Indians around Lake Nipissing that on the far shore of Lake Michigan there were people who lived by a sea that had a strange smell. To Nicolet it was clear that this meant salt water, and the people who lived there must be Chinese. In 1634 he led a flotilla of canoes across the top of Lake Michigan and turned southwest into Green Bay, believing that he was entering China, and he dressed for the occasion in a mandarin robe of embroidered silk—worn over frontier buckskins and moccasins. He landed at the foot of the bay in full regalia, firing salutes from flintlock pistols, and found himself sur-

123

rounded by Winnebago Indians, who were glad to see him but who obviously were not Chinese.

So the French learned that the lakes led into America rather than to the Oriental gateway, and they adjusted themselves to this knowledge and set out to do three things —trade for furs, save souls, and claim this limitless country for the Sun King. Up the waterway came soldiers and priests, government officials and fur traders, along with a swarm of men who went off on their own to live with the Indians, happily shedding the restraints of civilization for life in the deep wilderness. In 1671 a convocation of bemused Indians squatted by the rapids of St. Marys River, where Lake Superior's waters come down to the lower lakes, and listened without recorded comment while officials in formal attire unfurled the fleur-de-lis banner and claimed the American interior for Louis XIV.

As far as the history of the United States goes, these dates are ancient. The Recollets and then the Jesuits had a mission on Georgian Bay before Massachusetts was settled; they had crossed Wisconsin and traced the Mississippi to the Gulf before William Penn got his charter for a Quaker colony; and there were French settlers in far-off Minnesota before the American Revolution. The English who settled along the Atlantic coast inched their way inland generation by generation and farm by farm, taking their time about it, assimilating each plain and valley before going on beyond the next range of hills. The French went in fast, up the rivers and along the lakes, seeing Lake Superior before the English even saw the Alleghenies, ranging far and wide into lands which they could name and color with legends but which they could not hold.

They did set a pattern which was followed long after their day. They exploited the wealth of the Great Lakes country as if it were literally inexhaustible, and as they did so they profoundly changed the lives of the people who lived there. The wealth the French wanted was furs, and furs they got; getting them, they exterminated whole species of animals and turned Indian society inside out, compelling it to change or die. The native tribes had been almost wholly self-sufficient, hunting and fishing and farming and gathering in a way that kept their little communities in balance. The French thrust the modern world on them and in effect turned them into professional trappers who killed for the market rather than for their own use. When the first trader gave a red man a knife and a musket in exchange for a bale of beaver skins, Indian society began to die.

This pattern held good in subsequent centuries for the upper lakes rather than for the lower ones, and it may be that it was a pattern which the Great Lakes country imposed on the people who came in to possess it. The business of skimming off the wealth of the land without any thought for the final consequences prevailed on the upper lakes long after the furs and the French traders were gone forever. Perhaps the land of the upper lakes was made to be ravished. Certainly that is what happened to it.

It was different along the lower lakes. The shores of Lake Ontario and Lake Erie were taken over from the first by people who wanted to live there rather than by adventurers looking for quick profits, and the same was true of at least the lower half of the Lake Michigan country. The men who opened this land brought their plows with them, and their families, and the expectation of building a settled community. The land was fabulously rich, but they cultivated it instead of taking its wealth and getting out. The lakes were their highway, and they bordered the highway with farms and towns and cities, in southern Ontario and northern New York and Ohio, and westward into the great corn-hog belt; and at last the two nations, Canada and the United States, made a deepwater connection for this waterway with the open oceans, so that cargoes for and from all of the world moved along the waters where Indian canoe and French bateau once carried pelts of beaver and marten.

But the upper country was the *pays en haut,* as the French put it—the high country, the north country, frontier of a wilderness that was harder to tame, and what it offered was wealth that could be cut down or dug out and carried away forever. Here the settlers, the home-makers, came in the second wave and not the first. The lumbermen and the miners were ahead of them. Lumber camp and mining camp have no permanence; after they have taken what there is to take they disappear, and the settler has to do the best he can on what is left. So it was in much of the high country; the difficulty being that these hills which were so prodigal of iron and copper and tall timber were not really very good for anything else. Pine trees grow in sand, and iron and copper are found in rocks, and the man who makes a crop in sand and rocks gets a hardscrabble farm and little more.

The exploitation did not really begin until after the Black Hawk War of the early 1830's broke the power of the lake country Indians once and forever. Then the timber cruisers began to thread their way along the clear rivers of the northern half of Michigan's lower peninsula, going through incomprehensibly vast pine forests that seemed to offer an inexhaustible supply of timber. The population of the Middle West was increasing just then almost by geometrical progression, new cities were appearing everywhere and old cities were constantly growing bigger, and there was an unheard-of demand for lumber to build hundreds of thousands of houses. The lumber was at hand, waiting to be cut, clear white pine of surpassing quality and astounding cheapness. The timber cruisers marked it, and then the lumberjacks moved in, a muscular brigade in heavy boots, stagged woolen pants, and checkered Mackinaw coats, skilled in the use of the double-bitted axe and the long, flexible crosscut saw; directed by men who knew exactly what they wanted and who became known presently as lumber barons. There were State of Maine men by the hundreds, and French Canadians, who had been letting daylight into the swamps along the Kennebec and the Penobscot and who came now to woods where the pines rose fifty, sixty, or eighty feet before they bore any branches, perpetual twilight lying in the long aisles between the tall columns. These men went to work, and the logs went down the rivers to mill towns like Saginaw and Muskegon, the growing country to the south got the boards it wanted so badly, and the lumber barons grew rich. And the *pays en haut* began to lose the forest cover that it had had ever since the years just after the last glacier had melted.

It went by stages. First they cut just the pines that were handy to the rivers. Then the railroads came in, and logging branch lines went back into the hills for the pines that could not be taken out by water. Then, as the pines began to give out, the lumber barons went after the hardwoods that had been ignored earlier, the maple and oak and beech, and these were turned into logs and sent through the gang saws in the mills. Whole forests of young cedars were cut down to make fence posts, other forests went to make firewood for the cities or charcoal for blast furnaces, and little trees that were no good for anything else were cut up for pulpwood. It sometimes seems as if men then just hated trees.

Anyway, the "inexhaustible" forest was destroyed quite rapidly. In a little more than half a century the lumber boom was over—that is, the virgin timber was all gone—in Michigan's lower peninsula. It lasted somewhat longer in the Upper Peninsula, and in northern Wisconsin and Minnesota, because it started later in those parts, but it presently ended there too. For most of the cutover lands there began half a century of decline, with towns dying and farms being abandoned and people moving away, with thousands of acres of desolate land reverting to the state for unpaid taxes. A generation too late, the idea of conservation and reforestation took hold; the lake states are greener now than they were fifty years ago, and the forests are coming back . . . but they never will be quite like the forests that are gone.

Timber was one resource; copper was another. Under the barren rocks of the Keweenaw Peninsula, which curves out into Lake Superior about halfway between Sault Ste. Marie and Duluth, lay one of the world's richest deposits of copper—deposits so astonishingly rich that in many places they consisted not of copper ore but of pure copper.

An incredibly long time ago Indians mined this copper and used it to make knives, spearheads, axes, and other implements. They were pure Stone Age men, knowing nothing of smelting or casting; they simply hammered lumps of copper into shape just as if they had been working ordinary stones, although they understood enough about annealing to keep the tools they made from becoming brittle. It has been suggested that they may have been the first metal-users in all the world, and however that may be they were at least at it in remotest antiquity. Recent radiocarbon datings show that they were mining and using copper as early as 5,000 B.C.—close enough to the glacial period so that the topography of the lakes country has changed greatly since their day. Lake Superior rose far enough to put some of their sites three hundred feet under water, then subsided centuries later and exposed them for modern archaeologists to study. These copper workers vanished into mystery, at last, leaving among the less advanced tribes which succeeded them some knowledge that there was copper around Lake Superior and that useful things could be made of it.

To which knowledge the acquisitive American became heir, in the 1840's. He acted on it, with speed. Conservative Boston invested heavily, and the Keweenaw Peninsula became the center of a mining boom. Pursuing the veins where the metal lay in such richness, engineers drove deep shafts that sent laterals far out under the bed of Lake Superior. Miners from Cornwall, in England, were brought over to work in the diggings, and to this day there is a colorful Cornish overtone to some of the habits of speech in this part of the country. For a time Michigan supplied the country with most of its copper, and conservative Boston's investments paid off handsomely. Then, after a couple of generations, the cream had been taken off. The center of copper production shifted to new diggings in Utah and Arizona, and the Lake Superior boom was over. There are still copper mines there, and copper continues to come out of them, but it is a high-cost operation now. Shafts that go a mile deep and then fan out far under water are expensive to operate and maintain.

While they were looking for copper more than a century ago, men also found iron. They found it first in the Michigan Upper Peninsula, along the Marquette and Gogebic ranges, those worn hills left by primitive mountains that had been eroded down to nubs by the infinite weight of geologic time when the Rockies were just being raised. Then came the discovery that still richer deposits lay farther west, along the Mesabi Range in northern Minnesota. Like the other original resources of the Great Lakes country, these were truly fabulous. The veins lay so close to the surface, and were so deep and broad, that the miners worked in open pits, gouging out the ore with great power shovels, and it seemed that they would never get to the bottom of it. On this iron from the high country the prodigious American steel industry was based, the heart and center of modern industrial America. A canal was dug and locks were built at Sault Ste. Marie, where Indians once sat by the rapids to watch a ceremony performed for the King of France, and a vast fleet of steamers went shuttling through, year after year. This became the busiest canal on earth, carrying a far heavier traffic than Suez or Panama ever saw, thirty and forty and fifty million tons of ore in a year—the raw material for everything that was ever done by Detroit and Pittsburgh. Two world wars were fought and won on the iron that came down from Lake Superior.

No mining operation can go on forever. Sooner or later the veins of ore run thin and taper out; there is just so much mineral in the ground, and when it is gone it is gone for keeps. The Lake Superior ore is by no means gone, of course. The ore fleet still locks down at the Soo Canal through seven months of the year, and the long trains of short red hopper cars still come clanking down from the ranges to the long docks at Marquette and Escanaba, at Ashland and Superior and Duluth and Two Harbors; but the picture is changing. If the richest deposits are not worked out they are at least being worked 'way down, and the mining companies are spending big sums preparing to use the second-grade ores which formerly were ignored. Plenty of ore remains, but the easy days are about over. The recent opening of the deepwater canal to the ocean is an unmistakable sign that the steel companies are at least thinking about new sources.

The riches of the Great Lakes basin were not, after all, literally inexhaustible, as the firstcomers supposed; neither the furs nor the forests nor the minerals could last forever. What does last, however, is the waterway itself, the chain of lakes and rivers and straits by which these and other riches can be moved. The commercial fleets of the Great Lakes have changed mightily—the Algonquian birch-bark canoe and the six-hundred-foot steel freight steamer have nothing in common except that they float and will carry cargo—but they are still essential to the prosperity of the American interior. Modernized and specialized as the present-day carriers are, they still con-

tain a whiff of their wilderness origins. The skipper of a big steamer going west on Lake Superior for iron ore may be an integral part of the industrial process, but as he steams toward Duluth he knows that off to starboard there lies practically nothing but wilderness all the way to the North Pole. He lives in the very center of things but he lives also on the edge of the past, of the Stone Age itself, of the days when all of America's history was new. Not far to the north of his vessel's course is Isle Royale, a forty-five-mile-long island of rock and evergreens, a national park which is as wild and uncultivated now as it was when the Indians of prehistoric times went there for copper. (Some of their pits and implements are still to be seen there, untouched for no one knows how many centuries. Looking at these remains, one is compelled to wonder: how in the world did the Indian tribes, one or two thousand years ago, know that this island existed off beyond the horizon, how did they know there was copper to be had there, and how did they ever manage to get there in flimsy birch-bark canoes? One would like to know a good deal more about it.)

Isle Royale, to repeat, is still wild, and so is much of the mainland. Anyone who wants to see unbroken wilderness can see millions of acres of it along the Minnesota-Ontario border, running north from the western end of Lake Superior: the legendary Quetico-Superior region, preserved in something resembling its primeval condition by the Quetico Provincial Park just north of the border and the Superior National Forest just south of it. Some decades ago the lumberjacks got most of the original timber, but new growth came up to cover the scars and the area has never again been exploited. Instead the two governments have preserved it, and they have somehow managed to keep both the automobile and the airplane out of it so that it is wild and largely unspoiled right to this day. This is the fabulous "canoe country," filled with woods and streams and lakes which you cannot reach at all unless you go in by canoe—with a lot of portaging here and there—or go in on foot.

It has taken a struggle, by ardent conservationists on both sides of the border, to keep this wilderness unspoiled. The pressure to run automobile highways up to every lake and likely campsite is always strong and may eventually become too strong to be resisted; and there has been equal pressure to permit the establishment of a complex of fishing and hunting camps serviced by seaplanes, which would presently make the heart of this wilderness as accessible, and about as romantic, as the inner reaches of Central Park. So far, though, the line has been held, and this relatively unspoiled wilderness remains wilderness even though the fringes of it are hardly more than a day's drive from one of the world's largest industrial areas.

Cutting through this wild land is one of America's historic trails: the chain of rivers and lakes that lead from Lake Superior up over the height of land to the Lake Winnipeg area, coming up from Grand Portage on the big lake to Rainy Lake and Lake of the Woods. Here the Nor'Westers used to go with the huge canoe brigades that went on from the high country into the Saskatchewan and on to the Rockies, trading with far western tribes for skins long before the American Revolution. No place on earth today is quite as remote as the lands that lay at the western end of that trail were two hundred years ago, and although the colorful red-sashed *voyageurs* who opened the trail are long gone the country they crossed has changed very little indeed.

One of the surprising things about the Great Lakes basin is the fact that there are so many stretches of landscape that look now much as they looked before the white man came in. The Lake Michigan sand dunes, for instance, have the authentic stamp of primeval days even though Chicago is just over the horizon. The growing industrial complex at the southern end of Lake Michigan has encroached upon them, with steel mills and artificial harbors and railroad yards and enormous piles of iron ore, but a few miles away the world is all golden sand and blue water, with empty sky above and a pervading stillness that is broken only by the noise of the surf on the beach. This goes on for two hundred miles or more, culminating in the spectacular promontory of Sleeping Bear Point, up near Grand Traverse Bay—a five-mile flat-topped ridge of sand rising nearly five hundred feet above the lake.

Times are changing, to be sure. They started to change when the first canoe brigade went up past the St. Marys rapids and they have been changing ever since, and with the constant growth in population and the unending proliferation of hard-surfaced roads these parts of the lake shore are getting suburbanized. But there arc signs that increasing numbers of people want to keep this country as free as possible from the blight of overdevelopment. Back of the coastline there are woods and streams and lakes in profusion, and it may yet be possible to keep all of this from becoming nothing more than a weekend extension of Detroit and Chicago. Keeping this country open for the enjoyment of all Americans without at the same time getting it all cluttered up with real estate developments is going to be a hard job, but at least people are beginning to care about it.

The problem arises out of the strange characteristic that is inherent in the Great Lakes country: it lies close to the heart of the very summit of modern industrialization, and yet at the same time it contains something basically untamable and wild. The very conditions under which the heavy steamship traffic on the lakes is carried on serve to illustrate the point.

For if these lakes are in the highest degree beautiful they can also be exceedingly dangerous. In the course of the last century they have swallowed hundreds upon hundreds of ships and killed many thousands of men. They are usually peaceful enough in the summer, but in the fall and early spring they can become violent, whipped by tremendous gales that raise devastating seas; and the vessel tossed about in these storms always has a lee shore not far away—the mariner can never heave to and wait for a gale to blow itself out on the lakes.

This tradition goes all the way back to the beginnings. In 1679 the explorer and trader La Salle took tools, supplies, and workers past Niagara and built a square-rigger at the foot of Lake Erie, a sixty-foot, decked vessel with a high poop, christened *Griffin*. He sailed this to Green Bay, loaded it with furs, and while he went about his business in Wisconsin he sent the ship off to the lower lakes. It went out of Green Bay into Lake Michigan and was never seen again by anyone . . . first of the cargo carriers to go missing in a Great Lakes storm. There have been many others, since then; among them, the six-hundred-forty-foot steel freighter *Carl D. Bradley,* which was simply broken in half in a Lake Michigan gale in November of 1958, taking all but two of her thirty-five-man crew to the bottom.

The worst storm in modern Great Lakes history was perhaps the big blow of November, 1913, which wrecked forty ships and took two hundred thirty-five lives. This blow swept all of the lakes but hit Lake Huron the hardest; on that lake, second largest in the whole chain, eight up-to-date steel freighters were lost with all hands, and to this day no one knows just how or where those ships went down. They simply foundered, unseen in the darkness, like La Salle's *Griffin.* . . . Reflecting on the power of some of these storms, one is bound to shiver at the thought of the Indians centuries ago traveling all the way across Lake Superior in canoes to get copper from Isle Royale.

Under everything, the Great Lakes country has always had a harshness. If it offered untold riches it had a way of wrapping them in dangers, and in its industries of fur and lumber and ore and shipping there has always been a touch of man-killing violence. This has been a good country, a land of promise and great bounty, but it has never really been an easy country. It took pretty good men to master it.

An Animal Fair

f.53.

2

femele de les lan
auec ses trois petis
dune seule uentree.

French newcomers to America, canoe-ing up the St. Lawrence and Ottawa rivers, were men of action, bent on exploration and the gathering of furs. But the savage splendors of the wilds touched their souls, and many of them responded like poets and artists, sing-ing of the woods and waters, and drawing pictures of the birds and beasts. The wonderful sketches shown here were made about 1700 by a young wilderness traveler from Quebec, Charles Bécard de Granville.

The great beast with a long tongue (above) is a heavy-antlered moose, perhaps pawing the ground in rutting season. At left is a female of the species, with "little ones from the same litter." The decorative assemblage of birds at right includes a thrush (upper left), a swallow (4), a chickadee (5), and, in the center, balancing berries on its beak, "the bird with no name."

Rossignol 1

Loiseau a teste rouge P.42

t59

Loyseau bigaré de
poic epy le plemage est
beau

3

Loyseau sans
nom

4

5

Latardeve ou
mesange

Brondelle de
L'Amerique

Le bec
Crochu

129

From the time of its discovery (probably by Champlain), Niagara Falls took rank with the seven wonders of the world—a lure to any artist who sought to paint the great scenes of the New World. This view, more charming than most others, was done by the self-taught Quaker artist Edward Hicks, who visited the Falls in the year 1819.

In his autumn scene, Hicks made the cataract's spray seem like huge columns of smoke billowing above the viewers at the lower right. But the moose, beaver, eagle, and coiled snake, a touch of the paradise of the Garden of Eden, suggest the reactions of a later visitor, Charles Dickens, to whom the thundering falls gave " Peace of Mind, tranquillity, calm recollections of the Dead, great thoughts of Eternal Rest and Happiness . . ."

The Great Cataract

As they flow from Lake Erie, the waters of the Niagara River move faster and faster, gaining momentum over rapids until they approach the precipice. Then, with a stupendous roar, they plunge some one hundred sixty feet. This aerial photograph was taken above the twenty-five-hundred-foot-wide, horseshoe-shaped Canadian Falls; beyond Goat Island, which splits the river, is the one-thousand-foot-wide American Falls. Niagara was first described in 1678 by Father Louis Hennepin, who accompanied La Salle to the West. The explorer-priest was so overcome by the "vast, prodigious Cadence of Water" that he estimated the Falls to be more than three hundred feet higher than they actually were. But then, Niagara has always excited visitors to exaggeration—and sometimes to downright folly.

For, like Mount Everest, Niagara is *there;* and many of the brave, or crazy, have tried to conquer it. One celebrated daredevil was the tightrope walker Farini, pictured above in the act of maneuvering himself across the chasm with his balancing pole in 1860. Farini was trying to horn in on some of the fame that had already been accorded a French wire walker named Blondin, who in 1859 had terrified and dazzled crowds of watchers with a brilliant series of crossings, during one of which he had carried his trembling manager over the thirteen-hundred-foot-long cable. In later days, stunters went over the Falls—often to their deaths—in barrels, life preservers, and India-rubber suits. Today, Niagara's novelty as a setting for stunts is gone; but each year some three and a half million people still come to see the spectacle of nature that Father Hennepin once termed without "Parallel [in the] Universe."

133

The 1813 view above of Amherstburg, Ontario, just across the river from Detroit, shows the Shawnee chief Tecumseh (in headdress, lower right), soon after he had helped the British capture Detroit from the Americans. Eventually forced to withdraw by Perry's victory on Lake Erie (left), the British were finally crushed by William Henry Harrison.

Detroit Passage

The strategic location of the frontier post of Detroit, established by the Sieur de Cadillac in 1701 on the water link between lakes Erie and Huron, ensured that war would often mar its lovely setting. "The joyous sparkling of the bright blue water; the green luxuriance of the woods; the white dwellings, looking out from the foliage . . . all were mingled in one broad scene of wild and rural beauty." That was Detroit in May, 1763, as Francis Parkman described it. But soon afterward, the Indian leader Pontiac began his famous siege, and violence swept the area. In 1812 Detroit was a major goal of both the British and Americans, and once more the woods and waters of the region erupted in warfare.

From a sketch by Cah' Jas Van Cleve in 1870

In 1826 James Van Cleve left a clerk's job in Lewiston, New York, to ship out as purser on the Ontario, *the first American steamboat on the Great Lakes. Eventually he rose to captain, and in later years drew these water colors to preserve the memories of his almost forty years on the great inland seas. The view at left is of Lewiston, with Lake Ontario in the background, after he had first left home. The promontory above is Cape Thunder on Lake Superior, a landmark to Indians as well as steamers. Below are the Sault Ste. Marie rapids in Michigan; by 1870, when Van Cleve drew the scene, the rapids had been bypassed by the Soo Canal, which has since become one of the world's busiest waterways.*

This Indian map, drawn for La Vérendrye, helped him trace the passage from Lake Superior to Lake Winnipeg.

La Vérendrye's Canoe Country

West of Lake Superior, the Minnesota-Ontario border runs through a great wilderness of waters. Beginning in 1731, a French trader, the Sieur de La Vérendrye, spurred on by Indian tales of a river that would lead to the Pacific, blazed a canoe route through the area and emerged at Lake Winnipeg. For more than a century, La Vérendrye's route was used by fur men bound for western Canada. Today, as a result of efforts by Sigurd Olson and other conservationists, it is unspoiled, the silence of many parts of it protected even from the intrusion of airplanes, save those flying on fire patrol (above) or on other essential missions.

Cirrus
Lake

Kasakokwog
Lake

Pickerel
Lake

QUETICO
PROVINCIAL PARK

Sturgeon
Lake

MALIGNE RIVER

Poohbah
Lake

Lac
La Croix

Ag
La

Crooked
Lake

Basswood
Lake

ELY-BUYCK ROAD

Snow L
Lak

Moose Lake

Cummings
Lake

Trout
Lake

Burntside
Lake

ELY

White Iron
Lake

Bald
Eagle
Lake

Vermilion
Lake

David Greenspan

RT 1

RT 1

▲ CAMPGROUND ACCESSIBLE BY AUTO
△ PICNIC GROUND

140

Ontario's Quetico Park, and the United States's Superior National Forest which enfolds the protected Boundary Waters Canoe Area, contain much of La Vérendrye's watery wilderness. There are so many lakes (more than five thousand on the American
side) that it is difficult to name them. After noting such bursts of inspiration as
Gabimichigami, Sea Gull, Rose, Knife, Flour, Snip, Seed, Rat, Ham, Parent, East

BOUNDARY WATERS CANOE AREA
SUPERIOR NATIONAL FOREST
MINNESOTA

N

Northern Light Lake

Saganaga Lake

Whitefish Lake

Arrow Lake

North Lake

Gunflint Lake

Greenwood Lake

Elton Lake

CANADA

UNITED STATES

Brule Lake

SUPERIOR

Lake Alice

Lake Insula

Devils Track Lake

Isabella Lake

NATIONAL FOREST

Parent Lake

GRAND MARAIS

RT U.S. 61

LAKE SUPERIOR

Bearskin, and Nina Moose, one comes upon a group in the Insula Lake Route called quite starkly 1, 2, 3, and 4. But all of them are beloved by canoeists and fishermen, who find the cold waters filled with trout, bass, and northern and walleyed pike. As Sigurd Olson wrote: "For once in your life, the bass are waiting. . . . This is fishing for fun and fun alone, the kind of sport found only in primitive waters."

141

The Voyageurs

Canadian voyageurs, *making a typical portage, are seen in this 1867 drawing.*

Until well into the nineteenth century, the water routes from Montreal to the West echoed to the songs of the French Canadian *voyageurs,* hard-toiling employees of the fur companies. They are gone now; but the northern lakes and rivers are still marked by the signs and legends of this colorful breed of frontiersmen, who wore red caps and sashes, blue cloaks, and deerskin leggings, sang romantic and bawdy songs to the beat of their paddles, and let their hair hang long (against mosquitoes). Carrying supplies that were destined for fur trading to posts as far distant as the Arctic Ocean and the mouth of the Columbia River, and bringing back packs of beaver pelts, they knew every rapid, carry, and cape, like Michigan's Keweenaw Point on Lake Superior (left), as if it were their home.

A contemporary painting, Canoes in a Fog, *by Mrs. Frances A. Hopkins, shows a fur flotilla.*

Michigan's nineteenth-century Cliff copper mine (above) is contrasted with a modern open-pit iron mine in the Mesabi (left).

Copper and the Mesabi

In the ancient past, perhaps from five to seven thousand years ago, Indians on the borders of Lake Superior had picked up lumps of copper from the ground and hammered them into lance points and other useful and decorative articles. The habit died out; but in 1665 Father Claude Allouez, a wilderness priest on Lake Superior, wrote that he found "pieces of pure copper, of ten and twenty pounds' weight," glimmering in the water. Such tales of mineral wealth waiting to be exploited at the western end of the Great Lakes were generally ignored until the nineteenth century, when the demands of America's industrial society stimulated the opening of copper mines in the region. The Cliff Mine went into operation on the Keweenaw Peninsula in 1845, and in four years its rich deposits of pure copper were creating fortunes. But the mine eventually played out, and in 1910 it was shut down, leaving a large hole in the landscape.

Before that time, a new discovery in Minnesota had eclipsed the copper finds in Michigan and Wisconsin. In 1890, "Seven Iron Men" of Duluth—timber cruiser Leonidas Merritt and his brothers—struck rich and easily accessible masses of iron ore in the Mesabi Range. Open-pit mines bit into the earth; a railroad was built to the head of the Great Lakes; and ever since, Mesabi iron, carried in ore ships to Buffalo, Cleveland, and other ports, has provided much of the sinew for American industry.

The protective vegetation of the Indiana and Michigan dunes attracts a variety of birds, including the marsh hawk (top) and sharp-tailed grouse. The ground cover at Sleeping Bear (below) helps to build the dunes: as the west winds sweep in from Lake Michigan, the clusters of shrubs and grasses catch and anchor the sand.

The Sand Dunes

Along the southern and eastern shores of Lake Michigan, unscarred stretches of beach and sand dunes are fighting for their existence. There, where the wildlife is still untouched and vegetation grows in its natural state, the inlander can walk along the shore in a cool breeze from the lake, or bask on the sand (so fine that he can ski on the dunes) and know the pleasures of a protected ocean beach. But the needs of expanding industry and the plans of developers are crowding in. The bulldozers of neighboring steel mills have overrun large areas of the lovely Indiana Dunes; and farther north, at Sleeping Bear Dunes in Michigan, conservationists fear that they may not forever be able to reconcile the demands of summer real estate developers with protection of the area's unspoiled beauty.

The Fragrance of Pine

148

The white pine forests of northern Michigan, Wisconsin, and Minnesota were tall and deep and beautiful. "Over all," remembered one settler, "was the fragrance of pine." But a nation was growing, and loggers came in for white pine for houses and railroad ties. "There's more timber here than we could cut in a thousand years," they said. There should have been; but it was long ago, and before the time of scientific tree farming. The loggers went to work; and by 1900 the vast white pine forests of the Midwest had almost entirely disappeared—a conservation lesson hard learned.

The photograph at left, taken during the 1860's, shows a log drive on Minnesota's Rum River during the height of intensive cutting. In another half century, lumbering and fires had left scenes like the one above in Michigan. A use for the white pine is seen below: ties for the transcontinental Union Pacific Railroad, under construction in 1867.

JOHN SZARKOWSKI

150

Michigan's Isle Royale

It is very quiet here, as quiet as it may have been before there were any men at all on the North American continent. As the visitor stands on a grassy point of Isle Royale National Park, watching the twilight deepen the color of Moskey Basin (left), he knows that he is in a special place. Isle Royale seems to culminate the remote wild quality that is one of the two paradoxical faces of the Great Lakes. Here, in the same state as Detroit, no automobiles are allowed, and no roads have been cut through the hardwood and evergreen forests. Isle Royale is one place where Americans are forced to take up walking again. There are good places to hike: more than eighty miles of foot trails lead past interior lakes and to easily climbed peaks like Mount Lookout-Louise, which on clear days offers a distant view of the Canadian mainland. The lakes, full of pike, perch, and walleyes, are one reason why fishermen come to Isle Royale; some twenty-five miles of unspoiled trout streams are another.

On Lake Superior, northwest of Michigan's Upper Peninsula, Isle Royale was probably the site of the earliest use of copper by ancient Indians, and prehistoric copper diggings can be found scattered through the island. In the nineteenth century miners worked here again. But they abandoned the last mine in 1899 and went back to the mainland, leaving Isle Royale a Lake Superior sanctuary for the lover of nature and solitude.

The abundant wildlife on Isle Royale either swam from the mainland or, like the moose, originally crossed over on the ice. At the right an Audubon print (c. 1830) of an angry red fox, one of the island's most common species.

AUDUBON, *Quadrupeds of North America*, VOL. 2, 1851

V

THE
PRAIRIE
AND
PLAINS

By PAUL ENGLE

An awesome landmark of the plains, and the first United States National Monument (created in 1906), Wyoming's Devils Tower, a volcanic monolith with fluted sides, rises like a giant stump 1,280 feet above the Belle Fourche River.

The wide heartland is a country of no tremendous hole in the ground, of no towering peak or range of peaks. This is not scenery in the spectacular sense, but quite simply the greatest area of useful land in the world. You could plow an unbroken furrow (save for skipping lightly over a few rivers) from eastern Ohio to western Nebraska and from the Texas Gulf coast to Canada, and never be much more or less than one thousand feet above sea level. But this does not mean that the land itself is level everywhere. Grove and stream, low hill and shallow valley, make endless small changes in their apparent endlessness. On a hot summer day the landscape will seem to quiver as if it were in perpetual quiet motion.

The furrows would intersect near Lincoln, Nebraska, where the continent begins to tilt upward toward the Rockies. West lies the open range, the short-grass country of the drier plains. East lies the intensely cultivated tall-grass country of the prairies.

This is the place of exuberant soil, where dirt is not a sterility of disintegrated stone, nor a nuisance in the eye, but the source of life. You could plant the seeds of many grains in those furrows and harvest a crop fifteen hundred miles long. This is one of the wonders of the world: if God, man, or geological chance were to create somewhere an area of an earth most suitable for sustaining and nourishing manlike creatures, the result would be the same plain and prairie landscape that now gently rolls and undulates from eastern Ohio to eastern Colorado.

This is the place of the long, sideways look, because all of the powers that made the landscape were horizontal. What lies under these moderate hills and plains is not hard granite rock created out of fire, but the water-formed limestones, sandstones, and shales, earthlike and soft. For hundreds of miles they run in their flat, seldom-tilted beds, cropping out along streams and roads as cliffs that crumble into the soil that overlies them.

Since dirt is the mild substance and marvelous wealth of this land, it is appropriate that the rock that holds it up should be sedimentary, formed not by a molten upthrust from deep in the earth, but by a gradual settling of the gradually dissolved particles under an inland sea. This prairie-plain landscape, in certain lights, has the look of endless water endlessly moving, in the manner of an ocean. You are standing on what was once the floor of an ocean.

Over this ancient area came a modern (Pleistocene) sea, a staggering wave of ice, grinding down hills, filling valleys. The rocks it carried underneath, out of the igneous mass of the Canadian north, acted like a giant rasp, tearing the country into smoothness. It was a plow of ice, preparing the land for the later plow of steel.

The limit of glaciation is a long semicircle running down the Ohio River and up the Missouri to Great Falls, Montana. The horizontal push of the ice ground up rock and tree, producing a sediment of soil and leaving in this fertile dirt huge boulders of granite ripped from the old continental rock all of the way back to Hudson Bay. These boulders are everywhere in the glaciated country, standing hard, dark, and threatening in the mellow fields.

Nearly all streams in this long arc of land flow east, west, or south, but the Red River between Minnesota and North Dakota runs north. Once there was an expanse of water here larger than all of the Great Lakes combined. It has been named by geologists Lake Agassiz. It once drained southeast and continued far north of Winnipeg. The Red River drains this lake bed, where now the flowing wheat fields replace the underwater plants.

Another remnant of early time is the Pipestone National Monument in the southwestern corner of Minnesota, where originally clay had been deposited with sandstone above. Under pressure and heat this produced catlinite, a red stone easily worked. For hundreds of years the Indians shaped their pipes from quarries here. So sacred was the place, no warlike acts were permitted, no matter how hostile the tribes may have been elsewhere. This is one of the few points in the prairie country where antiquity of geological time meets the antiquity of human activity and belief.

The glaciers were the decisive force in making the landscape of that wide region from Great Falls to Youngstown, Ohio. Most of the lakes have been scooped out by that great knife of ice. Low ridges rising out of generally level ground are often gravel, sand, and clay left by a melting glacier. Snakelike, curving lengths of sandy slopes may be eskers, dropped by streams under the ice. The fabulous, rich soil of Iowa is often the fine loam washed out from the front of the glaciers, the heavier rocks and sand having been left behind to the north. All of this southward thrust was funneled between the Rockies and the Appalachians.

This whole prairie-plain country, narrowing toward the Gulf of Mexico, is actually a tremendous funnel. The Great Plains descend eastward from the edge of the Rockies at a rate of roughly ten feet to the mile until reaching the Mississippi River. The Missouri from the west and the Ohio from the east pour their massive waters toward each other. In the middle is the shallow trough of the continent.

There is every sort of river. The phrase "too thin to plow, too thick to drink" could apply to many streams other than the Missouri. In eastern Wyoming the Powder River, so-called because the dark sand along its edge resembled gunpowder, is muddy and alkaline and was once described by a disillusioned viewer as "a mile wide, an inch deep,

Great Falls

MONTANA

NORTH DAKOTA

YELLOWSTONE RIVER

Bighorn River

Powder River

THEODORE ROOSEVELT NAT'L MEMORIAL PARK

Bismarck

Red River of the North

MINNESOTA

LAKE SUPERIOR

BIG HORN MTS

WYOMING

DEVILS TOWER NAT'L MONUMENT

BLACK HILLS

SOUTH DAKOTA

BADLANDS

Minneapolis

PIPESTONE NAT'L MONUMENT

WISCONSIN

WISCONSIN DELLS

LAKE HURON

LAKE MICHIGAN

MICHIGAN

SCOTTS BLUFF NAT'L MONUMENT

MISSOURI RIVER

PLATTE RIVER

NEBRASKA

Omaha

PILOT KNOB STATE PARK

WAPSIPINICON STATE PARK

IOWA

Chicago

LAKE ERIE

COLORADO

OREGON TRAIL

ARKANSAS RIVER

KANSAS

STARVED ROCK STATE PARK

ILLINOIS

INDIANA

OHIO

WABASH RIVER

OHIO RIVER

MISSOURI

St Francis River

MARK TWAIN NAT'L FOREST

Current River

KENTUCKY

CAVE IN ROCK

NEW MEXICO

OKLAHOMA

WICHITA MTS

PLATT NAT'L PARK

OZARK NAT'L FOREST

MISSISSIPPI RIVER

TENNESSEE

WHITE SANDS NAT'L MONUMENT

STAKED PLAINS

RED RIVER

OUACHITA NAT'L FOREST

ARKANSAS

CARLSBAD CAVERNS

TEXAS

ALABAMA

GEORGIA

MISSISSIPPI

BIG BEND NAT'L PARK

LOUISIANA

FLORIDA

N

RIO GRANDE

GULF OF MEXICO

Scale

0   50   100   150 Miles

155

and runs uphill." It runs out of the Big Horn Mountains, and rejoices to share the area with such other streams as the Crazy Woman, Wild Horse, and Little Powder River.

The Mississippi draws water from thirty-one states and two Canadian provinces, from the Idaho-Montana border to New York. At a distance, from a hill, on a December, dark day when driving sleet rasps the eyes, the Mississippi resembles the last push south of the ancient glacier. Like a gray and coiling length of ice it thrusts its cutting edge through the land, pushing the hills apart. In flood the Ohio, the Mississippi, and the Missouri have the remorseless power of the old glaciers, tearing down, piling up, spreading sideways, dragging trees, animals, rocks along with a fury of motion that can no more be stopped than the turning of the earth.

In Indiana the Wabash River flows across the state from east to west, while many smaller streams flow south to the Ohio. All of them are lined with trees and many flow through that high, hilly country, heavily forested almost as it was before the white man brought the reckless edge of his axe. It is here that you will find the town of Solitude, along with the Nancy Hanks Lincoln Memorial and the famous Santa Claus post office. Central Indiana is a till plain heavily glaciated, but the southwestern corner has kept its untouched wildness.

Starved Rock State Park rises on sandstone bluffs along the Illinois River. These were once white sand on the bottom of the great inland sea, but now are stained cream, orange, brown, gray, blue, green, by leached minerals. The valleys are so deep and angular, in the West they would be called canyons. Trees rare for the area grow here—white pine, red cedar, yew, arbor vitae. Six hundred species of plants flourish under skies where at night the uncommon great horned owl flies.

One of the landmarks, hazards, and reliefs to the westward-going wagon trains was the Platte River, running east against the flow of emigration. Its water would seep away in the sandy soil, but it always offered the coolness of a drink to men and animals, and the hazard of a river crossing. The valley of this river is edged with the delicate leaf of the willow, the thin twig and soft branch of the willow. The flat river creeps along its great bend in central Nebraska, north of which the sand hills make a wide, empty, haunting landscape, a flow of sand. But animals survive there, and the reflected light can be as intense at noon as if it came direct from the sun.

Under the surface of the prairie-plain country, below the obvious rivers, is the moving water that, like an invisible and gentle glacier, alters the earth and rock through which it moves. The sandstone beneath the Dakotas is perhaps one hundred feet thick. It turns up toward the west and emerges near the Rockies. Here rain enters and flows eastward, to become the clear cold water rising in the wells of Dakota farms. The water falling on and flowing over the surface sustains plant and animal life, while water under the surface sustains that human life clever enough to tap it. One reason for the wonderful fertility of the soils in the middle states of the Midwest is that they combine adequate drainage with adequate retention of moisture.

Water moving underground in a region of limestone will hollow out the porous stone, acting like a gentle glacier below the surface. Immense rooms have been hollowed out in the Carlsbad Caverns of eastern New Mexico. The evening bat flight is perhaps the most dramatic aspect of the caverns. One of the first men to discover the caves saw a great black cloud rising out of the ground and thought that the ground was on fire. In uncountable numbers the bats swarm upward out of the cavern's mouth to feed in the valley of the Pecos River, returning just before dawn, when they swoop swiftly down to hang all day in dense clusters on the walls and ceilings.

The area around the caverns is now a national park. From an observation tower one can see wide sweeps of desert country running off to remote mountains. The land between is cut with canyons and softened with grayish-green desert plants. In May the prickly pear, primrose, pepperweed, phlox and mallow, verbena and ocotillo, and the spiky yucca are all in bloom in an exuberance of colors. By summer's end drabness returns, but bursts of life are still to be seen in the pronghorn antelope—the fastest North American mammal—the white-tailed and mule deer, the jack rabbits and cottontails, all of them like scraps of the desert come alive and moving. Here the roadrunner bird pursues lizards and insects, seldom flying. This unique creature is a relative of the cuckoo and is the state bird of New Mexico. Birds flourish here: the mourning dove, tanager, oriole, grosbeak, quail, nighthawk, whip-poor-will, cave swallows. The spotted, striped, and hog-nosed skunk haunts the night that conceals it. There are primitive forms of life, wingless insects, gnats, crustaceans, which never leave the caverns.

The glaciers leveled hills and pushed their tops into valleys, forming the basic soil of the northern plain and prairie. Then winds blew a fine, brown soil out of the west, its grains held in solution by air rather than water and for this reason called "loess." North of Sioux City, Iowa, the loess deposits are one hundred feet high. If you have lived in the open country, where the winds can blow with such force and steadiness it seems that they come not from the inner country but from outer space, you will easily understand how moving air can carry the surface of the earth itself over long distances. For the winds of the middle region prowl the sky like invisible glaciers, pounding and crunching and transporting. In summer they can bring not the relief of a breeze to the burning face, but a greater heat, as if they were tipped with fire. In winter they can bring to the freezing face a greater cold, as if they were tipped with ice. In autumn they can bring to the grateful nose a harvest-heavy tang, as if they were tipped with the stems of cut hay and ripe corn. In spring they can bring so rich a scent, so lively a softness, as if they were tipped with life itself, that one believes that flowers could be fertilized not by pollen but by the simple air.

If one item alone were to be chosen as the most important power and aspect of the plain and prairie country, it would be the grass. This holds the soil in place (save when it is wrongly plowed up and the wind blows it away, to destroy the right balance and make a dust bowl of the land). This nourishes the animals that nourish men. It is grass that is always present to the eye looking at any corner of these states. It is grass that gives a rippling texture to the surface of the land. It is grass whose roots grip and control the ground. It is the grass that offers color to the landscape, from the first tentative green of April to the yellow of late summer and the brown of autumn. Nothing can stop grass, it will take root in a cracked rock and live on air alone. The tough and abundant cornstalk, which gives the midwestern fields their density and their grace, is simply an elaborate type of grass.

In the prairie states, pastures are green with grass. Fields of hay are tall and sweet with clover, timothy, and alfalfa. In the western plains the brown grass covers the ground like a sunburned skin. Yet this plant nourished the buffalo in those huge herds that shook the earth when they moved. It might also be said that the swarms of buffalo were a furred glacier whose teeth mowed the grass.

In early Nebraska, the grass actually housed man as well as feeding his cattle. He cut the tough sod and stacked it for walls to make "soddies" against the raging summer sun and the raging winter wind.

To preserve the look of the land where so many different native species of grass flourished before wheel and plow came to tear them, a few places still exist. Iowa has set aside several primitive prairie areas in northern and western parts of the state. Here yellow and purple coneflowers, black-eyed Susans, spiderwort, the New Jersey tea (whose leaves were used at Boston when British-imported tea was unpatriotic), phlox, butterfly weed, blazing star, and many others, proved to the eye how colorful the original landscape was. The Flint Hills region of eastern Kansas, seven

by thirteen miles, rising from the Blue River and rolling off north and east, has been proposed for a national park. Here is the big bluestem, which once grew so tall it would conceal a horse and all of its rider save his head. Here the untouched grassy slopes have another dimension lost to cultivated fields—the sense of spaciousness, grass-covered and without human change.

This is a country of trees, dense along the southern edges of Ohio and Indiana, huddled in wind-rounded groves in Iowa and Illinois (look how many towns on the map have "Grove" in their name), edging the wandering rivers of the western plains. Hickory, butternut, black walnut, drop into the bags of waiting boys. Acorns nourish the uncountable squirrels. Although you are never deep in forest, you are never out of sight of trees.

Groves of shade trees were welcomed by travelers on the prairie. This 1855 view shows covered-wagon emigrants resting under cottonwoods at the Council Bluffs, Iowa, crossing of the Missouri.

In a landscape extended so far toward the horizon, it is natural to let the eyes look to the edge of the earth and then lift upward to the unedged sky. For this is a wild country of clouds, moving in their fluffy whiteness or their threatening darkness, great, unstoppable glaciers crawling through thin air. In summer they may be livid with lightning, or soft with an emptiness made visible. They can glow as if the sun came out of them, or hang with such a leaden grayness it seems they will drop and smash the earth with their weight. But they are always there, moving as the earth moves, endlessly changing, endlessly beautiful.

After glaciers covered ninety per cent of Illinois, the trees came and were chopped down later for farms, so that much of the state is actually prairie made by men, a natural landscape that was artificially created. There are over ten thousand prehistoric Indian mounds in Illinois, including the longest earthwork in the world, Monks Mound, seven hundred ten feet wide, one thousand eighty feet long, on American Bottom, near East St. Louis. It is fitting that, in an area where the greatest feature is the earth, the one great and enduring monument should be the dirt itself, shaped by a dark and savage hand.

Iowa is the only state entirely in the tall-grass area. Without one startling natural feature, the whole state is a natural wonder of fertile soil spread over gentle slopes of a friendly size. It is likely that from the crest of Pilot Knob State Park on the northern edge one can see in every direction more useful land than from any point in the world. Here the earth looks the way a country should when it is given over not to dramatic places startling the eye, but to the quiet nourishing of life. In Iowa the typical fish is not trout or bass with glittering scales, but the ancient catfish, with its earth-colored skin instead of scales, heavily hanging in the pools of earth-colored rivers. Here the wooly mullein lifts its leaves, the blue, white, and purple wild asters persist, the yellow, dark-blue, and pale-blue violets bring the sky down into lengths of sheltering shade.

The Wapsipinicon State Park, where the river of that name flows around dark limestone cliffs hung with fern and softened with moss, just outside the town of Anamosa in eastern Iowa, has preserved the miniature wildness one finds along the rivers. These small areas of surviving stone and hills are not prominent in the landscape, because small, but they are abundant, rising up from the open prairie in an abruptness of tree and valley.

Because it has one quarter of the richest land in the whole United States, it is likely that the surface of Iowa has been more altered and shaped by man than that of any other state. Almost every inch of land has been fenced, and most of it planted or plowed. From a plane this rolling length of field after field runs off in every direction, making a mottled earth. Other states raise monuments to individual men, but Iowa is itself a monument to what man does when he combines soft soil with hard work.

Nebraska is the transitional state from prairie to plain, from the Middle West to the West, where tall grass gives way to short grass. There are rough regions of the state: Chadron State Park in the northwestern corner has deep ravines, high buttes, pine trees; Chimney Rock and Courthouse Rock were landmarks on the Oregon Trail, surviving splinters of rock, but they had their importance for the very reason that the country is everywhere else wide, sandy plain, giving them an unnatural prominence. Yucca begins to appear in Nebraska, cottonwood and willow become the frequent trees, the sunflower and goldenrod yellow the state from below as the sun does from above.

Although it has good farming areas, the characteristics of Missouri most conspicuous to the eye are water—in springs, rivers, lakes—and rock, in the many rugged areas. The Missouri River crosses the state west to east. The St. Francis and Current rivers rush from basin to basin through deep gaps. In Big Spring State Park is one of the largest springs in the United States, once flowing over half a billion gallons of water daily from a basin at the foot of a tall cliff of limestone, where water drops onto ledge, down onto the rocks, and then rushes off to join the Current River. The uplands here are full of underground streams, with springs bubbling out of the rocks at Mark Twain National Forest and Alley Spring State Park. In sight of water one walks above water.

The geodetic center of the United States, from which latitude and longitude are calculated, is on Meade's ranch in Osborne County, Kansas. The geographical center is on the Fort Riley Military Reservation. Kansas is one long field, grassy over its sand and loam soils, changing from corn in the east to wheat to short grass as it goes west four hundred miles. The sunflower grows seven feet tall in the east, knee high in the west, as the rains lessen. Immense fossil remains lie under western Kansas, toothed birds that dove under water, tiny horses, reptiles that flew. Today Kansas is a good deal more staid than that, the high plains of the west rather treeless, the low plains of the east cherishing the Middle West's over four hundred kinds of wild flowers, its clumps of trees, the whole state running out wide and often lonely-looking to the staring eye.

Of all the tier of transitional states, Arkansas has more varieties of land than any other. In the southeastern corner along the Mississippi, Spanish moss grays the southern air. The southwestern corner near Texarkana belongs to the arid cattle plains. In the northwest area are

Where the high plains meet the Rockies: Montana's Paradise Valley on the upper Yellowstone River

the grain fields and orchards of the Midwest. At Blytheville in the northeast the cotton fields begin. From El Dorado in the south to Magazine Mountain east of Fort Smith the elevation goes from two hundred eighty feet to twenty-eight hundred feet. Between these four corners is a country of many springs, of every tree, of the Ozark and Ouachita ranges, the only mountains between the Appalachians and the Rockies, with the Arkansas River dividing them. This rough country is lush in plants, with forty-seven kinds of oak, sixty of hawthorn, with wild cherry and plum, hackberry and cypress, twenty-seven varieties of orchid, the beech and tulip tree, pecans, jasmine, hibiscus, red haw, and phlox. The Ozark National Forest is an almost uninhabited area, keeping the dark light under trees that sent the earliest settlers out into the open spaces. Petrified tree trunks are so common in the extreme northeast corner, they are used as tombstones.

The Dakotas combine within their borders a surprising number of landscapes. North Dakota is the center of North America, equally distant from the Gulf to the Arctic, from the Atlantic to the Pacific. There are rich deposits of soil in the eastern portions, leading to the old saying that if you plant a nail at night, it will grow into a crowbar by morning. All the forces of nature—the upthrust from below, the sideways grind of the glacier, the erosion of wind and water—have worked on this land.

South Dakota is split by the Missouri River. East are the level plains, west are the tumbled badlands. The highest point above sea level east of the Rockies is Harney Peak, just over seven thousand feet. In the cave at Wind Cave National Park, there is a delicate boxwork where calcite has been deposited along the crevices. In Custer State Park, once a sea bottom, a herd of buffalo roams; there are mountain goats on Harney Peak, white-tailed and mule deer prowl the untroubled emptiness.

The Black Hills of South Dakota are a great dome pushed up from so deep in the earth that the rock is older than the Rockies, Alps, Himalayas, or Pyrenees. Concentric rings of later rock encircle it. The tall needles and spires of the region are from this ancient granite bubble, a hundred fifty miles long and seventy-five miles wide. In the Black Hills National Forest elk, deer, bobcats, beaver, have increased as protection has come and cover has grown back. The loamy plains run up almost to the turbulent western area. At Slim Buttes the limestone cliffs afford immense views across the open country, bringing the recent soils into close touch with the old rock.

North Dakota has its wild variety. The Badlands along the Little Missouri River are fantastically eroded ridges, hills, buttes, domes, cones, in brown, red, gray, yellow sands and clays from the ocean bottom. Here were once forest swamps, with tall trunks fifteen feet across. The

159

north and south divisions of Theodore Roosevelt National Memorial Park have centuries-old fires in coal veins, so that in winter steam rises. The Indians believed that the hills were on fire. There is a scoria lily, which opens its blossoms only after the sun has set, as if it had borne too much light and heat.

The states that run out eastward from the Continental Divide are the true West. The streams that flow here run through crumbled, washed-out rock, so that what you walk or drive over looks like plain but is actually the mountains broken up under your feet. The eastern two fifths of Montana are dry wheat lands, eroded, crisscrossed with waterless valleys, with hardly fifteen inches of rain. The Missouri and Yellowstone rivers flow toward each other and have an importance out of all proportion to their size because of the great value of water in such a land. Pompey's Pillar on the Yellowstone is two hundred feet high, and was climbed by William Clark in 1806. The lovely word "bitterroot" is found in the mountain, valley, and river of that name, and is the state flower. The Judith Basin, once buffalo country, is now a fertile grain and hay oasis in the arid region. (Romantically, it was named by Clark, on his journey to the Pacific in 1805, in honor of Judith Hancock of Virginia, who later became his bride.)

In eastern Colorado the long sideways rolling of the plains bumps up against the high mass of the Rocky Mountains. Here is the abrupt confrontation between level land and the Continental Divide. Here the burrowing owl and the desert horned lark, the plover, the western mocking bird, and the noisy magpie fly over the sparse grass that once fed the abundant buffalo (called by Coronado, "large humped cattle, maned like lions").

After living on or driving over or flying above these restless, wind-haunted plains, one should go up on the Front Range to see what the eastward-lying country is really like. Here is a long view of the short-grass country such as cannot be had from moving across it. Limited only by the eye's ability to penetrate the glistening air, one can see the many soils of Colorado, the chalky white, the sandy brown, the red and gray and black. After a few miles the works of man blur into the surface of the earth, leaving only a primitive spaciousness. Surely this is the way it looked when this terrain rose from the ocean, when wind replaced wave and fresh rain replaced salt water.

Standing on the young mountains and looking over the old plains, where the grass blurs the landscape into a single field as broad as the bending sky, one often sees the Colorado cony harvesting the patchy grass behind the rock piles. This he stores for the winter, for which he is affectionately known as the "haymaker of the heights."

Out of the Colorado mountains the South Platte flows northeast into Nebraska and the Arkansas flows southeast into Kansas. Between the willow-bordered streams a brown and sandy country flows off to the horizon, which shifts with every shudder of the ever-changing light. Yet there are seasonal colors here for the careful eye—the sand lily, the evening primrose, white star flower, devil's claw; the red, yellow, and orange blossoms of the cacti, the silver foliage and edible berry of the buffalo bush, the gray-green sage, aromatic when crushed between the hands.

In Oklahoma, larger than any state east of the Mississippi, the plains country turns rough and turbulent. In contrast to the arid land around it, the Platt National Park (in the foothills of the Arbuckle Mountains) has many springs, creeks, wooded valleys, and grassy hills. As in the Wichita Mountains Wildlife Refuge, with its wild turkeys, deer, buffalo, wild longhorn cattle, and elk, the presence of water makes possible the presence of life. Here the most scenic areas are those that are most unlike the typical broken, dry plains in most of the state.

Coming south from the sandy sweeps of Kansas, one finds in Oklahoma a fine triumph of rock. The Alabaster Caverns near the Cimarron River in the northwestern corner are hollowed by water out of the stone. Millions of bats issue in the summer and hibernate from first frost to March. The roar of underground streams may sometimes be heard. Crayfish are found in Blind Fish Cavern, and have become in the loud darkness both transparent and blind. The sides of Glass Mountain are covered with crystalline gypsum and gleam in the crystal light.

The great gypsum area of the southwestern plains is in the White Sands National Monument of southern New Mexico. Here the fine grains of the stone have been blown into wavelike ripples, with a perpetual motion altering each form by a gradual sliding. Between the Sacramento Mountains on the east and the San Andres on the west, the dunes make a shining desert, glaring by night or day. Here is the ultimate opposite of the wavelike prairies, whose motion is frozen into fertile fields.

How could Texas not have every climate, every temperature, every land form? It has every soil, from the black prairies of the east to the alkali of the west. It has the curving salt water coast on the Gulf, and the salt surface of its desert interior. The Rio Grande is a river of extremes, from a thinness of water that is barely wet, to its mad floods. The temperature may drop fifty degrees in thirty-six hours. The state seems waterless to the eye, and yet three fourths of the people live on underground water from wells and springs. The earliest remnants of geological time are here, and the latest. The altitude ranges from fifty feet above sea level at the Gulf to almost nine thousand in the trans-Pecos mountains. Much of Texas looks difficult for living things, and yet it has four thousand kinds of wild flowers, almost seven hundred varieties of birds, five hundred fifty sorts of grasses. There are three kinds of jack rabbits, five varieties of cottontails, two kinds of marsh rabbits. The coyote is everywhere, howling his rage at not being a more dangerous animal. The armadillo shuffles through the hills, bearing quadruplets, always of the same sex. The flying squirrel startles tree and air. All four of the deadly snakes found in the United States are in Texas: rattlers, moccasins, copperheads, coral. The best-known lizard is the horned toad. It is illegal to kill the mockingbird, which is the state bird. The trees are from both the Atlantic and Pacific areas: oak, juniper, pine, fir, cypress, mesquite, along with the native cactus—yucca and maguey. Yet here is no ordinary yucca, for in the Big Bend National Park, where the Rio Grande bends north through several canyons, old sea bottoms pushed up by granite, there are many yuccas.

Texas is the state where the western plains explode. The Staked Plains, barren, malevolent, best described by a town's name, Levelland. The Palo Duro Canyon State Park, on the Prairie Dog Town Fork of the Red River in northwestern Texas, spectacularly breaks up the plains country with its wildness of gashed earth, tree, running river, and living green. At first this may seem too unique to be called Texan, and yet it is this very possession of every unusual place that is ordinary in the state. And people have admired it—why else would they name their towns Happy, Earth, Blessing, and Sublime?

Most of the structures built by man in the prairie-plains area have simply added an unnatural aspect to the landscape. But in this great territory of moderate rain and wide dryness, a remarkable return to nature has happened. The rivers have been dammed. In a sense this has made the region even more natural, the wider water providing more shelter and feed for aquatic creatures than before.

Through the Dakotas, the Missouri along much of its length is as much lake as stream, beginning with the Gavins Point Dam near Yankton in the southeastern corner of South Dakota, and continuing with the Fort Randall Dam and the vast Oahe Reservoir above the Oahe Dam. In North Dakota the Garrison Dam has backed up water over a hundred miles, almost to the Montana line.

The Fort Peck Dam in northeastern Montana has created long lakes not only on the Missouri, but along the Musselshell and the Little Dry. In eastern Wyoming there are the Keyhole Reservoir, on the Belle Fourche before it runs into South Dakota; and the Glendo Reservoir, on the North Platte below the Pathfinder and Seminoe reservoirs, on the same river. Farther downstream in Nebraska the North Platte above the Kingsley Dam has a recreation area unusual in the state.

In northeastern Kansas the Tuttle Creek Reservoir along the Big Blue River offers a body of water such as the state has never seen before. Missouri has not only the writhing Lake of the Ozarks on the Osage River, wriggling one hundred twenty-nine miles like one of the hooked fish for which it is famous, but the Table Rock Reservoir and Bull Shoals Lake, running down into Arkansas. In northeastern Oklahoma the little Neosho has been dammed to form the Lake of the Cherokees and Lake Fort Gibson. On the Salt Fork of the Arkansas, the Great Salt Plains Reservoir enhances the area of the Great Salt Plains Wildlife Refuge. On the Oklahoma-Texas line the Red River has been dammed to make Lake Texoma, with a long branch running up on the Wildhorse.

On the Brazos in Texas the Possum Kingdom Reservoir, Lake Kemp on the Wichita, Lake Travis on the Colorado, have all brought expanses of water where once there was only one sustained expanse of dry country.

These lakes have permanently altered the aspect of the landscape, as well as the recreational activities of the people living in reach of them. They are bringing back wild creatures—fish, game birds, and the citizen contemptuous with beer can and paper plate. Yet it is a marvelous thing that, as the thickly settled coastal and Great Lake areas go on snatching land out of nature, the plains are busy returning land and river to nature.

So the wooded prairie runs west to the grassy plain, and the plain runs west to the mountain, which stares down at the hot land from its cool height: a decent country, useful for decent men, a lived-in country, nourishing life in an abundance never seen on the earth's wrinkled surface before. It is a wide region, wide as the sky above it. As our knowledge expands our sense of the terrifying reaches of the sky, no matter what strange ways of matter or life we may find out there, will any planet have on it as heartening a range of soil and crop, of grass and grain and animal?

A French traveler, Charles Lesueur, sketched these settlers in a keelboat on the Ohio in 1826.

The Deep Woods of Ohio

In the early days, the country of the Ohio River Valley, rolling west of the Appalachians, was a vast, unbroken forest. But colonizers like Manasseh Cutler boomed it as a "garden of the universe," and after the Revolution a torrent of settlers pushed through the dark woods on horseback and along the open rivers in canoes, rafts, flatboats, and keelboats. With axes and hard work, they cut clearings and put up cabins, and as more settlers arrived, the woods gradually disappeared and became an open countryside of prosperous farms. Today it is difficult to envision the hardwood forest that once blanketed much of this section of the rich, agricultural Midwest.

Ohio River traffic in 1821 is seen above. The engraving on the opposite page shows a stand of sycamores in Ohio in 1841.

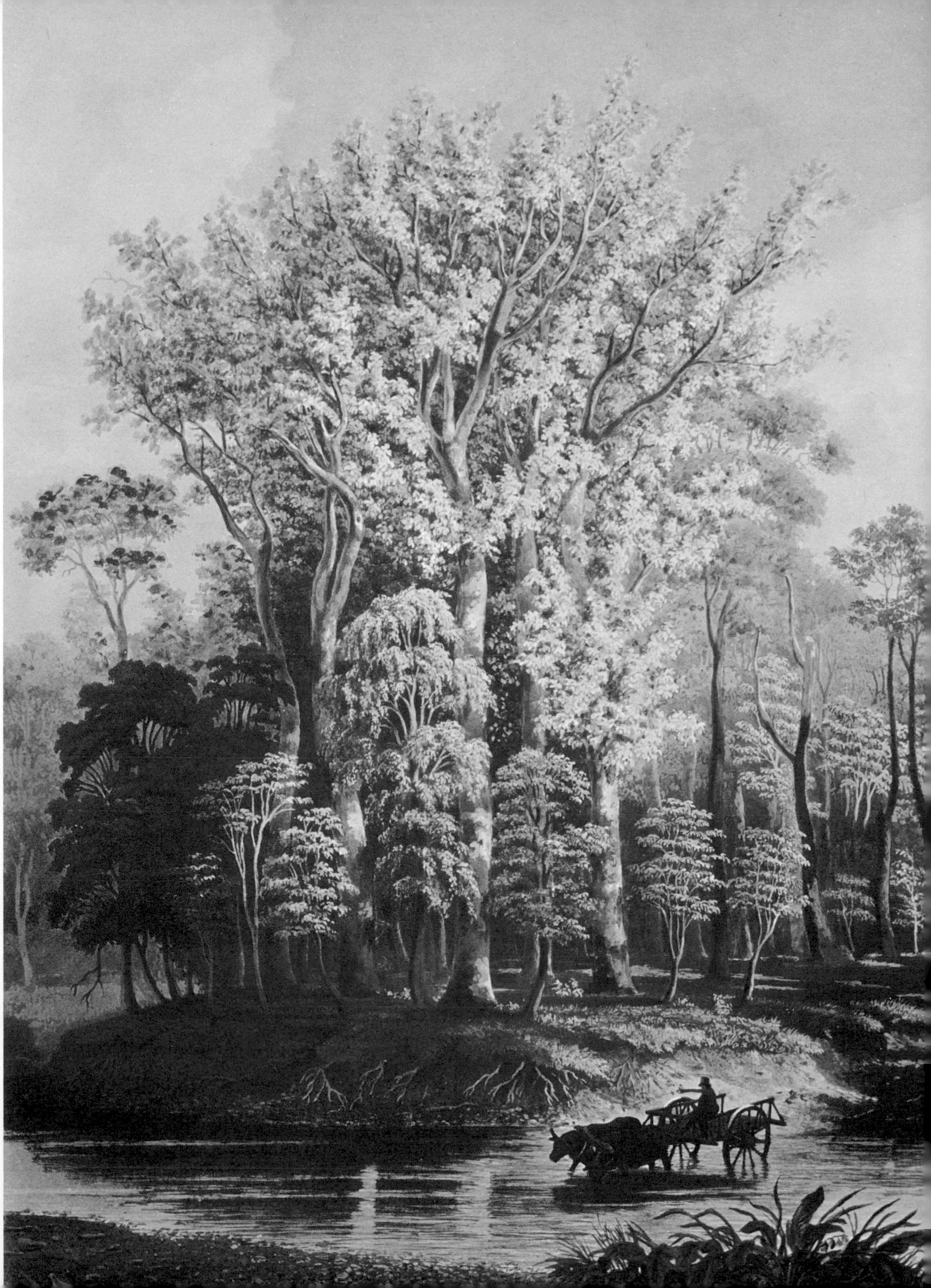

STOKES COLLECTION, NYPL

Cave in Rock

The first Frenchmen on the Ohio had called it the "beautiful river," and American travelers who went down it in the nineteenth century in flatboats and steamboats echoed the sentiment. "Nothing . . . can surpass what was now above us and around us," mused the frontier preacher, Timothy Flint, who descended the river in a "large skiff" in 1815. The long stretches of wide, clean sand bars, with wild geese, swans, sand-hill cranes, and pelicans stalking along them, the "infinite varieties of form of the towering bluffs; the new tribes of shrubs and plants," and the "ancient and magnificent forests, which the axe has not yet despoiled," all combined to make the voyage the "very element of poetry" for him.

There were exciting curiosities along the river, also, to break the reverie of dreamers and provide vivid paragraphs in letters written home. The most famous was Cave in Rock, a 160-foot-deep cavern near Shawneetown, Illinois. Though one traveler thought it a perfect retreat for monks, the cave acquired a dread reputation as the lair of river pirates who pounced on passing craft and robbed the crews and passengers. One of the most notorious was Samuel Mason who lured victims to the cave with a sign at its entrance that advertised: "Liquor Vault and House for Entertainment." In time, the pirates passed, but the cave is still an object of romance to those who travel on the Ohio River.

The imaginative view (right) of the discovery of Cave in Rock, its interior filled with Indian skeletons and pictographs, was painted in 1850. Earlier, the Swiss artist Carl Bodmer recorded the scene of the rock from the river as he had steamed past it in 1833 (left). Below is a photograph of the cave's entrance today, visited by tourists going by on the river.

A Midwestern prairie farmer of the nineteenth century, with scythe, whetstone, and sun-creased eyes

Rich, Black Earth

To every farmer who first came on them, extending farther than the eye could see, the open prairies of the Middle West were an unsurpassed wonder. After leaving the dark woods of Ohio, it was like stepping suddenly out of doors on a bright day. There were no trees to cut down, no stumps to plow around, and the soil was deep, black, and rich. "Bruised by the brushwood and exhausted by the extreme heat we almost despaired," wrote one westering settler as he approached the Illinois country in 1816. "A few steps more and a beautiful prairie suddenly opened to our view . . . lying in profound repose under the warm light of an afternoon's summer sun."

It took a while, and determination and labor, to work the open country into prosperous farms. Some settlers even avoided the areas without trees, fearing that they might be too sterile for crops. But the black earth lived up to its promise and rewarded those who settled on it. Today, thriving farms, like the one in Iowa at right, continue a tradition of yielding the most abundant crops the world has ever known.

Harper's Weekly, 1868

An 1868 sketch by Theodore Davis in Harper's Weekly *shows oxen helping farmers break the prairie sod.*

The days of Huck Finn come to life in the painting, Rafting Downstream.

Mark Twain

The Mississippi

Whoo-oop! I'm the old original iron-jawed, brass-mounted, copper-bellied corpse-maker from the wilds of Arkansaw!—Look at me! I'm the man they call Sudden Death and General Desolation! Sired by a hurricane, dam'd by an earthquake, half-brother to the cholera, nearly related to the small-pox on the mother's side! Look at me! I take nineteen alligators and a bar'l of whiskey for breakfast when I'm in robust health, and a bushel of rattlesnakes and a dead body when I'm ailing. I split the everlasting rocks with my glance, and I squench the thunder when I speak! Whoo-oop!"

Ever since its exploration in 1673 by Marquette and Jolliet, the Mississippi has been many things: fur traders' route from New Orleans to Canada; a national boundary; Jim Bowie fighting with a knife under the bluffs of Natchez; Island No. 10 and Vicksburg; the fire-spitting race between the *Natchez* and the *Robert E. Lee*; floods over the levees; and barges bound for Pittsburgh, the Great Lakes, and Fort Benton, Montana. But the enduring image is the 2,350-mile-long Father of Waters itself, the mile-wide tide, pictured opposite between Wisconsin and Iowa, and personified in the boast of Mark Twain's river raftsman in *Life on the Mississippi*: "Whoo-oop! Stand back and give me room according to my strength!"

169

The first (and weirdest) photograph ever made of a tornado (above) was taken on the plains of Miner County, South Dakota, August 28, 1884.

170

No catastrophe of the elements provided more dramatic scenes for the artists of America's illustrated weeklies than the great twisters of the Midwest. Views of people rushing for "cyclone cellars," and of humans, animals, and buildings hurtling through the air were gripping fare. The drawing above is of a 1902 storm. At right, an 1884 tornado is seen in the act of blowing away Jamestown, Ohio.

To the Storm Cellars!

It was a tornado that whirled away Dorothy and Toto from their Kansas farm; and to most Americans who remember their childhood reading and have never experienced the terror of the phenomenon themselves, a tornado is still something associated with the *Wizard of Oz*. But generations of prairie dwellers have known the "screaming, hissing" funnel as an all too real demon that wrecked farms, carried away buildings, and killed families. Usually appearing on clouded days during the spring and summer, the fearsome twisters made the possession of storm cellars a necessity in the open country.

"[The] glorious Wisconsin wilderness!" sang John Muir, the Scottish-born conservationist who came to Wisconsin in 1849 as a boy of eleven. "Young hearts, young leaves, flowers, animals, the winds and the streams and the sparkling lake, all . . . rejoicing together." To the traveler who has seen all of America, Wisconsin can be a surprise. In large parts of the state, there is a carefully composed look to the land, matched nowhere else in the nation. The high, green hills, colored outcroppings of rock, parklike stands of trees, and reflective waters of streams and lakes seem almost to have been set in place by an artist. Beauty can be found at frequented sites like the Wisconsin Dells; but one can also rejoice at the loveliness of a thousand unhailed settings like the one near the Mississippi River in this photograph by Paul Vanderbilt.

172

PAUL VANDERBILT, WISCONSIN STATE HISTORICAL SOCIETY

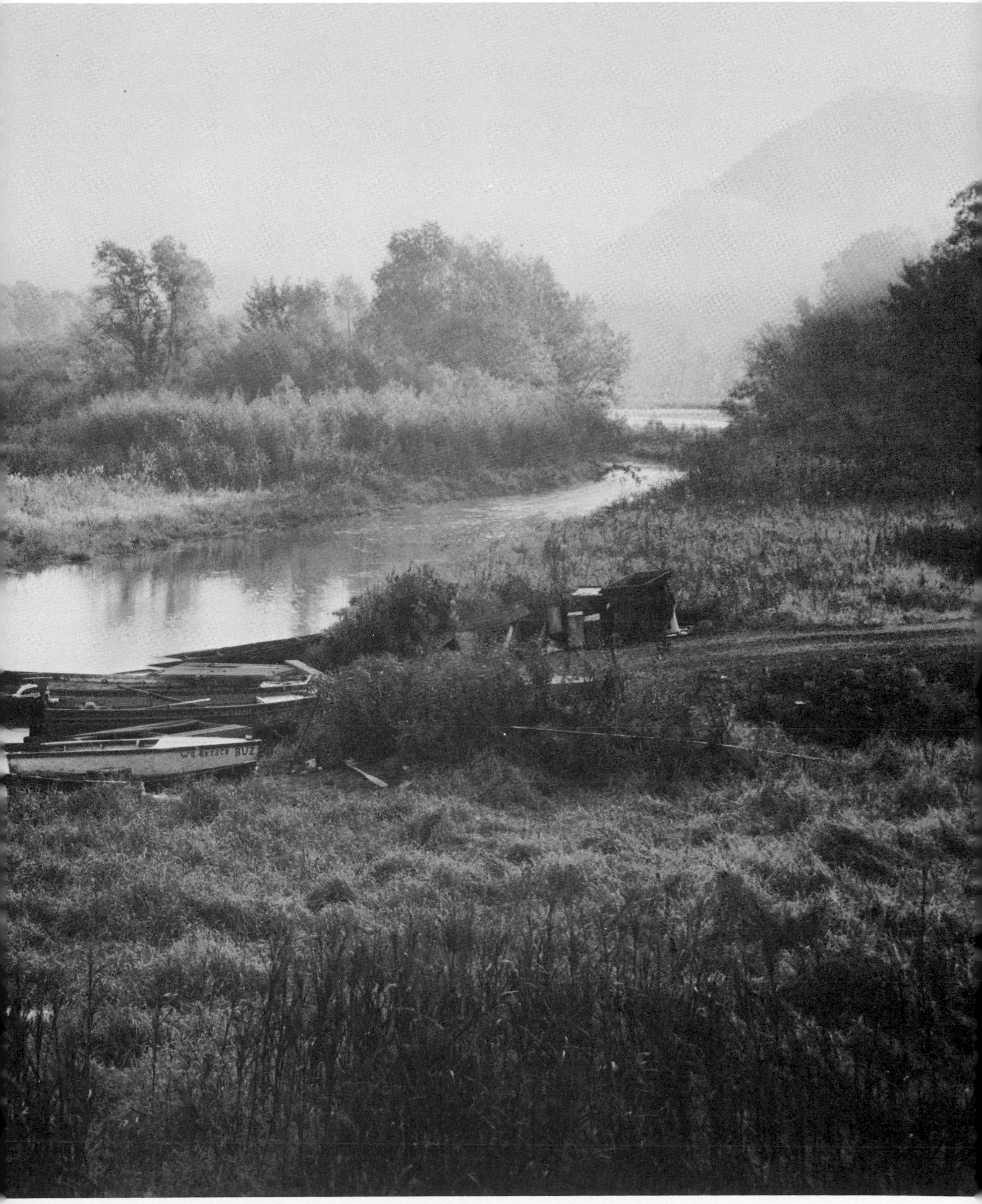

The border country was a meeting place of different Indian cultures. Under white pressure, bands of Sioux and other Indians migrated from the woods to the plains and changed their ways of life. They gave up canoes, agriculture, and semipermanent settlements, and adopted horses, buffalo hunting, and skin-covered tipis which they moved from place to place. The Indians who stayed in the border region, like the feathered Cree below, employed elements of both cultures. Sometimes they hunted buffalo on the plains; sometimes they lived like Easterners.

Western Minnesota's Pipestone Quarry, painted in 1848 by George Catlin, provided tribes with the red stone for their pipe bowls.

The Edge of the Plains

In 1800 the British fur trader Alexander Henry emerged from the watered woodland through which he had been traveling and gazed upon the Great Plains. The entire aspect of the country had suddenly changed. "[The] eye is lost in one continuous level westward," he wrote. "Not a tree or rising ground interrupts the view." Henry was in the Red River country of North Dakota, in a borderland that later rang with history. Métis, French Canadian half-breeds, who traded between Winnipeg and St. Paul in creaking, high-wheeled "Red River carts" (seen above in a photograph of the 1860's), tried in 1870 and 1885 to create an independent Indian and half-breed state. Their armed uprisings were finally crushed, and their leader, Louis Riel, was hanged.

175

One of the West's most fanciful maps (below) was published in 1703 by
the Baron Louis de Lahontan, who had ascended the Mississippi to the
Minnesota. Everything after that was imaginary, but for years explorers and cartographers accepted his description of the "Long River."

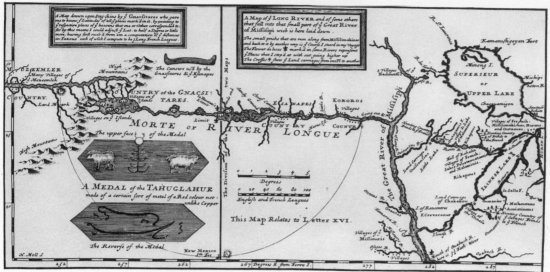

Eroded formations like these in Nebraska's Toadstool Park were often the source of rumors of strange country.

The Land of Rumor

When the United States acquired the Louisiana Territory in 1803, much of it was a region of mystery. French and Spanish explorers and traders had probed parts of its treeless plains and eroded badlands, but had left more rumors than hard facts. There were mountains of "solid rock salt," peaks of glass that shined in the night, rivers of brine and yellow rocks, silver mines, and ground that smoked from fires. A map made by Indians and sent to President Jefferson in 1805, "a little incredible," showed a volcano on the Yellowstone River. It was left for Lewis and Clark and those who followed them across the plains to set the rumors at rest—and prove some of them true.

177

Jack Rabbit

Squirrel

Striped Chipmunk

Black-tailed Deer

178

American Antelope

First Drawings of the Plains

These water colors of an Indian camp on Nebraska's Platte River (below) and of various animals, including the fleet antelope, which Lewis and Clark had described to the nation, were among the first drawn by an eyewitness on the plains. They were done by Titian Ramsay Peale, who accompanied Major Stephen H. Long's expedition to the Rockies in 1820. Long's report dashed popular interest in the region, calling it "almost wholly unfit for cultivation," and Peale's delightful drawings of this "Great American Desert" have remained largely unpublished and forgotten.

George Armstrong Custer

Pa Sapa and the "Thieves' Road"

From the dusty plains, the forested hills rising in the distance looked black to the Sioux who were migrating westward in the eighteenth century. But when they trailed into the trees and up to the pinnacles (left), they found a paradise of flowered parks and thirst-quenching waters. In time they came to venerate South Dakota's Black Hills and called them *Pa Sapa,* the sacred grounds. By solemn treaty in 1868, this heart of their plains homeland was barred to white men "forever."

But, spurred by rumors of gold, Lieutenant Colonel George A. Custer invaded the Hills in 1874 with twelve hundred men. As they rode through *Pa Sapa,* Custer and his party were enchanted by the "profuse display of flowers," which they picked from their saddles. The beauty of the area did not blind them to the object of their search; and Custer's triumphant report of gold "from the grass roots down" started a stampede that the government could not halt.

The miners' rush into the Sioux's sacred grounds led to Custer's own doom. When the government was unable to force the Indians to sell *Pa Sapa,* it ordered the Army to put them on reservations. Though troops eventually succeeded in securing the Black Hills for the white man, thousands of Sioux, fighting fiercely for their country under Crazy Horse, Gall, and Sitting Bull, first had the satisfaction at the Little Bighorn on June 25, 1876, of slaying Custer and many members of his Seventh Cavalry, who had opened the "Thieves' Road" to their *Pa Sapa.*

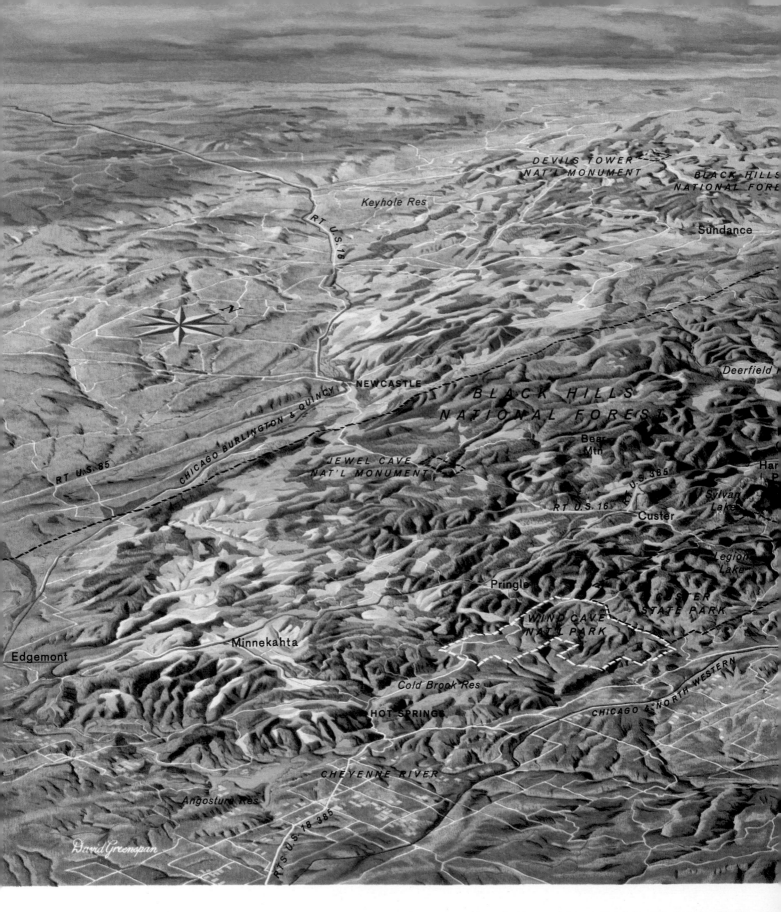

The labels visible on the map include:

DEVILS TOWER NAT'L MONUMENT

BLACK HILLS NATIONAL FORE[ST]

Sundance

Keyhole Res

RT U.S. 16

Deerfield

BLACK HILLS NATIONAL FOREST

NEWCASTLE

Bear Mtn

CHICAGO BURLINGTON & QUINCY

JEWEL CAVE NAT'L MONUMENT

U.S. 385

Har[ney] P[eak]

RT U.S. 85

RT U.S. 16

Custer

Sylvan Lake

Pringle

Legion Lake

CUSTER STATE PARK

WIND CAVE NAT'L PARK

Minnekahta

Edgemont

Cold Brook Res

HOT SPRINGS

CHICAGO & NORTH WESTERN

CHEYENNE RIVER

Angostura Res

RTS U.S. 18 385

David Greenspan

182

In 1874 Custer had written that the "natural beauty" of the Black Hills "may well bear comparison with the fairest portions of Central Park [in New York City]." Today this green oasis in the plains, formed when a batholith with a granitic core was slowly thrust from the earth's interior long before the creation of the Rockies or the Himalayas, is one of America's most popular recreational areas. The great busts

BLACK HILLS

WYOMING   SOUTH DAKOTA

RT U.S. 14

Belle Fourche

Belle Fourche
Res

Spearfish

Terry
Pk   Central
City
Lead   Deadwood

Sturgis

INTERSTATE 90

Silver
City

Pactola Res

Sheridan Lake

Mt
hmore

RAPID CITY

Keystone   RT U.S. 16

T RUSHMORE
T'L MEMORIAL   CHICAGO & NORTH WESTERN   INTERSTATE 90

RT 79   CHICAGO MILWAUKEE ST PAUL & PACIFIC

RT 40

Hermosa

CHEYENNE RIVER   BADLANDS
NATIONAL MONUMENT

Sheep
Mtn

of Washington, Jefferson, Lincoln, and Theodore Roosevelt carved by Gutzon Borglum
on the side of a mountain at Mount Rushmore National Monument help attract more
than a million people annually. But most come, also, to view the country's largest existing
buffalo herd in Custer State Park, the pinnacles and spires in the vicinity of Harney Peak, and the caves, lakes, and vast meadows of wildflowers that charmed Custer.

183

T. R. in the Badlands

Once a steaming marsh inhabited by prehistoric reptiles, the weird peaks and gullies of South Dakota's
Badlands (left) were eroded by centuries of running
water. Cutting up western parts of both North and
South Dakota, the broken country was thought by Indians to be an abode of evil spirits and was called
"les mauvaises terres à traverser" by French Canadian
fur trappers. In 1864 General Alfred Sully referred to
the Badlands as "hell with the fires out."

And yet, nineteen years later, a young "Eastern
punkin-lily," come west to improve his puny frame
by hunting buffalo, stepped off a train at Little Missouri, North Dakota—and shortly fell in love with this
"land of vast silent spaces." Theodore Roosevelt
nourished both his soul and body in this usually
avoided part of the American frontier. Badly in need
of a change after the loss of both his mother and wife,
as well as a political defeat in 1884, he made a second
trip to the Badlands and soon wrote his sister that he
was "well hardened" and that "the country is growing
on me, more and more; it has a curious fantastic beauty
of its own." Later, he wrote of life on his ranch near
Medora, North Dakota: "We worked under the scorch-
ing midsummer sun, when the wide plains shimmered
and wavered in the heat; and we knew the freezing misery of riding night guard . . . In the soft springtime the
stars were glorious in our eyes each night before we fell
asleep; and in the winter we rode through blinding blizzards . . . ours was the glory of work and the joy of living."

The western Roosevelt in 1884

Roosevelt's Elkhorn Ranch, now a national monument, fronted North Dakota's Little Missouri.

Buffalo, Buffalo!

Again and again that morning rang out the same welcome cry of *buffalo, buffalo!* . . . At noon, the plain before us was alive with thousands of buffalo,—bulls, cows, and calves,—all moving rapidly as we drew near; and far off beyond the river the swelling prairie was darkened with them to the very horizon." Twenty-three-year-old Francis Parkman was embarked on the most thrilling adventure of his life: a buffalo hunt on the Arkansas River in Colorado. It was 1846, and on the great, open plains, like those pictured above one year later by H. G. Hine, the frail, intellectual Parkman (like Theodore Roosevelt) would prove his mettle against the American West.

Borrowing a gun from his Canadian guide, Parkman rode down a hollow toward the densely packed animals. "In a moment I was in the midst of the cloud, half suffocated by the dust and stunned by the trampling of the flying herd; but I was drunk with the chase and cared for nothing but the buffalo." After a furious fight with a wounded beast, during which Parkman ran out of the correct size ammunition and had to use fringes from his shirt for gun wadding, he felled "a stout yearling bull." That night, as the future author of the *Oregon Trail* lay down to sleep, he heard across the prairie the "hoarse bellowing of the buffalo, like the ocean beating upon a distant coast."

Francis Parkman

187

Successor to the Buffalo

"The buffalo is gone, and of all his millions nothing is left but bones. Tame cattle . . . have supplanted his vast herds and boundless grazing grounds," wrote Francis Parkman forty-six years after his hunt. Today, the plains' great carpet of rich grass that once fed buffalo is the domain of Herefords (above).

189

An evening bivouac of fur traders on the banks of the upper Missouri, 1834

"Far Away, You Rolling River"

The thrilling descriptions that Lewis and Clark and other early travelers had written about the country high up "the wide Missouri" filled many Americans with a desire to see what that romantic land of wild animals, Indians, and fur trappers looked like. To the millions of people who could not make the trip themselves, some of the most popular views were those of the Swiss artist Carl Bodmer, many of whose pictures were published as colored engravings and were copied and recopied by other artists. Bodmer went up the Missouri in the American Fur Company's steamboat *Yellowstone* in 1833 with a Prussian naturalist, Prince Maximilian of Wied. His original paintings, some of which are reproduced on these pages, included faithfully accurate renditions of Indian life around the fur posts, as well as of the scenic grandeur of the country along the Missouri almost as far west as present-day Great Falls, Montana.

View of the junction of the Missouri and Yellowstone rivers, June 25, 1833

The weirdly eroded "white castles" on the Missouri in Montana, July 25, 1833

In 1837 Chimney Rock looked like this to the Baltimore artist Alfred Jacob Miller.

Hiram Scott had been dead less than ten years when Miller painted his bluffs.

Chimney Rock today shows the work of erosion since 1837.

Scotts Bluff is now a national monument of the Trail.

Landmarks of the Oregon Trail

To the impatient motorist who hurries across the United States, the Great Plains can seem a monotonous part of the trip. But to the person who knows his American history, the highway that follows the original Oregon Trail in Nebraska and Wyoming can bring the romance and color of pioneer days vividly to life. In this former country of roaming bands of Arapaho, Cheyenne, Pawnee, and Sioux Indians, travelers can still see the principal natural landmarks that stood up above the trail and excited the wonder and curiosity of those who trudged slowly past them in long trains of covered wagons.

During the great westward migration across the plains, these landmarks—Courthouse Rock, Chimney Rock, Scotts Bluff, Independence Rock, and Devil's Gate—made the way easier. It was good to know how far one had come, and also exciting to see with one's own eyes the "great natural curiosities" that earlier travelers and authors of "emigrants' guide books" had written about. Chimney Rock was described by almost every traveler; but one of the first was a fifty-six-year-old New York Congregational missionary, Samuel Parker, who in 1835 traveled west with a fur caravan to select mission sites for the Indians of "the Oregon country." In July his party camped near one of "nature's wonders . . . called the chimney," wrote the divine in his widely read book, *Journal of an Exploring Tour Beyond the Rocky Mountains,* "but I should say, it ought to be called beacon hill." Parker climbed to the base of the column and observed "some handsome stalactites, at which my assistant shot," thus helping the process of natural erosion that through the years has been eating away the formation.

Scotts Bluff, twenty-five miles west of Chimney Rock in Nebraska, also attracted comment, not only as an object of nature, but because of the legend of Hiram Scott, the fur trader, for whom it was named. In 1828, sick, and abandoned by his companions to die alone on the plains, Scott crawled sixty miles to the bluffs, where others found his bones the next year.

ABOVE AND BELOW: SOLOMON D. BUTCHER COLLECTION, NEBRASKA STATE HISTORICAL SOCIETY

Homes on the Range

"I am looking rather seedy now
While holding down my claim,
And my victuals are not always served the best;
And the mice play shyly round me
*   as I nestle down to rest*
In my little old sod shanty in the West."

By the end of the nineteenth century, large parts of the former buffalo range that had once been called a desert were dotted with the homes of thousands of farm families, drawn there by the Homestead Act of 1862 and various government and private land offers. But if—as the 1884 Northern Pacific flyer on the opposite page promised them—they would become "first families, and leaders, socially and politically," there was pioneering of a new and difficult kind first to be endured. In a country that had few trees for building materials, a generation of "soddies" acclimated themselves to the plains and raised homes of blocks of "the national soil."

Newly arrived settlers usually began with dugouts like the one above, inexpensively scooped from the sheltered sides of draws. One Nebraskan estimated in 1872 that his fourteen-foot-square home cost him $2.87½—and that included the luxury of a glass window. But the dugout was dank and cavelike, and many a woman burst into tears when she first saw her new home on the plains. The next step was a move aboveground into the comparative comfort of a sod house. Though they provided good insulation against summer heat and winter cold, they were an agony to the housekeeper. The turf roof leaked, sometimes for days, and women had to cook pancakes on buffalo chip fires under umbrellas, while families dispensed with evening prayers because it was too muddy to kneel. But these Americans, below or above the ground, knew how to brighten their homes with such touches as swings, bird cages, and pots of flowers. And eventually a family might live in an elegant structure like the two-story sod house at the far left, which boasted a circular, walnut staircase.

195

BOTH: U.S. DEPT. OF AGRICULTURE

The forward edge of a massive dust storm of the mid-1930's rolls in to blind and choke a town on the plains.

Dust clouds like this one drove caravans of "Okies" and others westward on highways, searching for new homes.

Harvest of Waste

Little by little," wrote John Steinbeck in *The Grapes of Wrath,* "the sky was darkened by the mixing dust, and the wind felt over the earth, loosened the dust, and carried it away. . . . The dawn came, but no day." For decades the families who had settled on the plains had planted and planted and done nothing to protect the valuable topsoil. In 1931, as a drought became worse, the soil began to lift; in 1933 it was blowing in great dust storms; and by the next year, from the Dakotas to Texas, thousands of impoverished families, like the one in Oklahoma in Arthur Rothstein's memorable photograph below, were filling roads to California and elsewhere, fleeing from what had become a terrible, sand-covered Dust Bowl.

GEORGE HUNTER

Dust storms can return to the plains; but man has profited by the misery of the 1930's and with modern practices of soil conservation can take better care of the open land. Wind strip cropping, seen above in Montana, in which wheat alternates with fallow, arrests wind erosion.

Beyond the buildings a shelter belt of trees and shrubs, planted by the farmer, also protects against the strong winds. Other methods to conserve precious water, like contour tillage, make the plains more productive than ever, and the farms a beautiful part of the landscape.

199

Canyon in the Plains

In 1805, the same year that Lewis and Clark journeyed to the Rockies, François Antoine Larocque, a French fur trader, traveled across the plains with Crow Indians and near the present border of Montana and Wyoming came on a great, winding chasm. From its brink, he looked far down at the Bighorn River and wrote: "The sensation of dizziness felt while surveying the river from the summit of these rocks is frightful." Climbing an eminence, he gained a larger view of the eroded cleft in the plains and the land beyond it. "One there sees the Big Horn river wind across a level plain of about three miles width and can follow its course for a great distance, not far from its point of meeting with the Yellowstone."

In later years, American trappers used the Bighorn as a fast way to get home with their furs. Launching bullboats, like those of the Hidatsa women drawn by Rudolph Kurz at Fort Berthold in 1851 (below), they floated across the plains to the Yellowstone and Missouri. The tub-shaped craft, made of buffalo hides stretched over a willow frame, was described by Washington Irving as "a slight bark to navigate these endless rivers . . . [yet it] is surprising what rough shocks and thumps these boats will endure . . ." But no one rode them through the Bighorn canyon. Though Jim Bridger dared the chasm in 1825, running its twenty-one mile course on a raft and living to tell about it, other trappers gave it the name "Bad Pass" and portaged around it. Today, dam-builders have closed the canyon and ended its challenge to modern Bridgers.

When There Were No Fences

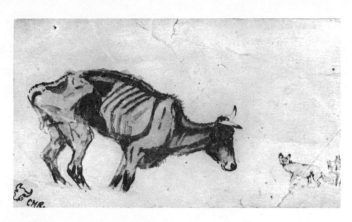

A reminder of the winter of 1886–87, when thousands of steers died in storms, this is perhaps the most famous cattle picture ever made. Charlie Russell, the cowboy artist, sent it to his employer, who had asked how the herd had fared. The title, Waiting for a Chinook, *was later changed to* Last of the 5,000.

The 1908 photograph of XIT Ranch Texas ponies in Montana (above) was made after an era had closed, but its view of a drive across the plains evoked in many an old-time stockman a wish for the return of lost days. "We used to trail cattle up from Texas and double our money on them," reminisced a pioneer cowman of the 1870's. "We didn't mind the distance. The range was free and there were no fences . . . " For a brief and colorful day, after the buffalo and Indians and before the railroads and barbed wire, the plains were the setting for long drives across the land, like the one below on Montana's Milk River. There were stampedes, blizzards, and high rivers to worry about, but no obstructions to bar the way from Texas to Canada.

The Big Bend

ANSEL ADAMS

On the southern edge of the great central tableland of the United States, the Rio Grande curves past the Big Bend National Park. The plains here have given way to desert and to mountains so rugged and weirdly shaped as to be almost magical in their spell. During its winding course, the river, photographed at right by Ansel Adams, flows through a shimmering land of more than a thousand varieties of plants, where peccaries, kit foxes, and other desert creatures live undisturbed.

In places, the river has cut through majestic canyons, including the Mariscal, Boquillas, and Santa Elena, whose walls rise up to 1,500 feet above the water. But above them, in forms like castles, soar the Chisos Mountains (once called enchanted by the Spaniards), with 7,000-foot-high peaks and views of the big and eerie wilderness.

WILLIAM A. BARDSLEY

High above a canoeist, an eroded arch on the wall of Santa Elena Canyon resembles a tunnel portal.

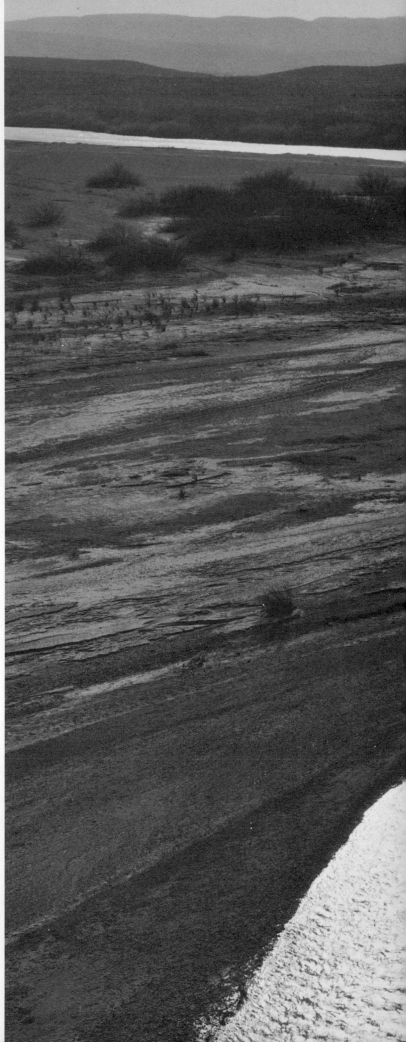

An amazing display of crystalline lime-stone formations, ranging from the bulb-ous and grotesque to the most delicate and lacy (below), encompasses the visitor who makes his way through the corridors and chambers of Carlsbad Caverns. The underground maze was discovered in 1901 by a miner, James White, who was attracted to the site by a great swarm of bats, and who marked his way through the various rooms with smudges and a reel of string so that he could find his way out. Though some 23 miles have since been explored, the full extent of the caverns is not known.

ABOVE AND BELOW: JACK R. WILLIAMS

206

ANSEL ADAMS

Caverns and Sand Dunes

No one knows for sure when or why the Spaniards gave it the name, Llano Estacado, the Staked Plains. A member of Coronado's party was in this broad, flat land along the Texas-New Mexico border in 1540 and wrote: "The country is like a bowl, so that when a man sits down, the horizon surrounds him all around at the distance of a musket shot."

There are strange and beautiful wonders throughout this corner of the United States, as intriguing today as they were to the men who first happened upon them. North of the Staked Plains is Texas's Palo Duro Canyon, and to the southwest, across the fabled Pecos, is the highest point in the state, the rugged Guadalupe Peak (8,751 feet).

In the Guadalupe Mountain foothills are the Carlsbad Caverns of New Mexico, the world's largest and most fantastic limestone caves—a national park since 1930. The forming of the caverns began some sixty million years ago, when the same movements of the earth that raised the Rocky Mountains broke up a limestone reef that had bordered a shallow inland sea. Ground water entered the breaks, creating small fissures in the limestone that grew into larger cavities and finally into the underground rooms and corridors that exist today. Another earth movement at a later date replaced the water with air, while rain seeping from aboveground entered into solution with the limestone and formed the multitude of stalagmites and stalactites that make the caverns an especial delight to visitors.

West of the caverns is another wondrous area. Swept by the wind into a flowing sea of white gypsum, the dunes of White Sands National Monument sprout spikes of yucca (left) and are covered with playful shadows when the sun lowers in the late afternoon.

207

Gates of the Mountains

On July 19, 1805, after a long journey up the Missouri, across the seemingly interminable Montana plains, Lewis and Clark came on this scene. Here, through the river's mist, just north of present-day Helena, was the first recorded view of the Rockies by Americans. ". . . from the singular appearance of this place I called it the gates of the rocky mounatains," wrote Lewis.

VI

THE

GREAT

MOUNTAINS

By WALLACE STEGNER

". . . one of the guides paused, and, after considering the vast landscape attentively, pointed to three mountain peaks glistening with snow . . . These remarkable peaks were known as the Tetons; as guiding points for many days, to Mr. Hunt, he gave them the names of the Pilot Knobs."

Washington Irving (*Astoria,* 1849)

When Thomas Jefferson sent Captains Lewis and Clark into the unmarked West to test the extent of Louisiana and find the way to the South Sea, both he and they believed that a single portage, possibly of no more than one day, would carry them from the headwaters of the Missouri to the headwaters of the Columbia. But the mountains did not turn out to be a simple wall that, once it was scaled, showed travelers or bears its other side. Lewis and Clark reached what they then called the "Rockey Mountains" (the Big Belts south of Great Falls, Montana) on July 16, 1805. On August 10, at the junction of Prairie Creek and Red Rock Creek, just north of modern Dillon, Montana, they reluctantly gave up the attempt to go any farther by water, and began their "portage." Turned back by the impassable canyons of Idaho's Salmon River, they went up the Bitterroot Valley and across Lolo Pass in the early snow. ("Several horses Sliped and roled down Steep hills which hurt them verry much   the one which Carried my desk & Small trunk Turned over & roled down a mountain for 40 yards & lodged against a tree, broke the Desk the horse escaped and appeared but little hurt.") Gaunt on a diet composed mainly of horse meat, coyotes, and crows, they made it over the pass and got salmon and camas bulbs from the Nez Perce, additions that laid the whole company out with dysentery. Nearly two months after taking to horses, they cached their saddles and put their dugouts in a river again. That was on October 6, where the Clearwater meets the Snake, the site of modern Lewiston, Idaho. Eighty-two days into the mountains, the explorers still had a month of mountains between them and the Pacific, which had once seemed just over the range.

Obviously, if they had known their way they would not have taken so long. The point is that, not comprehending the complexity of the ranges that tossed in crest and valley all across the West, they were bound to lose themselves; an important result of their exploration was the demonstration that the Shining Mountains were not simply a barrier range, but a whole system of ranges, a vast zone. By now, we understand that they are not even one system, but three long chains, roughly parallel: the Rockies, the Sierra-Cascades, and the Coast Ranges.

Perhaps because they were the first mountains encountered by Anglo-Americans working westward, and because they throw up all along the western edge of the high plains a broken, romantic front crowned with snow peaks, the Rockies have become for millions of Americans a synonym for mountains and the West. And certainly they are the most impressive both as fact and as symbol. Though it is customary among geographers to put their southern ex-

tremity at the Spanish Peaks, near the Colorado–New Mexico border, it is only by an arbitrary act of nomenclature that we can distinguish them from the broken ranges that continue down across the Southwest, across the volcano-crowned plateau of Mexico, and through Central America, to lift again into the magnificent Andean crest of Colombia, Peru, Bolivia, and the Argentine-Chilean border. From Alaska to Tierra del Fuego it is all one great cordillera, the longest mountain system in the world. Even if we cut it off at the Spanish Peaks, it stretches from the 37th parallel of north latitude to the 70th, well beyond the Arctic Circle, and at its widest it spans from Denver to Salt Lake City, an airline distance of four hundred miles.

The frontal wall of the Rockies runs due north across Colorado and into Wyoming. From the Laramie Range it turns north-northwest, and the whole system, narrowing as it goes, holds that direction through Wyoming, Montana, Alberta, British Columbia, and Yukon Territory, until at the far northern edge of Alaska, facing the Arctic Ocean ice, it curves around westward in the Brooks Range. Deep in south-central Alaska, where the crests come into a final tight coil south of the junction of the Yukon and the Tanana, is Mount McKinley, aloof, colossal, locked in ice.

Thus it is convenient to speak of the American, the Canadian, and the Alaskan Rockies. We shall speak only of the first and third, especially the first.

To name the ranges of the American Rockies, the peaks that crown them, the canyons that cut them, and the passes by which they were crossed, is to recite a climactic chapter of American adventure. Though every major range except the Uintas runs roughly north and south, our great trails—and our imaginations—run west, across them. Sawatch and San Juan and La Plata, Front Range, Gore Range, Laramie Range and Wasatch, the Wind Rivers and Gros Ventres and Tetons, the Big Horns and Absarokas, the Beaverheads and Sawtooths and Bitterroots, the Salmon River Mountains and the Coeur d'Alenes—they lift as surely into the air of myth as into the high blue of the mountain sky. And though other passes in other mountains have seen dramatic happenings—notably Donner and Carson and the other Sierra passes through which the Gold Rush poured—it is the image of an American on a pass in the Rockies that ignites our imaginations: Lewis and Clark struggling over the Lolo, the exploring fur traders under Robert Stuart struggling east, or Jed Smith riding west across the easy plateau of South Pass, where later half a nation would cross. It was the Rockies that first challenged us, and we have never quite got over thinking of them as the single mountain barrier between the western edge of the plains and the Pacific Ocean.

But farther west, separated from the Rockies in the south by the Great Basin deserts and in the north by dry plateaus and scablands, the Sierra-Cascades form a second system. It is shorter and simpler than the Rockies, but it is not minor. The Sierra Nevada begins at Tehachapi Pass, above Bakersfield, California, and runs a little west of north for four hundred miles. Just south of Mount Shasta it interlocks with the southern Cascades, which in turn reach northward, lifting a splendid series of volcanic peaks, Hood, Rainier, Baker, above a well-watered and heavily timbered and in a few places still-unspoiled wilderness, until the system is pinched out between the Rockies and the Coast Ranges in British Columbia. The shortest of the three western mountain systems, the Sierra-Cascades are still more than a thousand miles long. They have, in Mount Whitney in California, the highest American peak outside of Alaska, and in Rainier a peak less than a hundred feet lower. They contain the most magnificent conif-

213

Colorado's Snowmass Mountain towers above fishermen on a tranquil lake in the Holy Cross National Forest.

erous forests in the entire world, and some of the most magnificent mountain rivers, cascades, falls, and lakes.

And westward still farther, so far west that in places the ranges are all but submerged in the sea, and show only their island tips as in the Channel Islands off Santa Barbara, lie those very new, still-growing, generally disregarded, but most impressive continent's-edge mountains, the Coast Ranges. Impressive not simply because they are in many places spectacularly abrupt; and not simply because beyond Vancouver Island they put out to sea, so that you sail between them up the Inside Passage; and not simply because in Mount St. Elias, on the border of Alaska and the Yukon Territory, they push up an 18,008-foot peak that tops everything in North America except Mount McKinley in Alaska and Mount Logan in Canada. Impressive because lively to live with: the little Coast Range peak called Black Mountain that I see from my bedroom window is less than twenty-five hundred feet high, but it has grown several feet and moved several feet northward during my lifetime, and if the San Andreas Fault should slip a little, it could grow a few more feet tomorrow, or take another step in its journey up the coast.

Start at the bottom of California and fly north and you fly along the intricate waves of the continent's western wall: San Jacintos, San Gabriels, Santa Anas, then the east-west Santa Monica Range that projects Catalina and other islands into the sea. Then the entangled Santa Susana, Santa Ynez, San Emigdio, and Santa Lucia ranges, the last of which dominates the coast for a hundred miles south of Monterey Bay in what is loosely known as the Big Sur country. These were the mountains first called the Sierra Nevada. Juan Rodriguez Cabrillo, sailing up that impetuous coastline in 1542, wrote in his journal: "All the coast passed this day is very bold; there is a great swell and the land is very high. There are mountains which seem to reach the heavens, and the sea beats on them; sailing along close to land, it appears as though they would fall on the ships." That is one of the earliest impressions of any of our western mountains; and though the name Sierra Nevada was later moved to the greater range inland, the Santa Lucias remain as terrific as Cabrillo thought them.

Northward the short narrow ranges still stretch on, the most seaward of them hiding in their canyons groves of coast redwoods: the San Luis Range, the Gabilans, the Santa Cruz Mountains, the Diablo Range. San Francisco Bay is a valley sunk between them and flooded by the sea. Still farther north are the Klamath Mountains, made up of the Rogue River, Siskiyou, and Scott ranges, plus the wild tumble of ridges, cut by deep sea-hunting rivers, that are called the Trinity Alps. Then the Umpquas, clothed in spruce, and then the Olympics thrusting their peninsula nearly to Vancouver Island to enclose the incomparable harbor of Puget Sound. John Meares, running through the Strait of Juan de Fuca in 1778, while his countrymen were still having it out with the blue-coated Continentals of General Washington, saw that snow-cluster spiking the southern sky, and named the highest peak of it Olympus because it seemed a fit home for the gods. And from the Olympics go still more ranges, shore mountains and sea mountains, up the islanded coast, to turn the corner at their highest point in the St. Elias Range and curve on out as the Aleutian chain, separating the North Pacific from the Bering Sea and making a causeway toward Asia.

All of these, with the Sierra-Cascades and the multiple waves of the Rockies, make up our Great Mountains. From any part of the West, some crest of one of the systems will be a brown or lavender or white or smoke-blue tracery on the sky. Literally, the mountains make the West—make its air and its climate and its economy, provide the resources of minerals, timber, scenery, and most especially water by which it lives, create not merely the basic conditions of life but the special beauty and excitement and view that western living so often contains.

Except for the coastal strip from the northwest corner down about to San Francisco, the West is an oasis civilization, concentrated in the irrigable valleys. But valleys are as legitimately a part of the mountains as the peaks are—you can't have one without the other. More than that, everything that makes the valleys what they are comes from the highlands: advantages and disadvantages, the aridity of the rain shadow and the mountain streams that counter the aridity, the diurnal and seasonal winds that make the climate bearable, and sometimes those winds that make the residents want to exchange their local land for a cool corner of hell.

There are mighty creature comforts to be derived from a nearby mountain. It is pleasant to be able to flee a heat wave and by driving fifteen horizontal miles and one vertical one to cross all the life zones between Upper Sonoran and Arctic-Alpine, to exchange horned toads for Clark's nutcrackers and swap hundred-degree smog for thin, pure air straight off a snowbank. It is pleasant, from late fall until late spring, to have skiing in your back yard, as people in Denver, Boulder, or Colorado Springs do, or Salt Lake City, or Missoula, or Jackson, Wyoming. It is most agreeable to be within hours of back country, perhaps raw wilderness, with its camping, back-packing, fishing, and

hunting. These are reasons why you do not hear Westerners murmuring about the place where they live, or see them taking off for Florida or southern California when they draw their last pay checks at sixty-five. They owe much pleasure to their mountains. But they owe more than pleasure. The whole quality of their life is controlled from upstairs as if there were thermostats.

All of the Great Mountains in the United States proper lie in the latitudes of the prevailing westerlies. The winds that blow in off the Pacific loaded with moisture are forced upward and cooled by the first high land they strike. Even the lowest coast hills are to some extent rain catchers, and all throw some sort of rain shadow. Living on the east side of the Santa Cruz Mountains, I get five or six inches less rain each year than the crest only a few miles west and fifteen hundred feet above me. But I get two inches more than Palo Alto, down in the valley. And what is apparent here is spectacularly obvious on the Olympic Peninsula. The precipitation that may approach two hundred inches high up on the west side of Mount Olympus shrinks to twenty inches in the Sequim Valley thirty-five or forty miles farther on to the eastward.

However much rain it drops, the wind passes on, leaving a rain shadow in the mountain's lee, until it strikes the higher wall of the Sierra-Cascades, where it is sharply cooled so that it unloads again. Since the season of heaviest precipitation is winter, much of this moisture falls as snow. Four feet of snow in a single storm is not uncommon in either the Sierra or the Cascades. And again the wind passes on, this time wrung dry, across the second rain shadow. An inland valley town such as Boise, Idaho, gets an average rainfall of only eleven inches a year, and the Great Basin deserts in the rain shadow of the Sierra get less than six. Across the great dry heartland of the West the winds actually pick up more moisture than they drop, and when they strike the successive waves of the Rockies they are ready for a final milking. The habitability of the Great Salt Lake Valley is due entirely to the extra two or three inches of precipitation that the Wasatch squeezes out of the passing westerlies. It is so important, in fact, that a few years ago when California was planning to seed the clouds over the Sierra to help the snow-pack, the Salt Lake City Chamber of Commerce threatened a suit for the theft of moisture properly belonging to Utah.

From the Rockies the westerly winds, having watered in their fashion the entire West, sweep on out over the plains bone-dry. The rain shadow of the Rockies reaches nearly to the Missouri River; and the rain-bearing winds of Nebraska and Kansas come not from the west, but from the south, from warm wet air of the Gulf of Mexico.

215

The West is a vast club sandwich, three layers of mountains moistened on one side, dry on the other, and with dry or desert valleys between. The water that is life comes from the mountains, and crops thrive or perish depending on the heaviness of the winter snow-pack and the date and rate of the spring runoff. When human ingenuity is applied to ensure a more dependable flow for the streams, the dams that impound the water are as high up as possible, to get the greatest head and the smallest evaporation. Every valley in the West except those west of the Cascades lives off water caught and stored in the mountains. The high land is like a lightning rod that discharges the atmosphere, but to make a better analogy we would have to think of the lightning rod as being piped into storage batteries, from which can be drawn a steady flow of power.

Mountain water. Also mountain winds. In the Salt Lake Valley the conjunction of mountains and lake produces a regular back-and-forth flow of air, down the canyons at night, up the canyons in the morning. Those are relatively blessed breezes, and as dependable as the sea breeze and land breeze that they resemble. The Santa Anas of southern California, scorchers full of desert dust, get less praise. And the chinooks of the Northwest can be either lifesavers or death dealers, according to the season. The chinook is a foehn wind. It comes in off the Japan Current warm and wet, drops its moisture and loses some of its heat against the Cascades or Rockies, and comes down the eastern slope dry, still quite warm, and gaining temperature at the rate of one degree Fahrenheit for every four hundred feet of lost altitude. In winter it hits the plains as a great gusty blast of warm dry air that has been known to gobble a foot of snow in a night and leave the prairie nearly dry. It is what starving cattle and anxious cattlemen wait for and depend on to clear the snow off the range. It can raise the temperature fifty degrees in a half hour, and what it does to the spirits, after weeks of cold and blizzards, is like the effect of a happiness pill. But when it comes in August, hotter than one hundred degrees, and shrivels the heading wheat in the milk and scorches the eyes in farmers' heads, it is another thing. They don't call it a chinook, then, though it is. They won't admit it's the same wind as the one they pray for all winter.

Geology may be, as Henry Adams said, no more than history carried a little farther back than Mr. Jefferson. It can be an exciting history to read, and most visitors on their first trip to the West follow the example of John Burroughs and catch an acute attack of geological fever. Sometimes it can be serious enough to make us pontificate learnedly about Devonian metamorphics, about isostasy and intru-

sives and cross-bedding and nonconformities and plural erosion cycles, while in fact most of us characteristically confuse the periods of geologic time and could not tell orthoclase from the second ice age. Nevertheless there is one kind of geology, however amateur, that is useful to anyone. That is structural geology, and it is useful because it helps anyone to *see.*

Stand on the bank of the Green River near the Wyoming-Utah line and look at the broad hump of the Uintas running east and west across the river's course. Though the center of the range has been split like a ripe plum skin and cut into alpine peaks, including in King's Peak and Mount Agassiz the two highest in Utah, it is apparent even at a glance that the Uintas were originally one great dome, like an enormous Quonset hut or the Mormon Tabernacle; and that they have been raised across the existing river's course like a log across a circle saw, so that the river has literally sawn them in two. Float into the mountain at Flaming Gorge and you can see the strata bending up smoothly out of the river's bed, curving up almost vertically and then flattening out toward the dome. Float out the other side, out the mouth of Split Mountain Canyon, and you see the same strata, one after another, dipping down under in a smooth and perfect monocline, or fold. You can see remnants of the same sort of fold in the "flatiron" rocks back of Boulder, Colorado, or in the Denver Red Rocks Park—sedimentaries that once lay flat and even, but have been humped up and then eroded from the top until only the bases or stubs are left, leaning inward against the range's granite core.

Folding, generally complicated by faulting, is one way of making mountains. Stand on the plain before Chief Mountain, east of Glacier National Park, and you can see another way. Here you are standing on strata—never mind the geological names and dates—that are much younger than the mountain that sits on top of them. Though you may not see it clearly, Chief Mountain is the product of a thrust fault; the whole mountain mass has been lifted and shoved eastward several miles over the top of the prairie, like an ice pan pushed up and stranded on a shore, or a tar bucket slid across a roof.

Or stand on the rim of the Aquarius Plateau in southern Utah, a rim that provides one of the most magnificent views in all America, and look southeastward across the Waterpocket Fold to the high knobs of the Henry Mountains. They were the last mountains in the United States to be discovered—Major Powell saw them from the Colorado on his exploration of 1869, and his brother-in-law Almon Thompson hunted them out and mapped them the next year. Appropriately enough, they were a new kind of mountain. Laccoliths, G. K. Gilbert called them in his classic monograph, bubble mountains, humps pushed up by liquid magma that never did break through the crust, but hardened in place like a bunch of marbles under a rug.

Or confront one of those ranges that show us the overwhelming mountain fronts—the Sierra Nevada from Owens Valley, the Tetons from Jackson Hole, to a lesser degree the Wasatch above Salt Lake City. These are fault-block mountains, formed as one great block pushed up above a shear or fault line to form a bold cliff on the faulted side, and tilted so that the summit slopes back gradually. Once the block is elevated, erosion begins busily tearing it down, cutting it into canyons and peaks and ridges. But the faulted side, even when eroded into alpine forms, remains violently abrupt. From the Owens Valley you look up nearly ten thousand feet to the highest peaks in the Sierra; from the Antelope Flats under the Tetons you look

from an altitude of eight thousand feet to almost fourteen thousand on the horn of the Grand Teton, and the lift is so abrupt that the anxious wives of rangers can gather back of the cottages of the park headquarters at Moose and high above them watch rescue parties led by their husbands bring down the climbing casualties.

If you want your mountains sheer, order them created as fault blocks. If you want them symmetrical, have them built up into cones by successive lava extravasations, as the great Cascade peaks have been. If you want them layered, have them made out of untilted, unwarped sedimentary strata, as is the great pyramid of Timpanogos, above the Heber Valley in Utah. If you want them spiked and alpine, have them carved by water and frost out of hard granite or metamorphics or lava rock. If you like them rounded into great bosses, with U-shaped valleys and sheer cliffs, as at Yosemite, arrange to have glaciers run over them for a few hundreds or thousands of years.

However they are made—and observing how they have been made is one of the pleasures of seeing them—they all have similar effects on western climate and western life. The celebrated clarity of western air is a function of high altitude and dryness; the hard line between hot sun and chilly shade results from air too thin and dry for the diffusion of heat. The life zones through which we pass as we climb higher in the mountains are the product of an ecological adaptation and interdependence so intricate that even yet we understand only its rudiments. We only know that the deer depends on the cougar as much as the cougar on the deer: he is the agency that keeps deer from growing so numerous that they destroy their own forage. The great chain of life stretches upward and downward from the lowest enzyme in the soil to the city man sitting on his porch, and of all the dangers to the mountains, all the forces of change, there is none so disastrous as tinkering or exploiting or merely recreating man. He makes the forces of erosion look feeble; he changes the landscape more than the glaciers did. And yet he can learn, under provocation, to put his imagination to the purpose of preservation rather than destruction. He may ultimately come back, by the long road of ruthless continent-busting, to some sort of altered but essentially natural balance with the natural world.

Because most of them rise out of arid lands—indeed, to a degree cause the arid lands—and because until the jeep and the pestilential mountain-climbing scooter called the tote gote they were hard to get into, and because America has learned the hard way that something of the continent's plenty must be saved for the future, the Great Mountains hold the bulk of our reserved timber, our protected water-

The parallel rock walls of Devil's Slide, celebrated by pioneers traversing Utah's Weber Canyon, were once horizontal beds of limestone separated by shale. In a period of geological turmoil, they were upturned, and now rise forty feet aboveground. This picture was taken by T. H. O'Sullivan during an 1869 geological survey.

sheds, our surviving remnants of wilderness, and our rescued wildlife, as well as the grandest of our scenery. For better or for worse—and history is certainly going to say for better—a large part of the West has remained in federal ownership and has thus been spared the worst sorts of exploitation. Over half of the area of the six Rocky Mountain states is federally owned: 47 per cent of California; 74 per cent of Utah; 87 per cent of Nevada; 99.7 per cent of Alaska. That means national forests, federally managed grazing lands, wildlife refuges, national parks and monuments. With all its manifest imperfections, federal ownership has saved for us a great part of what has been saved. Essentially, that precious mountain remnant is destined to be playground and source of renewal and refreshment for our increasingly jammed millions.

Even in the national forests, designed in the first place strictly for controlled-yield forestry, recreation has become a major function. Every accessible national forest area from the Tongass and Chugach in Alaska to the Pikes Peak and Grand Mesa forests in Colorado is a controlled outdoor playground; and the deep and difficult wildernesses that still remain here and there, the country that must be worked for, literally do re-create those who hunt them out. Glacier Peak, in the northern Cascades, is such a wilderness, pouring with bright water, jutting with glacier-carved peaks, richly timbered, remote, silent except for the hollow roar of the mountains, as magical a sound as the roaring of a shell at a child's ear. The Sawtooth Primitive Area in Idaho is another such place of peace, its horns and spires raggedly sharp, its glacial lakes, one hundred seventy or more of them, full of fish. I do not think a man has lived who has not fished such a lake as one of those on a chilly morning, with his breath white and his hands numb, and flicked out his silver doctor or white miller or coachman or McGinty across water with just the faintest wrinkle of a riffle on it, and seen the water break just at the point where the fly floats on the surface, and simultaneously felt that hard, impetuous, wild yank from down under, and been suddenly engaged, pole bent and line cutting water and wrist locked and thumb delicate on the brake of the reel. It is one of the ways, one of the better ways, to be fulfilled. And in the Sawtooth country the mosquitoes are so fierce in early summer that only the hardy—or the anointed—are going to be there.

Because they are all mountain wildernesses, and because mountains all smell pretty much the same, and campfire smoke mixes with pine and spruce and alder smell everywhere to produce the same heady mixture, and because the sound of mountain water pounding in the night, or the sight of your own footprints across a meadow blue with dew, has the same effect always on the heart and the spirit, what makes the Glacier Peak or Sawtooth wilderness a wonder and a healing is just as native to the Bob Marshall Wilderness in the Flathead and Lewis and Clark forests of Montana, or to the High Uintas Primitive Area in the Grandaddy Lakes Basin in eastern Utah, or to Evolution Valley in the High Sierra. But even the relatively accessible primitive or wilderness areas can teach anybody something about who he is and how he relates to the natural world. Walk up into the Maroon Bells above Aspen, Colorado, or into Desolation Valley above Fallen Leaf Lake in the Sierra, and in an hour, by the motion of your own legs, you can walk from the hot present into cool timelessness; you can get a legal separation from asphalt and smog and enjoy a brief love affair with club moss and ferns and shy wild things and stillness.

Except for the Glacier Peak and Sawtooth areas, and for the still-magnificent wild backlands of Alaska, all our sections of the most splendid mountain scenery are in the national parks. They are managed for "use without impairment," though that is increasingly hard to do, and a good part of all the major parks is still essentially wilderness. Accessible or remote, the parks make up a series of magnificent outdoor museums.

All the three Great Mountain systems have their reserves: Rocky Mountain, Yellowstone, Grand Teton, Glacier, and Mount McKinley in the Rockies; Sequoia–Kings Canyon and Yosemite in the Sierra; Lassen, Crater Lake, and Rainier in the Cascades; Olympic in the Coast Ranges. They give us mountains of every structure and every shade of climate, from the friendly Colorado Rockies, forested and amiable to around eleven thousand feet, to McKinley, condemned by both altitude and latitude to eternal ice. And they offer every sort of outdoor experience, from the simple pleasure of waking to birds and pure air to the scientific joy of studying the delicate ecological balances that hold the natural world together; from childish wonder at Yellowstone's fading volcanic activity to the expansive, chest-cracking, mind-clearing feeling of making it up any peak—it does not matter, Whitney or Grand Teton or only some walk-up mountain—and seeing the world all below you and knowing that your legs put it there.

From Cabrillo's first coasting view of the Santa Lucias in 1542, it was 328 years before all our Great Mountains were discovered and known. Always the mountains have been our landmarks, the things men steered by and toward; reading the journals of the explorers we mark the red-letter days when they saw an unknown peak or range. Steller sighting the white horn of Mount St. Elias from the Bering Expedition ship off Icy Cape in 1741; Louis-

Joseph, Chevalier de La Vérendrye, disappointedly being pulled away from the dark hump of the Black Hills on his "farthest west for France" trip in 1743; Matthew Cocking bringing the Hudson's Bay Company to the Blackfoot in the Alberta piedmont two years before the outbreak of the American Revolution; Father Escalante skirting the Uintas and coming through the Wasatch in 1776; Alexander Mackenzie, that ice-blooded continent-crosser, marking the face of a rock with vermilion and bear's grease at the mouth of the Bella Coola: "Alexander Mackenzie, from Canada, by land, the twenty-second of July, one thousand seven hundred and ninety-three."

More than three centuries of discovery and exploration, and by the time Almon Thompson worked his way in to the Henrys in 1870, parties of tourists were already visiting and camping among the smoking springs and streams of the Yellowstone Plateau, and around campfires laying the plans that would shortly flower in the first of our national parks. What Henry Washburn and Ferdinand Vandeveer Hayden did in 1872, with the aid of Thomas Moran's paintings and William Henry Jackson's photographs, was to electrify Congress with the scenic magnificence of the Yellowstone country, and persuade them that it should be preserved for all the people. The same thought motivates those who are still working for preservation of the remaining wilderness areas and the inclusion of the remaining great scenery into the national park system.

For though as a people we have been monumentally careless of the continent we inherited, we have begun to learn the lesson that only carelessness could have taught us: that what was once God's plenty will soon be shortage, and that if we want any of it for the future we have to take steps. America is a byword for careless waste; nevertheless it was America that created the national park idea that is being copied around the world.

Anyone who has walked through the spongy twilight of the Olympic rain forest, and seen young Sitka spruces clinging in a line to their nurse log, and watched the light glow incandescent green where sun touches a tree upholstered six inches deep in moss, will know why. Or anyone who has hiked a rocky trail over a twelve-thousand-foot pass, and felt himself as tall as the peaks that lift all around him. Or one who knows the druid silence of a sequoia grove, or the dark virility of Douglas spruce. Or one who has seen the granite pink with alpenglow, or watched morning come down a mountainside toward his chilly camp.

You do not have to back-pack into the Great Mountains to know them, though the more intimately you meet and endure them the better. You can get a great deal simply by looking: mountains are one of the things in life that can survive indefinite looking. And you can see some things you will never forget. A boy who puts up a bighorn ram in the Colorado Rockies loses his breath for a second in wonder, and that single moment can stay with him pure and uncomplicated for life. And anyone who finds himself high up on the eastward-facing wall of the Tetons in the late afternoon will see something by which he is likely thereafter to judge all great views.

Seen from anywhere, the Tetons are impressive. In the early morning, from Togwotee Pass to the eastward, they are a long-toothed flame across the West, lavender tipped with rose. On a day when Jackson Hole quivers with heat, they rise serene, cool gray and white, the very ideal of how mountains ought to look. But best of all is to see them only as shadow, as mock mountains; to come down from a climb, from Lake Solitude or down the pitch of Death Canyon on some belated homing, and see that whole familiar crest—the three Tetons, Teewinot, the square burliness of Mount Moran—projected as a shadow out over the Antelope Flats and the coils of the Snake River, the whole shadow-range lengthening eastward toward the Gros Ventres as the sun drops, stretching and stretching but miraculously keeping their recognizable shapes, still Teewinot, still South Teton, still Moran, until they climb the slopes of the Gros Ventres and are bent by the tilted ground, and then the tip of Grand Teton slips over the edge and is broken off, and then another peak, and another, until they are all truncated and only valleys of sun light the spaces between them, and then the whole huge shadow of the range heaves and crests and flows over the Gros Ventres and all of Jackson Hole is in gray dusk.

It is not something you would go seeking, perhaps. But once it has happened to you, you know it as an experience you value above most others. You have been made more alive by it. That is a gift that the mountains, any mountains, have it in their power to give.

Meriwether Lewis   *William Clark*

U.S. PACIFIC RAILROAD SURVEY, 1853-55, VOL. XII, BOOK I

Into the Shining Mountains

Farther north, Alexander Mackenzie had crossed the Canadian Rockies, and Peter Fidler, David Thompson, and other British fur traders had explored the eastern slopes. But prior to 1804, when Lewis and Clark started west, Americans knew little of the nature of the height of land beyond the plains that Indians sometimes referred to as the Shining Mountains. Most people could only conceive of it as another Appalachians, relatively easy to cross; but Lewis and Clark, who almost starved to death struggling over Idaho's Bitterroot Mountains, quickly discovered otherwise. In 1807 Zebulon Pike, exploring the southern Colorado Rockies past the Front Range and the peak that was later named for him (right), was almost swallowed in only a fraction of that vast part of the Continental Divide wilderness.

Zebulon M. Pike

The main chain of Montana's Rockies, through which Lewis found a short cut home (though the total mountain crossing still took almost a month), is viewed from the east in the drawing below. His route, considered the best one until the famous South Pass was discovered later, is near the left side of the picture. The drawing of the high, rolling Montana plains, just under the mountains, was made by John Mix Stanley, after a sketch by Gustavus Sohon. Both men were artists with a United States government survey party under I. I. Stevens, exploring a route between the 47th and 49th parallels for a railroad to the Pacific in 1853.

Donald McKenzie, known to his companions as "Perpetual Motion," was one of the ablest explorers of the West. After Astor's venture collapsed, he led British trapping parties, making known much of the geography of the country from Oregon to Wyoming.

Death in Hells Canyon

The trail to the fur-rich Northwest had been blazed by Lewis and Clark, and what they had found others would now conquer. The second expedition to cross the continent were Astorians, men employed by John Jacob Astor to implement his dream of a great fur monopoly, with a post at the mouth of the Columbia River. They followed the Lewis and Clark route up the Missouri in the spring of 1811, but reports of hostile Blackfoot Indians caused them to abandon the river and head across the plains of South Dakota and Wyoming on horseback. It was a decision they would regret.

Their journey became catastrophic when they reached the Snake River, called "the accursed mad river" by the *voyageurs* in the party. The tumultuous rapids, rampaging through deep canyons, ripped their canoes apart and threw the men into the raging waters. One man was drowned; the others, desperate with hunger and thirst, trudged across the Idaho desert. Then came Hells Canyon, a gorge some 6,000 feet deep in the midst of a mountain wilderness (right), previously unseen by white men. Frozen by cold and snow, blinded by fog, and crazed by hunger, the Astorians wandered through the nightmarish chasm. Men died, and others became deranged. A 300-pound former Canadian fur trader named Donald McKenzie proved his mettle by leading one group safely through the canyon. The others found a longer way, and eventually most of them straggled to the mouth of the Columbia, more dead than alive. The trek, a total of 3,500 miles, had been one of the most terrible in American history. Yet in 1819 McKenzie again dared Hells Canyon, making the only known upriver passage through the deep chasm.

Realm of the Mountain Man

A mountain trapper by Alfred Jacob Miller

In the 1820's and 1830's the wild and little known fastnesses of the Rocky Mountains were the home of a colorful and romantic breed of men. They were the "mountaineers," who trapped beaver along streams in the fall and spring, sold the pelts at rowdy summer rendezvous, and hibernated in lonely huts or in Indian camps during the winter. Hardy, resourceful, and treasuring the freedom of their wilderness existence, they roamed through rugged and majestic areas like Wyoming's Wind River Mountains (left) and came to know intimately the best routes and mountain passes, thus playing a crucial role in westward expansion.

Among them were Bible-toting Jedediah Smith, who found South Pass across the Rockies in 1824; Tom "Broken Hand" Fitzpatrick, who later led emigrant trains to Oregon; yarn-spinning Jim Bridger, who became an Army guide; Kit Carson, only five-feet-four in height, but a giant in courage, who showed paths to John C. Frémont's expeditions in the 1840's; and many others, most of whom died unsung in the mountains.

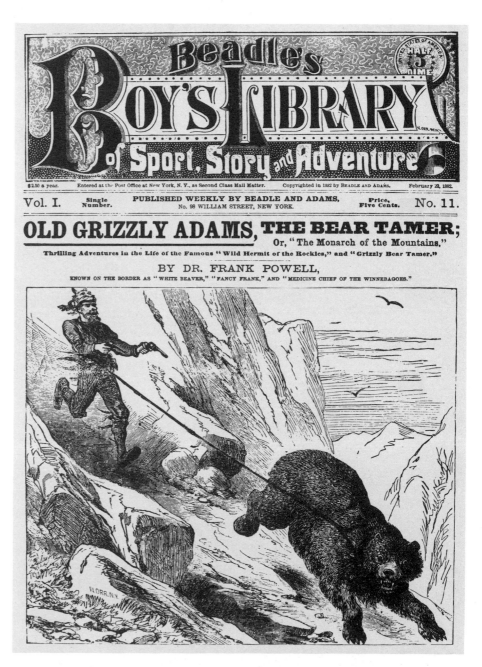

The powerful grizzly bear, now almost vanished from the American West, was once numerous on the plains and in the Rockies and was the terror of the mountain men— although not of the doughty hero of this dime novel who gained fame capturing them.

225

226

In his painting, Rocky Mountains, *the nineteenth-century artist Albert Bierstadt pictured an encampment of Shoshoni Indians amid a setting of mountain grandeur on the headwaters of Wyoming's Green River. Here, and in similar "parks" and "holes," the mountain men held their annual rendezvous at which they sold their beaver skins, bought gunpowder and alcohol,*

and engaged in shooting and wrestling contests with the Indians, as well as other more un-
restrained entertainments. In the background are the Wind River Mountains, one of which,
Fremont Peak (13,730 feet), was first climbed by John C. Frémont in 1842. He said of the
area: "It seemed as if ... Nature had collected all her beauties together in one chosen place."

227

Mapping the Rockies

Near the top of the ridge I emerged above timberline and the clouds, and suddenly, as I clambered over a vast mass of jagged rocks, I discovered the great shining cross. . ."

William H. Jackson had reached Colorado's Mount of the Holy Cross, and his photographs of that peak with its giant crucifix of snow thrilled Americans in 1873. Discoveries were not unusual to the men with whom Jackson was working, the dedicated members of the geological surveys who were exploring and mapping the vast territories of the West. Under Dr. Ferdinand V. Hayden, parties roamed mountainous Colorado for four years, 1873–76, scaling and naming peaks, and charting the area meticulously. Their hardships and problems were tremendous, but so were their enthusiasm and zeal. In the end, they produced volumes of useful reports on Colorado's flora, fauna, and geology, as well as an atlas of remarkable beauty and accuracy.

William Henry Jackson's famous photograph of the Mount of the Holy Cross

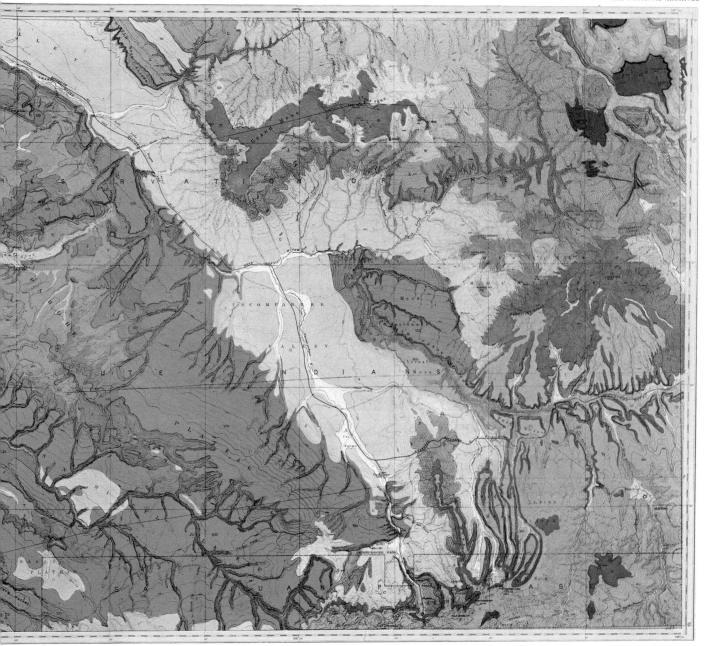

The Hayden Survey's 1877 Atlas, with its handsome maps of wilderness areas, was of great value to the newly admitted state of Colorado. Detailed maps like the one above of the Uncompahgres and surrounding regions in the western part of the state aided the development of natural resources and the building of railroads. Below is a Survey view of the La Plata Range, sketched from the west.

The Great Divide

Formed by the main chain of the Rocky Mountains, the Continental Divide extends in the United States across Montana, Wyoming, Colorado, and New Mexico, separating the waters of the Atlantic from those of the Pacific. This view of the Divide looks south (with Pikes Peak in the far distance) from Arapahoe

National Forest in Colorado, a state that has 54 mountains over 14,000 feet high and some 1,500 over 10,000 feet. From their huge snow masses begin the Platte, Arkansas, Rio Grande, and Colorado rivers, providing water to numerous states of the plains, the Great Basin and the Southwest, and to Mexico.

231

William H. Jackson recorded the early days of the mountain railroads in pictures like the one above of a train (the line is still in service today) hugging the side of Animas Canyon. He also photographed the trains passing over and under the Colorado Central bridge at Georgetown (below). At left is Otto Mears.

232

Railroads in the Rockies

In 1859 a gold rush brought miners streaming into the gulches and gorges of Colorado. A decade later the same rocky defiles echoed with the blasts of explosives and the shouts of work gangs, as pioneer railroad builders pushed tracks across impossible mountain country to connect the mining towns. Loss of life in accidents and bitter struggles for rights of way marred the era; but by 1884 General William Palmer's Denver & Rio Grande had flung down 1,600 miles of track, and other lines, built by men like Otto Mears (whose determined road building had earned him the name "Pathfinder of the San Juan"), were crisscrossing the state. Narrow-gauge locomotives, on tracks three feet wide, chugged up steep grades hewn from the sides of mountain walls, crossed canyons on high trestles, and descended into deep valleys. They brought in settlers, supplies, and luxuries for those who were getting rich, and they took out ore that was adding to the wealth of the entire country.

Splendors of Colorado

Colorado's natural wonders were once barriers to the builders of the nation. Today they teem with vacationers from all parts of the country. Among the most awesome attractions is the Black Canyon of the Gunnison (left), a sheer cleft in the land with walls of dark schist and black, pink, and gray granite. In the south, paralleling the Sangre de Cristos, are the Great Sand Dunes, a ten-mile-long sea of sand, constantly shifting into hills up to six hundred feet high. There are great plateaus, like the Grand Mesa, covered with lakes and forests; idyllic mountain valleys, like Estes Park and South Park; storybook peaks, like the Maroon Bells and Red Mountain; and Rocky Mountain National Park itself, its wilderness of many mountains dominated by Longs Peak (14,255 feet). But the greatest glory of all is the Colorado mountainside in fall, covered with long banks of aspen turned riotously yellow among the evergreens, their dry leaves rustling in the winds that precede the first snow.

The Majestic Tetons

To the Indians, they were "The Hoaryheaded Fathers" or "The Pinnacles." The Astorians, who used them as landmarks, called them "The Pilot Knobs," and the French trappers named them "Les Trois Tetons," the three breasts. Soaring from the floor of the great glacial valley in western Wyoming called Jackson Hole (for mountain man David E. Jackson), they are considered by many to be the most beautiful range of mountains in the United States.

Driggs

UNION PACIFIC

IDAHO

WYOMING

Rendezvous
Pk

Mt
Hunt

Buck Mtn
11,923

South
Teton

Nez
Perce —
Pk

Grand Teton
13,766

Mt
Owen
— 12,922

Mt St J
11,412

Teewinot Mtn
12,317

Jenny
Lake

JENN
LAKE LO

← TO TETON PASS

Phelps Lake

Moose ■

PARK
← HEADQUARTERS

RTS U.S. 187 89 26

Blacktail
Butte —

← TO JACKSON

GROS VENTRE RIVER

SNAKE RIVER

NATIONAL
ELK
REFUGE

JACKSON HOLE HIGHWAY

Kelly

Lower
Slide Lake

N

TETON
NATIONAL FOREST

▲ CAMPGROUND
△ PICNIC GROUND
■ ENTRANCE STATION

238

To the multitudes who visit its relatively small confines (some 500 square miles), Grand Teton National Park is a place of many soul-refreshing pursuits. One can fish for trout in Alpine streams and lakes, or ride a rubber raft down the Snake River through flats of desert sagebrush. He can hike along 233 miles of trails, probably coming upon a secluded waterfall,

GRAND TETON NATIONAL PARK

TARGHEE
NATIONAL FOREST

YELLOWSTONE
NATIONAL
PARK

Forellen
Pk

Bivouac
Pk

Eagles Rest
Pk

Ranger Pk

Mt Moran
12,594

TO
YELLOWSTONE PARK →

Leigh
Lake

JACKSON LAKE

Colter Bay

RTS U.S. 287 89

Signal Mtn

TETON PARK ROAD

JACKSON
LAKE LODGE

Signal
Mtn

Emma Matilda
Lake

Two Ocean
Lake

Pacific Creek

← RTS U.S. 287 26

*a colored carpet of wild flowers, or a moose browsing in a meadow. He can scale Grand Teton,
look for deer, or sail the vivid blue waters of Jenny and Jackson lakes. Or, from a thousand different vantage points, he can regard the changing colors and patterns of the breath-
taking rampart of peaks and acquire a memory of natural grandeur he will not soon forget.*

239

Members of an expedition of the 1870's watch Old Faithful erupt in this William H. Jackson photograph.

In the fall of 1826 a group of trappers wandered into a mountain-ringed, 7,500-foot-high plateau that the Indians called "the summit of the world." The next year, one of the men, Daniel T. Potts, sent home a description of what he had seen—the first written report of Yellowstone Park: "There is also a number of places where pure sulphur is sent forth in abundance. One of our men visited one of these whilst taking his recreation—there at an instant the earth began a tremendous trembling, and he with difficulty made his escape when an explosion took place resembling that of thunder. During our stay in that quarter I heard it every day."

It was hard for Easterners to believe such tales. John Colter had visited the region in 1807, but even his fellow trappers, used to western wonders, had hesitated to credit his yarns of spouting geysers, bubbling pools, and smoking hillsides. But the reports persisted, and serious exploration of the area began in the 1860's.

In 1870 an expedition under General Henry Washburn and Nathaniel Langford spent a month in the region. Around a campfire one night, excited by the sights they had seen, they proposed preserving the Yellowstone as a national park. It was an idea new to any country, but in time the Congress accepted it.

Walter Trumbull of Washburn's historic party sketched the Castle Geyser Cone.

Early views of the Yellowstone included the Upper Geyser Basin, Firehole River *(above), by John H. Renshawe, who visited the park in 1883, and Thomas Moran's water color of* Springs on the Border of Yellowstone Lake, *reproduced below.*

For All the People

William Henry Jackson, the great photographer of the West (above), had much to do with the realization of the dream of the Washburn-Langford party. Jackson had been photographing scenic regions of the plains and Rockies; and in 1871, when Ferdinand V. Hayden led the first government survey group into the Yellowstone, he took Jackson and his photographic wagon with him.

The next winter, congressmen, who were to be asked to establish the remote and little known region as a national park, found on their desks sheaves of wondrous photographs, like the one at the right of Upper Geyser Basin as seen from Old Faithful. The prints from Jackson's glass-plate negatives awed the legislators, as they did the people of the nation. In March, 1872, President Grant signed into law a bill creating the park. There were no appropriations, but some two million acres of spectacular beauty were "set apart as a public park or pleasuring-ground for the benefit and enjoyment of the people."

THO! MORAN 1872.

244

Thomas Moran's painting of the Grand Canyon of the Yellowstone shows why Indians referred to the river as one of yellow rocks. Moran, like Jackson, was a member of Hayden's 1871 survey party, and his paintings also helped convince congressmen to establish the park. This view of the canyon, 24 miles long and 1,200 feet deep, and of the Lower Falls, hung for many years in the Capitol.

245

There is no hunting in Yellowstone (or in any national park). Animals, like the moose at the edge of Yellowstone Lake at sunset (above), are there to be watched and enjoyed. Other attractions are not so easily protected against the thoughtless. Visitors who feed the bears endanger themselves, and make it difficult for the animals to provide for themselves at the end of the tourist season. Some persons who throw bottles and trash into geyser pools, like those below, upset the thermal plumbing and destroy or alter them. And the beauty of a hillside, such as that of Roaring Mountain with its fumaroles (opposite), can be destroyed by litter thrown by unmannered visitors.

Yellowstone Park Today

There are a thousand reasons in any generation why a park should not be established; but once it is, future generations live to bless the foresight of those responsible for what was preserved. Yellowstone, the first, is still America's largest and most fabulous park. Each year, more than a million and a half vacationers visit it, departing with memories of bears begging along the roads and Old Faithful obligingly erupting when it should. But there is much more to the park. There are hundreds of other geysers, shooting up from pools, cones, and flat land; fountain paint pots; mud volcanoes; steaming ponds exquisitely colored by the light and by the plant life they contain; and (shades of the pre-Lewis and Clark rumors from this magic land) a cliff of black glass (obsidian). There are hot springs and a naturally heated cave; petrified forests (as Jim Bridger said there were); many-hued limestone terraces; meadows; waterfalls galore; and canyons. There are numerous lakes, including Yellowstone Lake, 110 miles around and filled with trout. There are birds and animals of every sort, and forested mountains all about. Yellowstone is still unsettled; in 1959 a series of earthquakes created new wonders and changed old ones. A many-ringed circus of nature's spectacles, Yellowstone is a zoo without bars, a laboratory, and a playground.

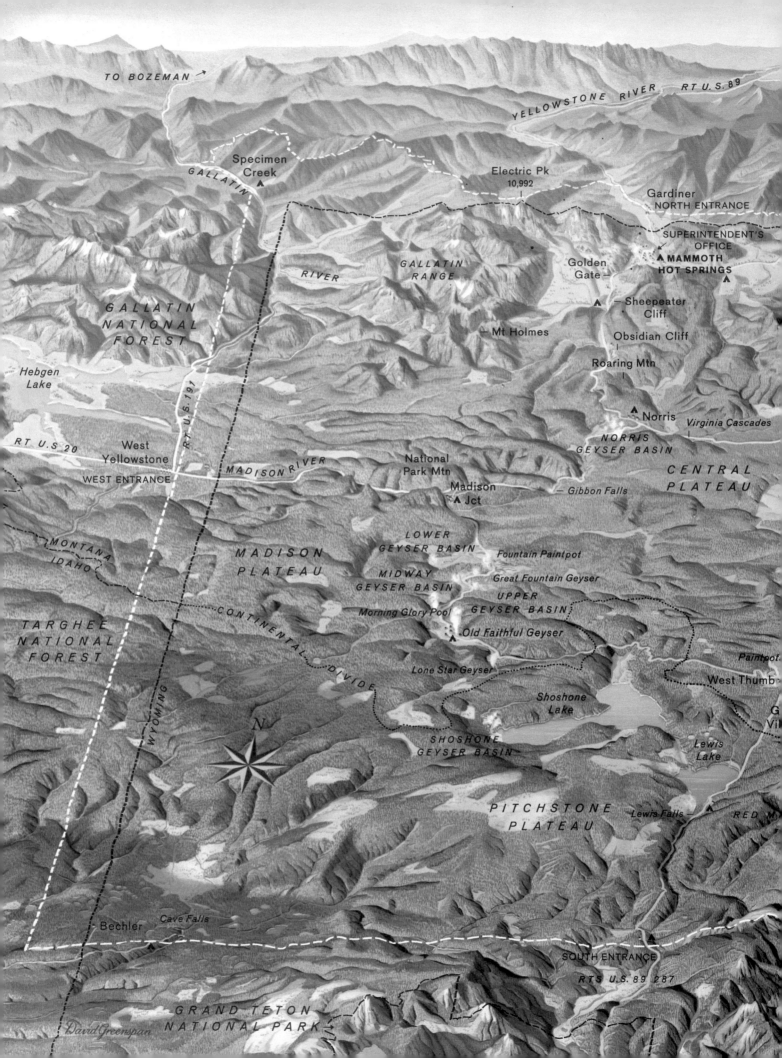

TO BOZEMAN

YELLOWSTONE RIVER   RT U.S. 89

GALLATIN

Specimen
Creek

Electric Pk
10,992

Gardiner
NORTH ENTRANCE

SUPERINTENDENT'S
OFFICE

GALLATIN
RANGE

Golden
Gate

MAMMOTH
HOT SPRINGS

RIVER

Sheepeater
Cliff

GALLATIN
NATIONAL
FOREST

Mt Holmes

Obsidian Cliff

Roaring Mtn

Hebgen
Lake

Norris

Virginia Cascades

RT U.S. 20

West
Yellowstone

NORRIS
GEYSER BASIN

CENTRAL
PLATEAU

National
Park Mtn

WEST ENTRANCE

MADISON RIVER

Madison
Jct

Gibbon Falls

MONTANA
IDAHO

LOWER
GEYSER BASIN

Fountain Paintpot

MADISON
PLATEAU

MIDWAY
GEYSER BASIN

Great Fountain Geyser

UPPER
GEYSER BASIN

Morning Glory Pool

TARGHEE
NATIONAL
FOREST

CONTINENTAL DIVIDE

Old Faithful Geyser

Paintpot

West Thumb

Lone Star Geyser

WYOMING

Shoshone
Lake

G
Vi

N

SHOSHONE
GEYSER BASIN

Lewis
Lake

PITCHSTONE
PLATEAU

Lewis Falls

RED M

Bechler

Cave Falls

SOUTH ENTRANCE

RTS U.S. 89 287

David Greenspan

GRAND TETON
NATIONAL PARK

The huge Garden Wall, seen above from the east, is a narrow crest of the Continental Divide, eroded by glaciers on either side.

Towering Granite Masses

Astride the Continental Divide, Montana's Glacier National Park reveals its own geological history clearly. Fossils of marine life recall the period when the area was an inland sea, and bands of different colors on the mountainsides tell of the layers of sediment that built up the water's floor. The gradual western slopes and the sheerness of Lewis Fault on the east relate the great pressures that thrust up the mountains, then moved them eastward with such force that they buckled. And the summits and glacial lakes (like Cracker Lake, seen from Mount Siyeh, right) are mementos of ice age glaciers that gouged and sculptured the region aeons ago.

WATERTON
LAKES
NATIONAL PARK

Mt Dungarvan

Mt Crandell

Waterton Lake

Mt Cleveland
10,448

CANADA
UNITED STATES

Kintla Pk
10,110

Upper Kintla Lake

Kintla Glacier

Carter Glaciers

Flattop Mtn

Rainbow Glacier

Longfellow Pk

Kintla Lake

Vulture Glacier

Heaven

Bowman Lake

Wolf Gun Mtn

Quartz Lake

Logging Lake

NORTH FORK FLATHEAD RIVER

FLATHEAD

NATIONAL FOREST

APGAR MTNS

LAKE Mc

APGAR VILLAGE

GL

N

GREAT NORTHERN RY U.S.2
TO KALISPELL RY U.S.2

David Greenspan

▲ CAMPGROUND
■ ENTRANCE STATION

Once the haunt of Blackfoot Indians, who called it "the backbone of the world," Gla-
cier National Park enfolds 1,500 square miles of great peaks, eroded valleys, lakes
in which icebergs bob, and ever-changing, ever-shrinking glaciers. Hugh Monroe, a
British trapper, was the first white man known to have visited the region (in 1816);
and railroad surveyors made tentative explorations into the mountains in the 1850's.
In 1885 George Bird Grinnell, an ardent naturalist, conservationist, and editor of

GLACIER NATIONAL PARK

Chief Mtn

Babb

Lower St Mary Lake

Mt Grinnell

Lake Sherburne

Swiftcurrent

Many Glacier

Going-to-the-Sun Mtn

Grinnell Glacier

R.T. U.S. 89

St Mary Lake

BLACKFEET HIGHWAY

Logan Pass

GOING-TO-THE-SUN ROAD

Lower Two Medicine Lake

TO BROWNING

Hidden Lake

Mt Jackson

Mt Logan

Mt Stimson 10,165

CONTINENTAL DIVIDE

Rising Wolf Mtn

East Glacier Park

Insight Mtn

Sperry Glacier

Harrison Glacier

Mt Pinchot

Two Medicine Lake

R.T. U.S. 2

Mt Doody

Mt St. Nicholas 9,380

Statuary Mtn

Summit Mtn

Harrison Lake

Marias Pass

Summit

Mt Grant

MIDDLE FORK FLATHEAD RIVER

FLATHEAD RANGE

Forest and Stream, vacationed there and fell in love with its wild beauty. His campaign to have it established as a national park was won in 1910, and today he is memorialized by the park's Grinnell Glacier, whose mass is 300 feet thick in places and deeply scarred with crevasses. To the north, beyond the border, is Canada's Waterton Lakes National Park, encompassing similar terrain. In 1932 the two areas were merged in Waterton-Glacier International Peace Park, a symbol of international friendship.

Crossing the Bitterroots, 1855, by G. Sohon

The Lure of the Wilderness

From this place we had an extencive view of these Stupendeous Mountains principally covered with snow . . . we were entirely serounded by those mountains from which to one unacquainted with them it would have Seemed impossible ever to have escaped. . ."

Idaho's Bitterroot Mountains have changed little since William Clark found them so formidable in 1806. Though a water-level highway now threads through the range, paralleling the high-country route that Lewis and Clark took, it is still easy to get lost and die in the huge mountains. Yet generations of Americans gained spiritual strength in such country, and thousands of persons still find refreshment and inspiration in the challenges of a wilderness vacation. Today, 1,239,800 acres of the Bitterroots (seen at right, looking north from 10,131-foot-high Trapper Peak) and adjacent land are preserved as the Selway-Bitterroot Wilderness, the nation's largest. There, and in similar reserves like Montana's Bob Marshall Wilderness, automobiles, lumbering, and other marks of civilization are forbidden, and man can gain a welcome respite from the pressures of modern life.

Big Game of the Rockies

Ᵽn the fall the best days come to the mountains. Then the colors are turning, and the air is crisp and exhilarating. At the base camps, doctors, clerks, and postmen arrive without wives and get into red shirts. In the morning, they're off to the high country and the animals. Some go for meat, some for a trophy, and some merely to try for a picture as good as the one below by Joern Gerdts of a mountain goat being one.

Though elkhorns for hat racks are now out (housewives probably never did like them), the elk is still a prize game animal.

Mountain sheep were once common, but now they usually stay above timber line and make the hunter climb to get them.

JOERN GERDTS

The wise and patriot chief, Joseph

The Home of Chief Joseph

Of all the Indians evicted from their homelands, none fought harder and more tragically for a country they loved than the Nez Percés of Chief Joseph, who occupied the beautiful Wallowa region of northeastern Oregon. Protected on all sides by lofty mountain ranges and deep chasms, including Hells Canyon, the lush, sparkling meadows of Wallowa Valley, with its gem, the glacial Wallowa Lake (below), provided delightful and easy living in the spring and summer. In cold weather the Indians descended into canyons like the Imnaha (left), where they lived in comfort, with abundant grass for their horses.

In the 1870's white men found a pass into the valley and began infringing on Nez Percé land. By a corrupt treaty, which Joseph's people had not signed, the Indians were ordered to leave the region. Joseph, a humane and statesmanlike leader, did all he could to avoid conflict, but other Nez Percés resisted and war broke out, culminating in an epic 1,300-mile fighting retreat by the Indians across Idaho and Montana to within only thirty miles of the Canadian border and safety. There, heartsick for his surrounded and suffering people, Joseph made his noble speech of capitulation in 1877: "From where the sun now stands, I will fight no more forever."

259

The Grand Coulee, with its dark, towering walls, is seen above in 1941, just
before storage waters were diverted into it by Grand Coulee Dam, the largest
concrete structure in the world. The main reservoir, Roosevelt Lake, has a
660-mile shoreline, and is now a national recreation area. The scene at right
of Summer Falls in the neighboring channeled scabland shows the layers of lava
that built up the Columbia Plateau. Below is a painting by James M. Alden,
who was with the Northwest Boundary Commission in the basalt region in 1860.

The Northwest Plateau

Between the northern Rockies and Washington's Cascades is a high arid region, the Columbia Plateau, with numerous features of geological interest, including the dry site of an ancient waterfall, a frothy lake of accumulated minerals and salts (Soap Lake), and the fifty-mile-long Grand Coulee with basalt walls up to one thousand feet tall.

The plateau was originally formed by lava flows, many of them issuing from vents in the earth. Floods gouged and channeled the land, and ice age glaciers ground across it. When the glaciers melted, a stubborn ice mass, the Okanogan Ice Lobe, obstructed the course of the swollen Columbia River, which cut a new channel, the Grand Coulee. With the breaking of the ice lobe, floods inundated the plateau, and the Columbia resumed its original course, abandoning the Coulee and the site of a waterfall. Today, the Coulee is partially filled again by a storage reservoir created by Grand Coulee Dam.

"Lynx Fasciatus," *the tiger cat of Lewis and Clark*

Science in the West

"One-Striped Garter Snake"

During the 1850's a notable group of expeditions, dispatched by the Corps of Topographical Engineers, explored the West along parallel lines, searching for the best route for a railroad to the Pacific. Attached to the various parties were American and European botanists, zoologists, geologists, and other scientists, who compiled the largest mass of data yet gathered about that part of the nation. In addition, artists with the expeditions sketched the flora and fauna, as well as the topography and the Indians, and in drawings like the ones on these pages, which were published by Congress in a series of governmental reports from 1855 to 1860, gave Americans a graphic look at some of the wonders of a part of the national domain that was still little known and regarded as exotic.

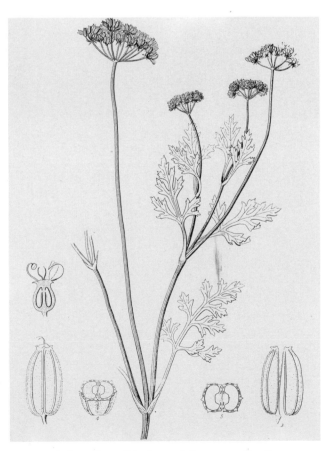

A flowering wild plant of the carrot family

Features of "the Northern Raven"

These drawings appeared with the report of Isaac I. Stevens, governor of the newly established Washington Territory, who led the northernmost of the railroad survey parties. His expedition traveled from St. Paul, Minnesota, to Puget Sound, exploring the area between the 47th and 49th parallels. Using the Lewis and Clark journals, his men found five passes across the northern Rockies, but another of the men, Lieutenant George B. McClellan, failed (to Stevens's disgust) to cross the Cascades.

"The Western Duck Hawk," seen in Washington Territory

Farms That Reach to the Sky

To travelers who thread their way through the torturous mountain-and-canyon geography of the Northwest, the bounteous farming country from Pendleton, Oregon, to the breathtakingly beautiful Palouse prairie of Idaho and eastern Washington (left) is a startling surprise. Composed in some places of rich silt up to eighty feet deep, believed to have been borne by the wind from more arid areas, the region receives rain in the fall and winter, just when it is needed, and has rarely known a crop failure.

The first settlers were uncertain whether or not the high plateau hills would be productive. But a gold strike in Idaho during the 1860's created a sudden demand for provisions, and in 1864 a Walla Walla farmer got thirty-three bushels of wheat to an acre from the uplands. The rush was on. With the use of gangs of horse-drawn hillside combines (above) and migratory threshing crews known as "bindle stiffs," the region became the breadbasket of the West. Today, golden wheat and pea fields billow across swells that cut off the horizon, or circle in contoured, colored strips around isolated stands of dark pines.

Mount Mazama

Oregon's Cascade Mountains, which stand as a barrier between the rainy coastal strip of the state and the broad, arid interior, were once—say the Klamath Indians—a battleground of the sacred spirits. The natives' legends tell of a cataclysmic struggle among the deities that lasted for seven terrifying days. The black skies were filled with flames, the earth trembled with mighty explosions, and fire and rocks hurtled through the air, destroying homes, villages, and forests. Finally one mountain, the throne of the spirit of the underworld, collapsed, and the war was over.

Geologists credit the Indians' legends to actual eyewitness accounts of the eruptions of Mount Mazama, a prehistoric, 12,000-foot-high volcano in southwestern Oregon that spewed out such a great volume of lava and rock through its top and fissures in its base that it collapsed and fell into its own crater more than seven thousand years ago. Indian artifacts, dating from before that period and discovered under pumice and lava, testify that man was indeed present when the eruptions occurred.

Now the basin of Mount Mazama is filled by Crater Lake (right), famed for its deep-blue color, the result of its unusual clarity and its depth of almost two thousand feet. Since 1853, when white men discovered it, the lake has awed visitors. In 1902 it became a national park, chiefly through the efforts of William Gladstone Steel, who was then appointed its first superintendent.

Crater Lake is the most stunning jewel of the Oregon Cascades. But there are other beautiful lakes, too, and majestic fir forests, tumbling waterfalls, and intriguing lava formations. Rising above all in the volcanic country are snow-capped peaks that have not completely blown their tops, including Mount Jefferson and the Three Sisters, each of them more than ten thousand feet in height. They were noble landmarks to early travelers between California and Oregon, one of whom, John J. Young, an artist with a government railroad survey group in 1855, made the drawings at the far right.

ALL: U.S. PACIFIC RAILROAD SURVEY, 1855, VOL. VI

Mount Pitt (now Mount McLoughlin) and the Klamath River

Three Cascade peaks: Mounts Jefferson, Hood, and Adams

Mount Hood (11,245 feet), as it appeared from Tygh Valley

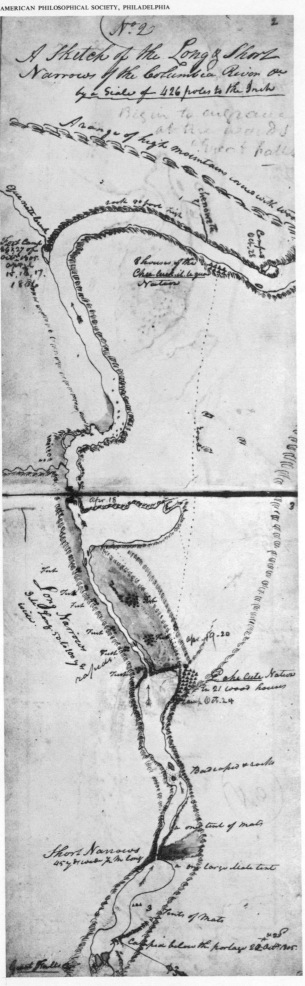

River of the West

In 1792, with the restrained enthusiasm of a New England Yankee, Captain Robert Gray, skipper of the *Columbia,* recorded the climactic moment of a great discovery in the Northwest: "We found this to be a large river of fresh water, up which we steered. Vast numbers of natives came alongside."

Other sea traders and explorers had earlier seen the broad mouth of the long-sought "River of the West." But like Englishman John Meares, who named it Deception Bay in 1788, they thought it only a coastal indentation. Gray, however, crossed the difficult bar and sailed fifteen miles up the river, whose headwaters began 1,270 miles upstream in the Rockies of British Columbia. He named the river for his ship and, after trading with the Indians, sailed away.

That same year Britain's Captain George Vancouver also found the river and sent one of his boats one hundred miles up it. Lewis and Clark came down the river in 1805, making maps of its principal features, like the area at the Dalles (left), and in 1811–12 Astorians arrived by land and sea and the British explorer–fur trader David Thompson completed a navigation of the river from its source to its mouth. All of these early visits provided bases for conflicting American and British claims to the strategic Columbia and the fur-rich Oregon country it drained.

For a time the British held sway. The North West Company, and later the Hudson's Bay Company, built posts along the river and its tributaries, and traders like Dr. John McLoughlin, whom the Indians called "the white-headed eagle," ruled the region as if it were a feudal kingdom. But there was more to the Columbia country than furs. The rivers teemed with salmon, the mountains were covered with timber, and the warm valleys were rich and fertile. By the 1840's, American settlers, lured partly by the glowing reports of missionaries among the northwestern Indians, were coming down the Columbia River by the thousands. As they poured over the land and built new homes, their numbers settled the issue and helped establish ownership of Oregon and the river for the United States.

The Oregon country, flanking the beautiful Columbia, awed Easterners with its majestic scenery, highlighted by snow-mantled peaks. Mount Rainier, as seen from Puget Sound (above), was painted in 1875 by Sanford R. Gifford, who called it Tacoma, after its Indian name. The mountain is the seventh highest peak in the United States (14,408 feet) and is encompassed by a national park of great Alpine beauty. Below is an 1853 view of Mount Hood from an Indian village on the Columbia, painted by John Mix Stanley. The Vancouver expedition named both peaks for British naval officers.

Where Rolls the Oregon

Celilo Falls, a great Indian fishing center, is now flooded by a dam.

When William Cullen Bryant referred to the Columbia as "the Oregon" in "Thanatopsis" in 1821, the river's banks were lined with Indian fishing settlements, and a way of life ten thousand years old was undisturbed. But in the 1830's, diseases, introduced by fur traders, began to wipe out whole villages and decimate others. Then came American settlers who took the Indians' lands away from them. Resentful natives made the passage of the Columbia a dangerous one, and many frightened pioneers were forced to huddle in the safety of blockhouses, like the one above at the Upper Cascades (photographed in 1867 by Carleton E. Watkins). When the Indians were finally crushed, some of the survivors were permitted to continue living along the river; today, however, the descendants of even those remnants are moving elsewhere, flooded out of their last villages by power dams.

271

An American Alps

Alexander Ross

In July, 1814, Alexander Ross, a Scottish fur trader, set out from the North West Company's post on the Okanogan River in northern Washington to make the first trip across the Cascades to the Pacific. Crossing "rugged and broken country," through forests so thick that he had to climb trees to see the sun, and over mountain terrain of "rocks and yawning chasms," he came within fifty miles of Puget Sound. But a storm, striking with unbridled fury, frightened away his Indian guide, and Ross was forced to turn back.

Today, the northern Cascades are still a little-traversed wilderness, blanketed with glaciers like Douglas Glacier on Mount Logan (left), squaw grass (below), and other Alpine splendors. Being considered as a new national park, the huge, Swiss-like region now includes national forests, a primitive area, and the Glacier Peak Wilderness Area.

RAY ATKESON

SIERRA CLUB, A. SCHMITZ

A jet's-eye view (at 40,000 feet) makes the forested heights of Washington's southern Cascades look like a crinkled robe.

The snow-covered peaks, formed volcanically, are Mount St. Helens (9,671 feet) and, farther away, Mount Adams (12,307 feet).

"You aren't a logger until you own a dollar watch and have your picture taken with a tree." With that effective sales pitch, Darius Kinsey, who migrated from Missouri to Washington in the late 1880's, carried his camera from one logging camp to another, taking dramatic photographs of the big woods, like those shown on these pages. He sold prints of his pictures, which sometimes posed men inside trees (upper right), to the appreciative lumberjacks for half a dollar.

276

Bulls of the Big Woods

In 1826 the botanist David Douglas was surprised and almost killed by Indians during his excitement while measuring a fallen Oregon tree 215 feet long and almost 60 feet in circumference near its base. In later years, land-clearing settlers cursed the Northwest's towering trees, but men who cut timber for a living regarded them as wonders.

As the harbors of the Columbia River and Puget Sound filled with ships waiting for lumber, sawmills went up in the woods, scaring Indians with their shrill whistles. Red-shirted loggers attacked stands of cedar, hemlock, spruce, and giant Douglas fir. The forests rang with the noise of saws and axes, the long wail of "timber," and the shouts of bullwhackers who drove the teams of oxen that hauled felled trees to the river over greased skid roads, trails of logs embedded in the earth. Power-driven engines replaced oxen after 1880, but the term "skid road" is still applied to those sections of towns where loggers customarily blew their pay on liquor and ladies.

Six yoke of oxen drag a felled tree along a skid road near Renton, Washington, in 1893.

The Olympics

Although they were first sighted from the sea in 1774 by the Spanish captain Juan Pérez, the Olympic Mountains, honed and sharpened by rain, snow, and glaciers, were not actually explored until the 1880's. When expeditions penetrated the wilderness of northwestern Washington's Olympic Peninsula at last, they recognized the aptness of the name that another viewer-from-the-sea, Captain John Meares of England, had given to the tallest of the glistening, snow-covered peaks in 1788: Mount Olympus, home of the gods.

Today, Mount Olympus (7,976 feet) rears above a 1,400-square-mile national park that includes a 50-mile-long strip of Pacific coastline. Established in 1938, the park contains dense, coniferous rain forests, constantly drenched by the outpourings of wet ocean winds that run into the Olympic Mountains. But there are also bright, springlike displays of wildflowers on Hurricane Ridge and other open slopes, and sparkling waterfalls in an area called the Enchanted Valley.

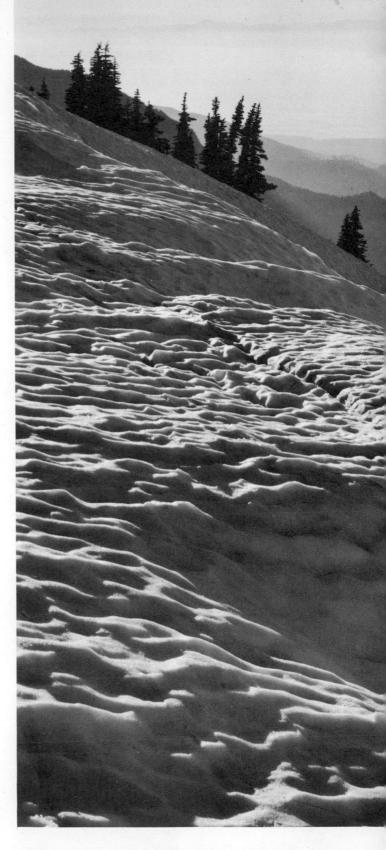

Inhabitants of the rugged wilds of Olympic National Park, photographed above by Ansel Adams, include deer, black bears, cougars, and Olympic marmots. Raccoons are often seen on the beaches, seals gambol on offshore rocks, and the nation's largest herd of Roosevelt elk, numbering about six thousand head, thrives on the hillsides.

ANSEL ADAMS

Water in its many forms—fresh, salt, liquid, frozen, and vaporous—gives the Olympic Peninsula its enthralling variety. There are more than fifty glaciers in the park, the longest of which is Hoh Glacier (left), extending like a giant tongue for almost four miles. Along the Pacific coast, waves pound against the rocks, and fog gives an eerie atmosphere to the bleak shore at Point of Arches (above), near Cape Flattery. And in the famous rain forests (below), moss-covered vine maples, Douglas fir, spruce, and hemlock grow to enormous size under an annual rainfall of some 140 inches. The floors of the forest are covered with ferns and wild flowers, and the ground and air are permeated with the heavy odor of lush, wet vegetation.

281

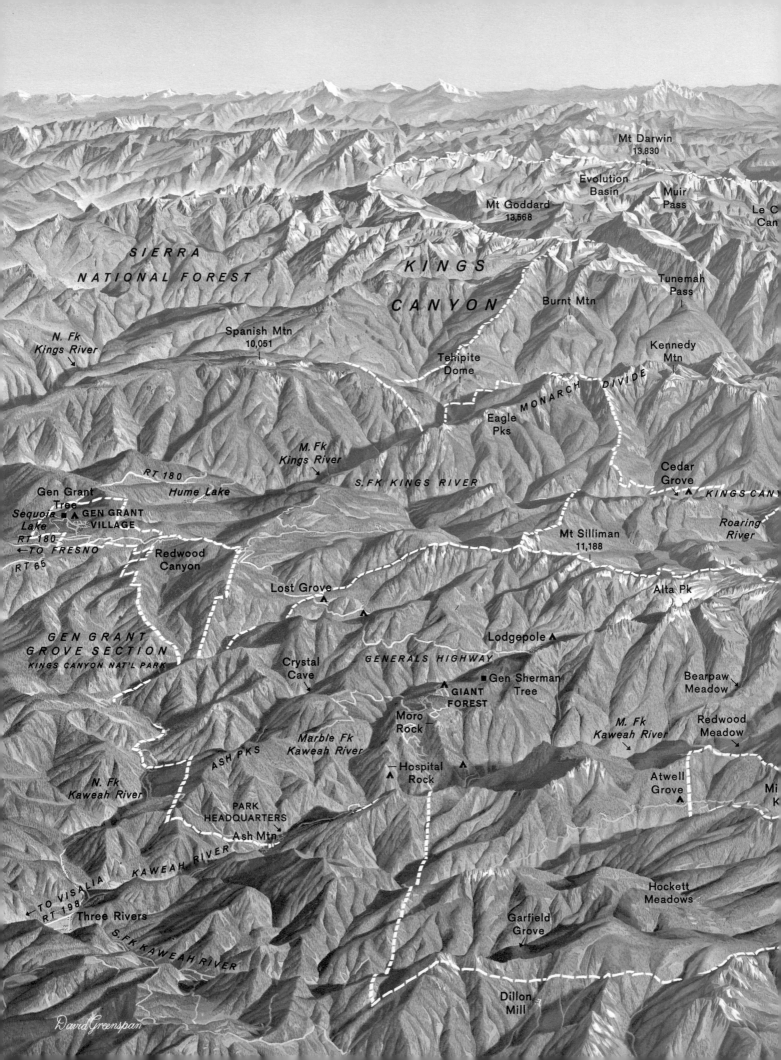

Mt Darwin
13,830

Evolution
Basin

Muir
Pass

Le C
Can

Mt Goddard
13,568

SIERRA

NATIONAL FOREST

KINGS

CANYON

Tuneman
Pass

Burnt Mtn

N. Fk
Kings River

Spanish Mtn
10,051

Tehipite
Dome

Kennedy
Mtn

MONARCH DIVIDE

Eagle
Pks

M. Fk
Kings River

S. FK KINGS RIVER

Cedar
Grove

RT 180

Gen Grant
Tree

Hume Lake

Sequoia
Lake

GEN GRANT
VILLAGE

KINGS CAN

Mt Silliman
11,188

Roaring
River

RT 180

TO FRESNO

Redwood
Canyon

RT 65

Alta Pk

Lost Grove

GEN GRANT
GROVE SECTION
KINGS CANYON NAT'L PARK

Lodgepole

Crystal
Cave

GENERALS HIGHWAY

Bearpaw
Meadow

Gen Sherman
Tree

GIANT
FOREST

Moro
Rock

M. Fk
Kaweah River

Redwood
Meadow

ASH PKS

Marble Fk
Kaweah River

Hospital
Rock

Atwell
Grove

N. Fk
Kaweah River

Mi
k

PARK
HEADQUARTERS

Ash Mtn

KAWEAH RIVER

Hockett
Meadows

TO VISALIA
RT 198

Three Rivers

Garfield
Grove

S. FK KAWEAH RIVER

Dillon
Mill

David Greenspan

SEQUOIA
AND KINGS CANYON
NATIONAL PARKS

Bishop

SOUTHERN PACIFIC

INYO
NATIONAL
FOREST

PALISADES Mather
Pass

Split Mtn
14,058

Mt Pinchot
13,495

Big
Pine

INYO
MTS

CIRQUE CREST

Mt Baxter
13,125

SIERRA

OWENS RIVER

Rae
Lakes

NEVADA

Paradise
Valley

Glen
Pass

Kearsarge
Pass

RTS U.S. 395 6

OWENS

VALLEY

Mt Brewer
13,577

Forester
Pass

Bubbs
Creek

Mt Tyndall

Independence

CLOUD

CANYON

Mt Barnard
13,990

Triple Divide
Pk

Mt Whitney
14,495

Stewart

Mt Langley
14,042

KAWEAH PKS

BIG ARROYO

Mt Guyot

Kern
River

CHAGOOPA
PLATEAU

Florence
Pk

Farewell
Gap

SEQUOIA

N

KERN
CANYON

Coyote
Pass

Coyote
Pks

SEQUOIA

NATIONAL

FOREST

▲ CAMPGROUND

The Work of Ages

The two contiguous national parks in the Sierra Nevada of California—Sequoia and Kings Canyon—contain high peaks, including Mount Whitney (14,495 feet), the nation's highest outside of Alaska, and deep canyons like that of East Creek (left). But the parks' unique glory are the giant and aged sequoia trees, the largest of which (the General Sherman Tree) is 272 feet tall, 36½ feet in diameter, and more than 3,500 years old. Protected against fire and lightning by their thick bark and remarkable ability to heal, the big trees (painted above by Albert Bierstadt) are also guarded by law against those who in a moment would undo the work of centuries and cut them down.

YOSEMITE NATIONAL PARK

Center Mtn

Matterhorn Pk

Quarry Pk

Mt Conness
12,561

MONO LAKE

Cold Mtn

TIOGA PASS ENTRANCE

RT 120

GLEN AULIN

INYO NATIONAL FOREST

Polly Dome

TUOLUMNE MEADOWS

lt nann

Tenaya Lake

Tuolumne Pass

Blacktop Pk
12,710

SUNRISE

VOGELSANG

Clouds Rest
9,929

Mt Lyell
13,114

MERCED LAKE

Mt Clark

Foerster Pk
12,058

Triple Divide Pk

SIERRA

Post Pk

Merced Pass

NEVADA

A VISTA CREST

Fernandez Pass

Sing Pk
10,552

N

BUCK CAMP

Chiquito Pass

SIERRA NATIONAL FOREST

▲ CAMPGROUND
▲ HIGH SIERRA CAMP

Mountain man Joseph R. Walker may have been the first white man to see Yosemite (in 1833), but it was not until 1851, when troops entered the valley on a punitive mission against Indians, that the region was explored. By 1855 the first tourists had arrived, and nine years later, when the valley became a California state park, it had been made famous by the writings of Horace Greeley and Thomas Starr King, the photographs of Carleton Watkins (opposite page), and the paintings of Thomas Ayres, Albert Bierstadt, and Henry Pratt, who made the above view of Yosemite Falls in 1854. The high country around the valley became a national park in 1890, chiefly through the efforts of John Muir, and in 1906 the canyon was added, forming Yosemite Park as we know it today.

"I'll Take Yosemite"

Stephen T. Mather of the National Parks

The history of the National Park Service is filled with the names of great benefactors like John D. Rockefeller, Jr. and Gilbert Grosvenor, whose efforts and gifts have conserved vast areas of the country unimpaired for the enjoyment of future generations. Of one man in particular, Stephen T. Mather, it has been said, "There will never come an end to the good he has done."

Mather, a Chicago industrialist, visited Yosemite National Park in 1914 and was appalled at the poor and unprotected state in which he found it. In anger, he wrote to the Secretary of the Interior, who replied by asking him to come to Washington and run the parks himself.

Mather took the job in 1915, and in 1917, after Congress had created the National Park Service, he became its first director. With an able assistant, Horace M. Albright, who later succeeded him and became one of the nation's leading conservationists, Mather labored tirelessly, at the expense of his health and his own funds, to build up the parks. He took writers and congressmen to the parks, inspired public support, and until his death in 1930, fought for laws and appropriations to improve old parks and establish new ones.

He worked for all the parks, but his favorite was Yosemite. "Yellowstone is a great place," he once told Albright, "but . . . I'll take Yosemite." His feelings were understandable, for Yosemite is awe inspiring. Its famous valley, gouged by glaciers and water, is lined with waterfalls like Bridalveil and mountains like the Three Brothers (seen in 1866 photographs, right). And beyond them, giving meaning to the Indian name Ahwahnee, "deep grassy valley in the heart of the sky mountains," is a wilderness of high meadows and more mountains.

To many visitors the most spectacular view of Yosemite is of its magnificent canyon, shown here in an Ansel Adams photograph in winter, when snow blankets the valley and powders the famous peaks. At the left is El Capitan (called "Rock Chief" by the Indians), which rises 3,604 feet and, although scaled a number of times, is still a formidable challenge to climbers. In the distance is Half Dome, round on one side, sheer on the other, and at 4,852 feet the highest point above the valley. At the right are the spires that seem aptly named, the Cathedral Rocks.

291

The Sad Tale
of Hetch Hetchy

In the early years of the twentieth century many Americans became conservation-minded. President Theodore Roosevelt camped out in Yosemite with John Muir and in the Yellowstone with naturalist John Burroughs, and became a staunch advocate of conservation. The Audubon Society, the Sierra Club of California, and other organizations dedicated themselves to the protection of fast-disappearing natural wonders, and garden clubs and civic groups worked to preserve local parks and green areas.

The significance of the conservation movement, as it would affect the future of the nation, was dramatized during the first decade of the century by a valiant but losing fight to save Hetch Hetchy Valley, a beautiful section of Yosemite National Park. In 1903 San Franciscans proposed damming the valley for a reservoir as a source of hydroelectric power. John Muir cried out in horror: "Dam Hetch Hetchy! As well dam for water tanks the people's cathedrals and churches; for no holier temple has ever been consecrated

to the heart of man." Many others, including J. Horace McFarland of the American Civic Association, Robert U. Johnson of *Century Magazine,* Frederick Law Olmsted, Jr., Stephen Mather, and members of the Sierra Club, joined Muir to oppose the measure. They fought until 1913 when, after much political maneuvering and conflict, Congress authorized the flooding of the inspiring valley—which, if it were still available, could have reduced the overcrowding that now handicaps the park.

Once a smaller version of the better known Yosemite Valley, with flowering meadows, magnificent rock formations, and lovely waterfalls (opposite page), Hetch Hetchy is now inundated in wet seasons, and is a wretched bed of mud and stumps when the reservoir is low (below). If the "rape" of Hetch Hetchy (since proved to have been unnecessary) has had any beneficial effect, it has been that conservationists ever since have used its memory to prevent similar invasions from destroying the natural beauty of other national parks.

Roosevelt and Muir in Yosemite National Park

U.S. PACIFIC RAILROAD SURVEY, 1853, VOL. V

This 1853 field sketch by a government explorer at Kings River was one of the first of the Sierra Nevada.

ANSEL ADAMS

The High Sierra

WILLIAM A. GARNETT FOR BANK OF AMERICA NT & SA, MUNICIPAL BOND DEPT.

The Sierra Nevada is filled with lore, not all of it pleasant. To fur trader Zenas Leonard, who struggled across the range in 1832, it was "a defiant wall of rock," with winds that "shrieked wild and high among the summit crags" and snow so deep that horses sometimes sank out of sight. In 1846 the grimmest tragedy of the overland emigration occurred when the Donner Party, trapped on its heights, resorted to cannibalism.

Today, the Sierra, some 385 miles long with an average width of 80 miles, is crossed by highways; and hikers and fishermen find relaxation on its high trails and lakes. Climbers scale Mount Whitney, the tallest United States peak outside of Alaska, and Lone Pine Peak (both seen at left overlooking Owens Valley), and vacationers play at 6,225-foot-high Lake Tahoe (above). But winter gales and snows still add to the Sierra's lore: in 1952 a train was snowbound for four days before its passengers were saved.

A Ranger's Life

The dwarfed wigwagger high on the treetop platform at left was one of the early rangers of the U.S. Forest Service. His job was to keep watch over Shasta National Forest in California for signs of fire, but other rangers, equally immune to high-country vertigo, protected national forests elsewhere. Roosts on tall trees and mountain peaks were vantage points for scanning large areas and spotting the first puffs of smoke that might erupt into giant blazes, like the one that ravaged Montana's Flathead Forest in 1910 (right). The rangers' communications systems were primitive, often merely semaphores or sun-flash heliograph signals. For transportation, they used horses and homemade vehicles, like the one belonging to the 1913 ranger (below), who fitted a twenty-horsepower Ford with flanged wheels and toured the forest on railroad tracks.

Conservation of the woods has been a concern of many Americans since 1626, when Plymouth Colony forbade the cutting of timber on public land without official consent. But it was difficult for most people, who saw trees growing everywhere, to realize the need for protective measures. In 1891 President Benjamin Harrison finally set aside the first forest reserves, and in 1905 Theodore Roosevelt created the Forest Service in its present form, with 734 employees under conservationist Gifford Pinchot.

Today, there are more than 150 national forests, covering some one hundred eighty million acres, or over one twelfth of the total area of the United States. Man's carelessness still causes scores of destructive fires each year (lightning starts some), and modern foresters fight them with an integrated system of smoke jumpers, radio, and ground and air equipment. But, with multiple use of the forests by loggers (under regulation), vacationers, and others, a ranger's life can be a varied round, from laboratory research to the supervision of camps.

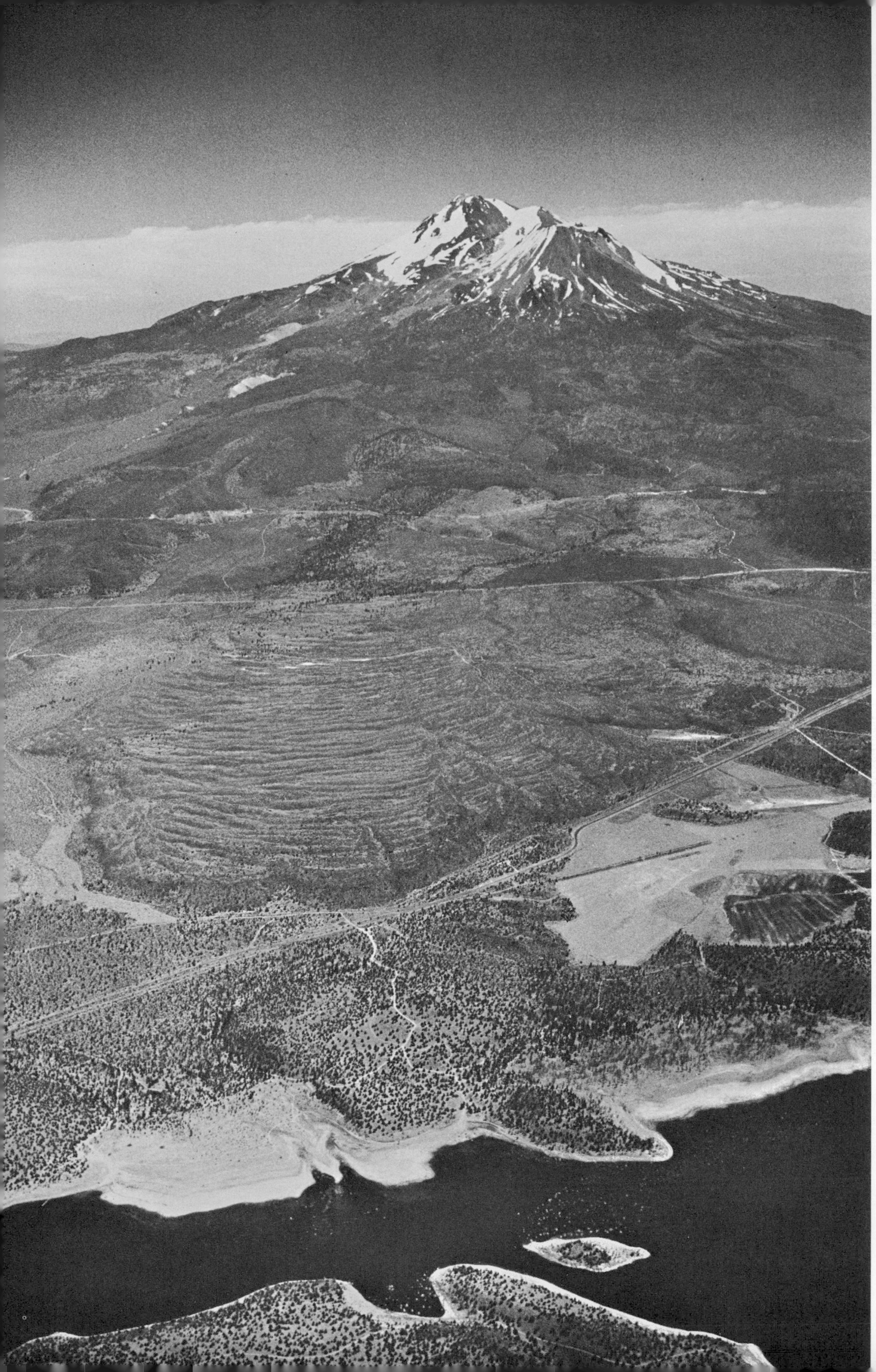

JAMES YARNELL

U.S. FOREST SERVICE

Land of Lava

When Mount Lassen, named for an early settler, began a series of thunderous eruptions in 1914 (above), Californians were reminded of the volcanic nature of their northern peaks. Lassen has been quiet since 1921, but the lava formations and smokes in Lassen Volcanic National Park bear testimony to the mountain's inner heat. Other state landmarks are the Lava Beds, composed of numerous caves of hardened lava near Mount Shasta (left), and the sixty-foot-high basaltic columns of Devil Postpile (below).

The red rocks of the Garden of the Gods in 1919

Mortals Among the Gods

Despite the efforts of conservationists, the needs and pressures of modern America continue to destroy scenic beauties and natural resources. The Garden of the Gods, a stand of tall red rocks at Colorado Springs, was once a lovely park. Men enjoyed it so much that they recently moved right in with swimming pools, tennis courts, roads, and homes (right). Realtors have similarly "developed" Lake Tahoe and the red mesas at Sedona, Arizona. In the Northwest, modern tree farming methods assure the reseeding of clear-cut blocks by adjacent trees that are left standing. But as the photograph of Washington's Olympic Range at far right demonstrates, the temporarily denuded sections and twisting logging roads have given the forest the look of the mange.

Elsewhere, streams have been polluted with waste and detergents, gulches fouled by mines, and grasslands grazed bare. Unrestrained by public opinion or laws, spoliation of these resources continues each year.

300

Mount McKinley

The Alaska Indians called it Denali, "the high one, home of the sun." But prospector W. A. Dickey, annoyed by rabid "cross of gold" Democrats in 1896, renamed the mountain in honor of the new Republican candidate for President, William McKinley.

Sometimes shrouded in clouds, sometimes completely exposed and shining with unbelievable brilliance in the full sunlight, the two-peaked giant, with a northern summit of 19,470 feet and a southern one of 20,320 feet, is the highest in North America, rearing above a neighbor, Mount Foraker (17,400 feet), the nation's third highest mountain. Through the efforts of naturalist Charles Sheldon, Mount McKinley National Park was established in 1917. Later the park was expanded to include some three thousand acres of spruce forests, tundra, and glacier-lined slopes, the home of grizzly bears, Dall sheep, wolves, and caribou.

Viewed from across Wonder Lake in this Ansel Adams photograph, the snow-mantled mountain and its foothills, easily seen from observation points reached by modern highway, are an unforgettable sight of the forty-ninth state, still the fortunate possessor of numerous other unspoiled scenic areas.

VII

THE
BASIN
AND
DESERT

By GEORGE R. STEWART

From the air, the arid country of the Southwest, worn and creased by erosion, is a sunlit and shadowed carpet of fascinating "what-is-its?" This is a tall butte near the Colorado River's Marble Canyon in Arizona.

Six hundred miles it stretches east and west, from the Rockies to the Sierra Nevada, and almost a thousand miles, north and south, from the lava fields along the Snake River to the saguaro-studded desert at the barbed-wire fence where the flags change. Altogether, it totals well over half a million square miles, close to a fifth of the whole of the old forty-eight states.

To draw a sweeping line upon a map, and to label with some name or number everything that lies inside—that is easy. But anyone may be puzzled to recognize the unity in the land itself. The flaming reds of Arizona's Painted Desert, what have they in common with the gray sagebrush valleys of central Nevada? The crags and cliffs and pinnacles of the Grand Canyon and Bryce and Zion, how can we include them within the line that also encloses the Bonneville Salt Flats and the dead-level Black Rock Desert in northwestern Nevada?

Yet unity there is, and to identify it we can repeat the title that Mary Austin, who usually wrote with a touch of poetry, gave to her book in 1903—*The Land of Little Rain.* Except for the higher mountain ranges, the region receives not more than ten inches of rain a year; a large part of it, less than five inches. In determining what people see and think—even what they feel and imagine—all over this half-million square miles, everything else is secondary to this basic dryness.

In the mid-nineteenth-century there was a favorite term—The Great American Desert. It lapsed for various reasons, but largely because it had been misapplied to an area east of the Rockies, which was grassland and not true desert. But America has a desert, and it is large enough to be called great. This is it.

A desert, to be sure, cannot be said to have rarity value. A remarkably large portion of the so-called good earth's surface is notable for deficiency of rainfall—the Sahara, Arabia and most other parts of the Near East, vast areas of central Asia, other vast areas of Australia, southern Africa, and South America. In fact, taking land surface the world over, we find as much desert as anything else.

But the American in the beginning looked upon his own desert country as something abnormal and shocking; and he has never wholly got over that idea. Why he had it, is easy enough to see. As an immigrant from the British Isles or northwestern Europe he came from gently hilly, tree-growing country, and so he took the Eastern Coast as normal, though actually such a broad-leaf forest is rather rare on the earth. He got a first shock when he came to the treeless, grassy plains, and a second one when he came to the great mountain-masses of the Rockies. But the third and final and most shaking shock came to the American when

he saw the dry country. He thought it unlovely, even horrible and hideous—inhospitable at best; at worst as treacherously and viciously dangerous as its own rattlesnakes.

Well on toward a century passed. Some Americans published books and articles about the desert, and many others, covered-wagon emigrants and railway travelers, scribbled in their journals, and the upshot of this writing was that the dry lands were ugly and horrible. At best they could supply, in a kind of incidental way, some fantastic phenomenon like the Grand Canyon.

About 1900 something shifted. Two books in particular symbolized the shift, and in themselves also did a little to help it along. One of these was *The Land of Little Rain,* already mentioned. The other was John C. Van Dyke's book published in 1901, and called merely *The Desert.*

The two writers were very different. Mary Austin had lived for several years in the dry country, at its western edge in California, just under the high wall of the Sierra Nevada. So her love of the desert might be discounted, as the special pleading of someone writing about a beloved local scene. But Van Dyke was an outsider. He was from New Jersey, a rather easygoing art critic with a gift for popularizing. Many people read *The Desert,* and they could not readily shrug off what such an Easterner had written in the voice of authority.

Now, after all, what is there to admire about this broad region? Why, after many years, did we shift ground and decide that it was not ugly and forbidding but was beautiful and even lovely?

First of all, I think, we came to appreciate its space. All countries, indeed, have space, but this one seems to possess and to display its spaciousness in a most striking manner. This is a trait that the early travelers noted, even though they seldom reacted aesthetically to it. But they constantly remarked upon the clear air, which made distant objects seem close. Sometimes this phenomenon got them into trouble. A covered-wagon emigrant, in 1841, saw some snow on a mountain, and decided it would be fun to go and get some. Instead of its being an hour's walk, he began to wonder whether he would ever get there at all. Being a determined young man he kept on, and reached the snow, but he had to stay out overnight.

This clarity of air, which impressed the pioneers so much, is certainly to be connected with the dryness, inasmuch as you will rarely, in the desert, find your view obstructed by a fog or an all-day drizzle. On the other hand, the air is often hazy with dust, and the spaciousness results in part from qualities other than clarity.

The dryness builds up the spaciousness in another way by reducing the vegetation. Often you can see for a long

distance because you are looking out across the top of the sagebrush and do not have the view impeded by trees. Moreover, the crest of a line of desert hills stands out more sharply and looks closer at hand because it presents a clear line of rock not made fuzzy by trees and bushes.

This matter of spaciousness, however, is tied up also with another basic quality of the whole area, what we may call its three-dimensionalism. We may again contrast the eastern United States. There you typically look down into the next little valley and over to the hill beyond it. Even

on a clear day you rarely see more than two or three miles. But much of the desert country is "constructed," as we may put it, of steeply rising mountain ranges with sweeping and open valleys between them. From one side of one range you look across the valley to the next range, and a view of twenty or thirty miles is ordinary. Looking up or down the valley you may see some peak a hundred miles off.

Moreover, this is plateau country with an almost level "floor" several thousand feet above sea level. The three-dimensional quality becomes evident as you look both

307

ways, up and down. The mountains rise sharply above the floor. The lower ranges lift their crests up two or three thousand feet; the most elevated peaks, eight or nine thousand feet. But the canyons—they have been called mountains in reverse, and upside-down mountains—have been eroded from the general level of the floor, and the bottom of the Grand Canyon is in places a mile down. In Death Valley National Monument the process has even gone beyond what we would think should be its limit. There, because of movements of the earth's crust, the bottom of the valley is nearly three hundred feet *below* sea level. Nevertheless the nearby ranges rise to over eleven thousand feet above sea level.

Though these desert peaks set no records for altitude, they include some fine mountains—Charleston Peak and Boundary Peak in Nevada, the San Francisco Peaks in Arizona, Pilot Peak in Utah. Little-known Mount Wheeler (13,058 feet) in eastern Nevada is now being considered as a new national park.

What are probably the most amazing glories of the whole area are connected with this three-dimensional quality. Only because of altitude that allowed water and frost and wind to work downward so far could we have had in the end such masterpieces of erosion as the Grand Canyon, Zion Canyon, Bryce Canyon, Cedar Breaks, and a hundred other such features not so widely known.

We must consider, also, the desert sky. The covered-wagon emigrants, caught in the inferno of the Salt Lake Desert, or the Forty-Mile or the Black Rock, had only curses for that sky, and we cannot blame them. Even now, on a summer day, most people care to see as little as possible of it and will probably note that it is nothing more beautiful than a dusty blue.

But, given better conditions, the Americans have learned to become lyrical about the desert sky. In the afternoons the high white cumulus clouds pile up in it, contrasting with an intense blue. It can suddenly, as a thunderstorm hits, turn a kind of green-black beautiful, even if a bit terrifying. It is best of all at sunset—or at dawn, if you care for that sort of thing. Mr. Van Dyke let loose his whole ample color-vocabulary on the subject—"chrome-yellows, golds, carmines, magentas, malachite-greens."

Anyone would gather, from all the eulogy, that this color furnishes one of the most important sources of appeal to the sight-seer. Over much of the desert, indeed, the prevailing tone is gray. On the other hand, there are certainly many areas that are brilliant with varied hues.

Again, one wonders how much of the fascination with the desert arises not from a sense of beauty but from a sense of strangeness. Approaching the desert from the east the American had a normal color standard for landscape. It should be green in spring and summer. In fall it should dull into yellows and browns, with a touch of red. In winter it would be brown or gray, except when it turned white. Moreover, except for the snow, nearly all the colors would be those of vegetation.

This superb panorama of the Grand Canyon was drawn in 1880 by William Henry Holmes, an artist with a government expedition.

The desert was different. There was very little seasonal change, except for an occasional powdering of snow. Much of the color was not vegetational, but was of rock, earth, or sand. Green was not important, and it would generally be a green that was on the edge of being gray. Red and black tended to dominate. The reds shaded off into pinks in one direction; in the other direction, into browns and even purples. For contrast, the rocks showed sharp bands of white and yellow.

The place names testify to the impression made by the colors. Straightforward pioneers named many a Red Rock and Black Rock, Black Mountain and White Mountain, and even Striped Rock and Striped Mountain. A more self-conscious later generation produced such flights of fancy as the Painted Desert, the Valley of Fire (for its redness), Rainbow Bridge, and the Great White Throne.

Not with colors only but in other respects also the interest of the Americans in the desert seems to spring from a fascination with the strange and fantastic.

Take the mirage. On the desert it is as common as a hot day. But many people from other parts of the country have never known a mirage, and some of them will even manage to drive U.S. 40 across the flats of Great Salt Lake without realizing what they have seen. Most people imagine that the mirage will show a file of camels, or a twenty-mule-team wagon, or at least a row of palm trees. It will not—unless you have a vivid imagination, and in that case you might as well stay at home and do your imagining there.

What you are likely to see is two things. First, at a distance there will be something that looks so much like a body of water that you may never be quite sure but that there is a little skim of water out there from a recent thunderstorm. Second, you will see the ends of the desert hills neatly curled up, so that you seem to be looking underneath them. Occasionally, the mirage can be more spectacular. Driving across the salt flat of the Black Rock Desert, I once saw an approaching car that seemed to be coming at me through the air like a low-flying airplane. (But the ordinary tourist should not be driving out on a place where there is no road.)

The mirage is only one of the desert's many phantasms. The American has rarely experienced volcanic action, but in the desert he can see much of its effects. Moreover, because of the dryness, it is not obscured by greenery, but often looks just about as it must have looked many millions of years ago. Neat little cinder cones, each with its recognizable crater, are scattered about in many areas, and Sunset Crater National Monument in Arizona takes its name from a notable example. Lava Beds National Monument in California preserves various volcanic formations. Craters of the Moon National Monument in Idaho has not only craters, but also lava flows, caves, and tunnels. In fact it has just about every manifestation of volcanic activity except an active volcano.

In much of the dry country fantastic land forms are so common that only a few of the most notable have been

The view, seen from Point Sublime, appeared in Clarence E. Dutton's 1882 Tertiary History of the Grand Cañon District.

made into national (or state) parks and monuments. In most regions Shiprock in New Mexico and Monument Valley in Utah would be hailed as natural wonders. And whoever heard of the City of Rocks in southern Idaho? It was a notable landmark on the California Trail, and even yet you can find the names of forty-niners chiseled on the rocks. These rocks were big as houses and were spread thickly over an area of several square miles. So it seemed a kind of city, and was thus named. There was even a great dominating mass rising up with twin spires that could be called Cathedral Rock. But the City of Rocks has not been set aside as a preserve, and even to get there you have to go some miles off a paved road.

Or take another kind of curiosity. In Petrified Forest National Monument in Arizona we are fortunate to have preserved what is doubtless the best of its kind. But there are others. A geologist friend once took me into another one, which does not even have a name, or a road that you wish to tackle in anything less than a jeep. The petrified wood was lying around everywhere. You stooped to pick up what looked like an old bit of pine wood— and it turned out to be stone!

Cliffs—they run for miles! The map makers strained to get colors enough to name them—the Brown Cliffs, the Roan Cliffs, the Orange Cliffs, the Vermilion Cliffs.

These cliffs are most prominent in the great eastern area of the desert. Dryness has little to do with forming the cliffs, though except for the dryness they would be largely obscured by vegetation. The reason for the cliffs lies deep in the geology of the country. The prevailing rock is sandstone, which has been raised high above the sea without losing its original horizontal bedding. Because of this bedding, the rock tends to weather off in great chunks, which break away so as to form the perpendicular, high-rising walls.

As for the prevailing redness, there is some argument about its origin. Some think it the result of rocks formed from laterite, the typical red soil of a wet tropical country. Others consider that the red rocks were originally desert sands, and are thus an indication that aridity has been a long-time feature of the area. The spectacular petrified sand dunes of Zion National Park are certain evidence of desert conditions at one particular place and time.

Desert vegetation also aids in producing an interesting landscape, as the names of three national monuments testify—Organ Pipe Cactus, Saguaro, and Joshua Tree. In addition the Forest Service has established an area for the bristlecone pine, now believed to be the oldest of living organisms. Again, we can maintain, the fantastic quality strikes people most forcibly.

On the salt flats, on the sheer cliffs, on some of the lava flows, vegetation is lacking. Over the dry country, in general, we properly think of vegetation as scanty. But such a judgment is quantitative, as if unconsciously we were using as criterion the number of cows to be pastured on a township. Considered qualitatively, the desert displays both a large number of species and a great variety of form and appearance.

Only a few species are so common as to tend toward monotony—sagebrush to the north, mesquite to the south, on the higher lands the juniper and the little piñon pine. But go a little higher still, and suddenly you enter a world of big yellow-barked pines, as on the Kaibab Plateau along the north rim of the Grand Canyon.

Elsewhere also, for special reasons, the prevailing growth changes sharply. Here it may be prickly pear; here, desert holly. Sagebrush does not grow in salty soil, and so around the edges of the dry and intermittent lakes you see greasewood, bright green and growing in hummocks, and farther from the salt pan come various little desert shrubs, such as the shad scale, beloved by grazing sheep, coral-colored in autumn.

Where the desert is most deserty, there the plants seem to grow most grotesquely. Sagebrush requires cold winters, and even mesquite has some limitations of soil and water. So, far in the south, the yuccas and the cacti take over. The Joshua tree is a yucca, a member of the lily family, though looking remarkably like a palm, and so-called by the Mexicans. As for cacti, they are various enough to constitute a whole flora in themselves, though certainly the giants among them, the organ pipe and the saguaro, are the most notable at dominating a landscape.

Desert flowers, also, for their brief moments, transform the landscape into far-spreading white or pink or yellow. You are privileged to dislike rabbit brush. (What it has to do with rabbits is uncertain.) It is a nondescript-looking shrub that moves into overgrazed country, replacing better plants. But in October mile after mile along U.S. 66 turns bright yellow when the rabbit brush flowers.

The mammals, birds, and reptiles rarely become a part of the landscape—perhaps a hawk or buzzard hangs in the air, seemingly motionless, over a sand dune, or else he gives scale and action to the view as he sails along a canyon rim. But most of the desert creatures, though as varied and curious as the plants, are happy to be inconspicuous.

They have adapted to the situation, and only a sentimentalist imagines them enduring a harder struggle for existence than wild animals do elsewhere. Many of them have neatly solved one problem by becoming nocturnal. Some of these are burrowers who have never seen the blazing and glaring sun. To them the desert is an always-cool place, dimly lighted by moon and stars—and so it has been to their ancestors through thousands of years.

Only the antelope are individually big enough and collectively numerous enough to become, in a few places, a significant part of the landscape. Such places are, unfortunately, among those visited by fewest people—the Hart Mountain area in southern Oregon, and the Sheldon Refuge in northwestern Nevada. There you can still see the graceful pronghorns in hundreds—their bodies such a yellow-brown that at a distance you think them less brown than yellow. Each shows conspicuously the white spots on the rump, so that you realize why their Mexican name is *berrendo,* "two-colored."

In these far-off places the herds give to the sagebrush slopes a sense of life and motion, and, we may say, some reason for being. Now, with adequate protection, the antelope are on the march, and soon we may see them in many parks. So it may be with other animals, too. Fifty years hence, we may hope, no desert crag will have to be without its bighorn sheep, supplying the viewer with a scale and with animate beauty. (Was Shiprock once Sheep Rock? It looks, indeed, very little like a ship. Perhaps it will be Sheep Rock again.)

Last, we may consider how people, also, have helped to create the desert scene. Modern man with his cities and the harsh lines of new-cut highways is too recent; the desert has not yet had time to absorb him, though undoubtedly it will. On the other hand, the work of the older desert dwellers integrates with the landscape. A Hopi village, such as Walpi, crowns its mesa with as much native grace as if it were a yucca or a weathered local rock—and indeed the houses are actually built of such rock. So also it is with Acoma and the Enchanted Mesa in New Mexico.

The still-older work of the cliff dwellers has become, with the passage of time, even more closely identified with nature. The ruinous condition of their buildings enhances the effect. The cliffs of Mesa Verde National Park are beautiful enough, but by themselves they would gain few second glances in that country of a thousand cliffs. When set off by ancient houses and towers, the cliffs become memorable. Canyon de Chelly is a natural wonder of itself, but its ruins make it a double wonder. So it goes also with the many others—Frijoles Canyon, Wupatki, Walnut Canyon, Montezuma Castle, and the rest.

Even these ruins have their links with the general theme of dryness. Except for dryness, the people would not have concentrated so much in canyons. Except for increasing dryness, these dwellings might not have been abandoned. Without continuing dryness, the walls and towers of

Utah's Bryce Canyon National Park was formed in recent geologic times when the land rose and broke into blocks, which were then shaped by erosion into ranks of dazzling pinnacles and spires.

unmortared stones would scarcely have stood through centuries, to attract their thousands of sight-seers.

But the emphasis cannot be entirely upon the unity of the area as one of low rainfall. There is also diversity. Physiographers, those scientists concerned with land forms and thus with scenery, divide the dry country into three provinces, and in one of these even the passing tourist can distinguish three subdivisions, well marked by the type of landscape and even of vegetation.

To the north, the Snake River country forms a part of the physiographic province known as the Columbia Plateau. Much of it is level plain, but everywhere with mountains on the horizon. The valleys are sagebrush-covered,

311

with some irrigated areas where sugar beets and potatoes grow abundantly. But the great mark upon the country is from its volcanoes, some old even by geologists' standards, some only a few thousand years in the past. The Snake has cut out a magnificent canyon through the black basalt, typical of the region. The canyon of the Bruneau is also a spectacular one.

The second great subdivision lies to the east. Roughly circular, it is known as the Colorado Plateau, but is named from the river, rather than from the state. Including southwestern Colorado, it also sweeps around to embrace all the adjacent parts of Utah, New Mexico, and Arizona, thus reaching from the Rockies to the Grand Canyon. This highly variegated and scenic region of cliffs, canyons, and colorful rocks includes three national parks (Grand Canyon, Zion, and Bryce Canyon), as well as several national monuments. It is, in fact, the sight-seer's paradise. The most remarkable landscapes of the dry country are concentrated in this region.

All of the west and south, much more than half of the area of the whole arid region, is included within what physiographers know as the Basin and Range Province. It totals about three hundred thousand square miles, not counting its continuation into Mexico. The unity of this vast territory, however, is more apparent to the scientist than to the tourist, and the latter is likely to see it according to three local variations of landscape and vegetation, which produce only subdivisions for the scientist.

Of these subdivisions the northernmost and largest is the Great Basin, stretching its vastness from Great Salt Lake to the Sierra Nevada and from middle Oregon to southern Nevada. To the physiographer its dominating regional trait is that the water, even when there is any to flow, drains "inward" to a large number of lakes or sinks, by far the largest being Great Salt Lake itself. The lake beds, many of them dry except after a thunderstorm, show up as salt pans, devoid of vegetation, dazzling white under the desert sun. In size they range from mere dried-up puddles to the Great Salt Lake Desert and the Black Rock Desert, each covering hundreds of square miles. These numerous lake beds and the few still-existing salt lakes constitute the region's most striking features, also providing a plain evidence of the rainier climate that existed as recently as ten thousand years ago. Some of the bodies of water—notably Pyramid and Walker lakes—are less often visited than they might well be, and are surprisingly beautiful, with their expanses of turquoise-blue water set among desert mountains and fantastic rock forms.

In general, however, the Great Basin is not highly scenic, and some would even term it monotonous. Chiefly it displays broad sagebrush valleys, separated by north-south-trending mountain ranges—as C. E. Dutton, an early geologist, termed them, "an army of caterpillars crawling toward Mexico."

Nevertheless, the region is constructed on a vastness of scale that cannot fail to be impressive to any sensitive traveler. It is strikingly empty now, but one feels that in other days it might have been a land of giants.

South and east of the Great Basin a tongue of high country reaches north from below the border, and is known as the Mexican Highland. To geologists and physiographers the region is not as distinct as it might be, and there is argument about its limits. To the tourist it seems to stand out rather clearly. Though beautiful in many parts the Highland is not a region of spectacular scenery.

As its name indicates, it is more elevated than the surrounding country, and so receives more rainfall, in many parts as much as twenty inches a year. It is, therefore, not desert, but is grassland or open forest country of big yellow pines. On the rainfall map of Arizona the Highland stands clearly marked—a long arm of higher precipitation extending across the state from southeast to northwest.

Like the Mexican Highland, the Sonoran Desert too, as its name indicates, is a northern extension of an area lying south of the border. The region is set off for the traveler, most strikingly, by its characteristic vegetation, which results from scanty rainfall—in many places, less than four inches annually.

Since the winters are warm, sagebrush does not flourish, and because of the dryness there is no grassland. The passer-by notes a thin vegetation, with much bare rock, gravel, and sand. He sees mesquite, Joshua tree, cactus of many kinds. There are also many drought-resistant shrubs and small trees, hard to name but often beautiful, such as the desert holly and the smoke tree. The national monuments have been established chiefly to preserve this bizarre vegetation.

The diversity of the dry country displays itself in many other ways than regionally—for instance, by season. Most Americans have a fixed idea that a desert is hot, doubtless because they usually travel across it during their summer vacations or else associate it particularly with a few places —like southwestern Arizona—that are winter resorts. But much of our dry country has bitterly cold winters, with thermometers falling to twenty below. Not continuous heat, but extreme change, is the rule. Desert stations may report a summer high of 110 and a winter low of –30.

But even the daily range can be extreme. At Black Rock Spring in northwestern Nevada I have been shivering beneath sweater and windbreaker on a September morning.

Then, as the sun rose above the rock, the effect was as if I had stepped in front of an open furnace. Within five minutes I had shed my heavy clothes and was suffering from heat and hunting for shade.

The whole desert country is a scenic heritage for the American people. Like most heritages it may be intelligently husbanded, and even enhanced, or it may be squandered. We have done something in both ways.

The establishment of the national parks and monuments is a major achievement. Private and semipublic interests have sometimes attempted to encroach upon these reservations; as population continues to increase, we shall have more such attempts. The growing and often intensive utilization of the parks and monuments, however, makes them of such economic value to the localities, as well as to the nation, that there is good hope of their preservation. At the same time the increasing pressure of people exerts some wear and tear on the parks themselves.

State parks, particularly such large ones as Anza-Borrego in California, will also, doubtless, be maintained and even extended. The national forests, though their primary function is not the preservation of scenery, actually help much toward that end. Some states also enforce good laws against the wanton picking of desert flowers and the breaking-off of branches.

Along the highways we have not done so well. Year by year the senseless billboards are gradually working out farther and farther from every town. The modest ones for "Joe's Service Station" and "The Ideal Restaurant" are not so bad. The large and blatant ones advertising national products would result, one would think, in nothing except bad public relations for the company involved.

Roadside litter, even in the vast "empty" spaces, is becoming a problem. U.S. 66 leads to several national parks, but that highway itself might well be created

National Garbage Dump Monument. I recently drove along much of it with a geologist who frequently stopped to examine formations. I found the roadside, everywhere, unsightly and disgusting with bottles, cans, wastepaper, half-eaten lunches, and other filth.

In some ways the desert is highly vulnerable to an advancing civilization. One threat has been, and remains, the construction of dams. Hoover Dam has flooded a part of the canyon of the Colorado River, and Glen Canyon Dam will do the same for another part.

Grazing, or overgrazing, is a deadly enemy to the old desert ecology. Curiously, in the last thirty years, the big lumber companies have changed from exploiters of forests to conservers of forests, but no comparable change has as yet come over the cattle and sheep ranchers. The rye grass, so tall that the early emigrants could not find oxen that strayed into it, has almost disappeared from along the Humboldt, though Rye Patch station preserves the memory. As the bunch grasses have been grazed off, the sagebrush has moved in, so that in the end the land probably carries fewer animals than it did at first. So also, in most places, the antelope, bighorn, and coyote have disappeared, and only the jack rabbit seems to thrive.

Yet there is an opportunity for hope. A desert is highly resistant. In spite of a population pressure such as we have not yet approached, the Chinese have made little encroachment upon the deserts that lie to their westward.

Of course, the Chinese cannot afford to drink beer and then throw the bottle away, or to go churning across the desert in a jeep just for fun, and thus bring about a hundred years of erosion in one day.

But the desert can survive even a great deal of such wanton abuse. It may still be there, looking much the same, even after Glen Canyon Dam is level-full of silt, and U.S. 66 shows but faintly beneath the blown sand.

Where Dinosaurs Roamed

A towering spectacle: Echo Park's Steamboat Rock

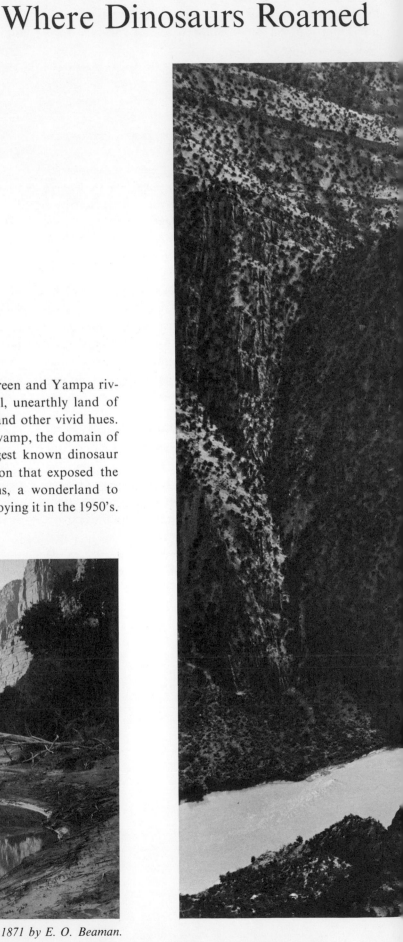

On the Utah-Colorado border, where the winding Green and Yampa rivers meet, is Dinosaur National Monument, a beautiful, unearthly land of upthrust mountains and polished canyon walls of reds and other vivid hues. Some one hundred forty million years ago it was a flat swamp, the domain of sluggish monsters whose remains form the world's largest known dinosaur fossil deposits. The same processes of uplift and erosion that exposed the dinosaurs' bones created the magnificent river canyons, a wonderland to boaters and conservationists, who kept a dam from destroying it in the 1950's.

Lodore Canyon, a gateway to Dinosaur, was photographed in 1871 by E. O. Beaman.

Downstream from Steamboat Rock, the joined waters of the Green and Yampa rivers surge past a mighty upthrust of exposed rock.

Ogden (above), for whom Ogden, Utah, was named, was followed by other explorers who saw many of the Snake country sights he had noted. Charles Preuss, with Frémont in 1843–44, drew the subterranean river gushing from the canyon wall of Snake River, and Timothy O'Sullivan, with the Wheeler Survey in 1874, photographed the Shoshone Falls.

Volcanic eruptions and lava flows across the plains created this lunar scene at Craters of the Moon National Monument.

Ogden's Snake Country

Mostly a dry arid sand plane covered with a Strong groth of wild Sage and prickly pears," the Snake River country (named for the Snake, or Shoshoni, Indians), which stretched across southern Idaho, was the bane of covered-wagon pioneers who had to struggle through it, suffering from heat and thirst, on their way to Oregon. The man who knew it best was Peter Skene Ogden, who explored much of it in the 1820's, when he led "Snake Country brigades" of Hudson's Bay Company trappers between the Columbia River and the vicinity of Salt Lake. Ogden's journals make interesting reading today, referring to pocked lava fields (now Craters of the Moon National Monument); the Big and Little Lost rivers, which vanish in the soil and reappear one hundred fifty miles away (upper left); and 212-foot-high Shoshone Falls, the Niagara of the West, whose roar Ogden could "distincly" hear from his camp on the plains some ten miles away.

The Elusive Buenaventura

Early Spanish maps showed it; Indians hinted of it; and fur traders *wanted* it to be there: the fabled Buenaventura River, which was supposed to flow from Salt Lake across the Great Basin to the Pacific near San Francisco Bay. There were good reasons for trying to find a waterway from the Rocky Mountain fur country to the Pacific. Travel on foot and on horseback over the difficult, arid terrain west and northwest of Great Salt Lake was hazardous and slow. And perhaps the river would be filled with beaver.

British and American trappers all looked for the Buenaventura. Ogden, instead, found the Humboldt (called Mary's, or Ogden's, River before Frémont gave it its final name), which disappeared in a Nevada sink. During the first

journey from Great Salt Lake to southern California through "a Country of Starvation," the American mountain man Jedediah Smith missed the Buenaventura, and failed also to find a sign of it on later trips that included the first crossing of the Sierra Nevada by a white man. In 1844 Frémont, who also looked hard for the river, concluded that it was a myth. Later explorers confirmed Frémont. In 1854, where the Buenaventura might have been, F. W. von Egloffstein, a topographical artist with a railroad survey party, drew these panoramic views looking westward across the Great Basin in Nevada, showing the bleak country about Mud Lake (above) and Mount Shasta and the northern Sierra (below). By then, it was certain that there was no Buenaventura to include.

Alkali and Rabbit Skins

Imagine a vast, waveless ocean stricken dead and turned to ashes; imagine this solemn waste tufted with ash-dusted sage-bushes; imagine the lifeless silence and solitude that belong to such a place; imagine a coach, creeping like a bug through the midst of this shoreless level . . . This is the reality of it." It was August, 1861, and twenty-six-year-old Samuel Clemens, primed for excitement on his first stagecoach trip into the Real West, had just entered the Utah-Nevada alkali desert west of Salt Lake—to find that his "stern thirst for adventure . . . did not last above one hour."

This part of the Basin is not amiable. Some of its "grim stillness" is reflected in the photograph above of Nevada's Carson Desert, taken in 1867 by Timothy O'Sullivan, a member of the Clarence King survey party, which was making a geological exploration along the 40th parallel. (O'Sullivan carried his equipment in the ambulance wagon shown on the desert.) The King group, which made important contributions to scientific knowledge of the West, was no more charmed than Mark Twain had been, and remembered the sterile region as "one of the most desolate and forbidding" it had to cross.

The alkali land was a bitter one, able to nourish only a few Indians, like the Paiute below. Although J. Goldsborough Bruff, who made the drawing during his trip across Nevada to California in 1850, labeled the Indian "Hostile & treacherous," the Paiutes were really a timorous people, scurrying in small groups around the desert like the rabbits they hunted for food and for skin robes. West of Carson Desert was Pyramid Lake (seen in another of O'Sullivan's 1867 photographs), whose cutthroat trout provided better fare than the natives' usual diet of rabbits and insects. In 1874 President Grant made the land around the lake a reservation, but white men had already claimed most of the watered areas. To show the land grabs, a Paiute, Captain Dave, drew the map above in 1885, with notes like "Mollon got ranch to close by the Lake."

H. V. A. von Beckh drew this view of Simpson's expedition crossing the "somber, dreary waste" of Salt Lake Desert.

"The snowy peaks of the Sierra Nevada . . . the water of Carson Lake beautifully blue," wrote Simpson of this scene.

Exploring the Great Basin

In 1859 Captain James H. Simpson of the Topographical Engineers led a sixty-four-man party from Camp Floyd, Utah, near Great Salt Lake, across the Great Basin to the Sierra Nevada to find a new and direct route between the East and the growing towns of California. It was a successful expedition, and Simpson's men (pictured above crossing the Carson River) were hailed for opening a new road across Nevada, "thus facilitating the mails and emigration." Simpson also gave the great interior country between the Rocky Mountains and the Sierra its classic definition, calling it "an elevated central region . . . pre-eminently a basin of mountains and valleys."

Jim Bridger, photographed in later life

Great Salt Lake

Hell, we are on the shores of the Pacific," Jim Bridger is said to have exclaimed late in 1824, as he spit out a mouthful of briny water from the lake he had just come on after riding down Utah's Bear River. Other trappers poured out of the mountains and soon coasted the lake to prove that Bridger's discovery was not an arm of the Pacific Ocean, but a great salty lake. In 1843 Frémont made the first scientific exploration of the body of water, determining its elevation at 4,200 feet. Frémont was impressed by the lake's "extremely beautiful bright-green color," but at times—depending on the light—Great Salt Lake can seem to be slate gray or, as the photograph at right shows, silvery blue.

The saltiness that caused Jim Bridger's oath results from the same process, evaporation, that has helped reduce the lake (now seventy miles long and fifty miles wide) to one tenth the size it was fifty thousand to one hundred thousand years ago—and it is still shrinking. Since the lake has no outlet, the minute quantities of mineral salt picked up by the streams that feed it become increasingly concentrated as the water evaporates. Today, the lake is some 25 per cent salt, enough to support the poorest swimmer.

The barren land beyond the lake, seen in this old view, once lay beneath the larger inland sea.

Wind, Sand, and Rocks

Southern Utah's terrain, a wonderland of brilliantly colored cliffs, canyons, pinnacles, arches, reefs, mesas, buttes, and bridges, has been called a living textbook of geology. Near Moab, the center of a post–World War II uranium rush, is Arches National Monument, where wind, water, sand, freezing, thawing, and other weathering have carved a host of spectacular formations from the red Entrada sandstone. In the monument's Devil's Garden (right), rows of upright bedrock slabs, or fins, some more than 100 feet high and less than 20 feet thick, overlook huge amphitheatres. Into the fins, wind-driven sand has cut 64 of the monument's 81 known arches, including 291-foot-long Landscape Arch, thought to be the longest natural bridge in the world. Delicate Arch (above), called by some "the schoolmarm's britches," rises gracefully some 100 feet high on the edge of a precipitous cliff of "slickrock" in another part of the monument, a perfectly proportioned example of advanced wind erosion.

Other national parks and monuments in Utah, including Bryce, Zion, Capitol Reef, Cedar Breaks, and Natural Bridges, contain unique formations of their own. At Zion National Park, the story of the past is written boldly on the face of Checkerboard Mesa (left). Ages ago, wind-blown sand carved the horizontal lines, which were later preserved in the stone when a sea inundated the region. The vertical lines appeared at a still later time, when an uplift in the earth's crust exposed the mesa to further weathering.

Double Face Rock rises above Canyonlands.

A Great New National Park

In 1961 Secretary of the Interior Stewart L. Udall, flying low over the juncture of the Green and Colorado rivers in southeastern Utah, got a thrilling view of what may well be the most spectacular wilderness in the United States (right). There, in a remote and stern part of the West, difficult of access, the Colorado River system has sliced through and stripped back layers of highly colored rock, which weathering has fashioned into a massive land of mesas, scarps, needles, canyons, spires, arches, standing rocks, and other eroded features.

Conservationists were quick to echo Udall's enthusiasm for the region, and today the National Park Service proposes to preserve a large part of it as the new Canyonlands National Park, containing some of the most breath-taking scenery and important geological values in the country. With travel through the area heretofore hindered or barred by the canyons, steep cliffs, and arid, rugged terrain, much of it is still poorly known, and some of it has not yet been explored. But recent reconnaissance groups, using helicopters, jeeps, and horses, as well as adventuring by foot, have come on numerous wonders, including huge arches of unsurpassed beauty and panoramic views more stunning than those at Grand Canyon. Parts of the new park will be kept in their wild state, but roads and trails will make many of the area's grandest features accessible to the visitor.

CANYONLANDS

Green River

Crescent
Jct

Deadman
Pt

HORSESHOE CANYON

MINERAL CANYON

Upheaval
Bottom

HORSETHIEF CANYON

Upheaval–
Dome

TAYLOR CANYON

The Ne

ISLAND IN THE SKY

Green River

Grandview
Pt

DEADHORSE CANYON

Junction
Butte

Panorama
Pt

HORSE CANYON

WHITE

*ORANGE
CLIFFS*

Elaterite
Butte

*THE
MAZE*

Candlestick
Spire

*ELATERITE
BASIN*

Doll
House

Confluence

*THE
FINS*

*LAND OF
STANDING
ROCKS*

Spanish
Bottom

*CATARACT
CANYON*

Devils
Lane

Colorado
River

IMPERIAL VALLEY

Ruin
Park

David Greenspan

GYPSUM CANYON

BEEF BASIN

Devils Garden

ARCHES NATIONAL MONUMENT

Delicate Arch

Double Arch

RT U.S.160

Park Avenue

Tower of Babel

MOAB

Dead Horse Pt

KANE SPRING CANYON

HATCH PT

Colorado River

LOCKHART BASIN

Standing Rock Basin

RUSTLER CANYON

Indian Creek

HARTS DRAW

Elephant Hill

SQUAW FLAT

Cave Spring

North Sixshooter Pk

LOST CANYON

Salt Creek

South Sixshooter Pk

sler rk

Druid Arch

Virginia Park

Tower Ruin

HE NEEDLES

Angel Arch

HORSE CANYON

DAVIS CANYON

East Fork

West Fork

▲ CAMPGROUND
△ PRIMITIVE CAMPGROUND

N

There are enough natural spectacles in Canyonlands to use up a visitor's whole summer supply of film. Expansive rimtop views make it hard to leave such overlooks as Grandview and Panorama points (Dead Horse Point, a Utah state park, also scans a part of the area). A bouncing jeep ride over Elephant Hill into serene Chesler and Virginia parks, tucked among banded pinnacles, alcoves, grabens, ridges, and pockets of the Needles (right), is unforgettable. There are superb, newly discovered arches, like Druid Arch (above) and Angel Arch, and perhaps others not yet found. On the Island in the Sky is the awesome, multihued Upheaval Dome, and far below, a ride on the rivers takes one past ever-changing canyon walls to fearsome Cataract Canyon. In the region west of the rivers are the Land of Standing Rocks and, for the venturesome, the unexplored canyon network called the Maze.

332

Narrow rock fins in the Standing Rock Basin

The beautiful Angel Arch, with its winged angel, glows at sunrise.

The Mormons' view before hurtling down to the river

Hole in the Rock

The Explorer Scouts making their way beneath the huge cliffs of southeast Utah's Escalante River (left), one of the tributaries flowing into historic Glen Canyon of the Colorado River, are inheritors of a spirit of tough adventure that typified pioneers in that big rock country. There is no more beautiful part of the Colorado than Glen Canyon, but the rugged terrain guarding it was a formidable obstacle to early travelers.

In 1776 Father Escalante's expedition managed to cross the river by hacking steps with axes in the canyon wall. One hundred three years later, another epic occurred in the canyon when a group of Mormon families, on their way to found a colony in the San Juan country, were stopped by a rock barrier more than 500 feet above the Colorado. Finding a cleft in the rim, they blasted and chiseled a hole wide enough to admit their wagons. Then, with one man at the reins and others tugging at ropes behind, they drove through the hole and straight down the cliff. Somehow, they all made it safely, crossing the river and the brutal terrain on the opposite bank. Today, waters from the new Glen Canyon dam are inundating much of this historic country.

335

In 1909 a Paiute first guided a white man to see Rainbow Bridge, and the U.S. Geological Survey photograph at right was probably taken the same year. In an echo of the unsuccessful Hetch Hetchy fight, conservationists recently tried in vain to secure protection for the 309-foot-high bridge (tall enough to span the Capitol in Washington) from reservoir waters backed up by the new Glen Canyon dam.

The Four Corners

The vast plateau where Utah, Colorado, Arizona, and New Mexico meet is a big land of chromatic beauty and wild solitude. Long before the first white men arrived, the Four Corners region was the home of Basket Maker-Pueblos (Anasazis, or "the ancient ones," as modern Indians call them). They planted corn along streams in deep, red-rock canyons and built stone apartment-like dwellings high in the recesses of canyon walls. In the thirteenth century they abandoned the area and drifted elsewhere, but their homes remain almost intact today at Mesa Verde and numerous other sites.

In one of the canyons they left, almost hidden in the mountainous "slickrock," is Rainbow Bridge, to many the most moving single work of nature in the United States (left). And forming another chasm, not far distant, are the Goosenecks of the San Juan River (above), where water travels six miles and covers—as the crow flies—one.

337

A Navaho warrior of the Kit Carson era

Navaho Country

The tall buttes and spires that rise in isolated splendor from the floor of Monument Valley (right) have been seen as the background of many western movies. But never has the celluloid image been able to reflect the area's real beauty. This is Navaho land, a country astride the Utah-Arizona border, where mountains are still sacred, true values of life still have meaning, and chants and poetry maintain spiritual contact with nature and keep the world in harmony.

The Navahos and white men were enemies for many years; but in 1863–64, an army under Kit Carson invaded the stronghold, Canyon de Chelly, and starved the Navahos into submission, burning their crops and killing their sheep. After four years of exile in eastern New Mexico, they returned to their present home, where more than 80,000 of them now struggle to develop their reservation's resources.

Joseph Heger drew this view of Canyon de Chelly when it was still a Navaho citadel.

Powell on the Colorado

Powell's second expedition (photographed below at its starting point, Green River, Wyoming, by E. O. Beaman, a member of the party) was more leisurely than the first, and gave him a chance to examine the river's features, including Marble Canyon (seen above in a picture made during the survey), and the terrain of the surrounding country. Powell, at right with an Arizona Indian, later wrote a farsighted report, warning the nation that the arid Southwest required a new policy of land development, involving planned irrigation and clusters of small farms with guaranteed water rights.

One of the most dramatic adventures in western exploration occurred in 1869, when a daring group of men under Major John Wesley Powell, a one-armed veteran of the Civil War, made the first trip down the Colorado River through the Grand Canyon. Powell's narrative of the voyage, telling of roaring "mad waters"—huge swells, rapids, eddies, and whirlpools—of "grand, gloomy depths" beneath walls "more than a mile in height," of towering rock formations (above), and beautiful side canyons full of surprises, is suspenseful reading. But his trip, since duplicated by others, was more than a quest for thrills. On this and a second voyage down the river in 1871–72, he mapped one of the last great uncharted regions in the United States.

341

Mt
Sinyala ▲

HAVASUPAI
INDIAN
RESERVATION →

HAVASU CREEK

AZTEC
AMPHITHEATER

COCONINO PLATEAU

Havasupai ▲
Pt

Walapai ▲
Pt

Mescalero ▲
Pt

Shiva
Temple

HERMITS
REST

COLORADO RIVER

Isis
Temple

Pt
Sublime
▲

GRAND CANYON
VILLAGE

Hopi Pt

Buddha
Temple

A.T. & S.F.R.R.

PARK
HEADQUARTERS

Yavapai Pt
7,000

BRIGHT ANGEL CANYON

■ RT 64

Mather Pt

RT U.S. 180

TO WILLIAMS

Yaki
Pt

SOUTH RIM

Grandview
Pt

Wotans
Throne —

Cape Royal
7,876

Horseshoe
Mesa

Vishnu
Temple

GRANITE GORGE

Jun
Tem

EAST RIM DRIVE

Apollo
Temple

Solomon
Temple

TUSAYAN
MUSEUM

Desert View
■ 7,450 ▲

Comanche
Pt

N

RT 64

TO CAMERON

David Greenspan

The romantic engraving below of Grand Canyon, made from an 1858 field sketch by F. W. von Egloffstein, who served as Ives's topographer, was one of the first attempts to picture the great gorge, and reflected the awe with which the members of the expedition viewed the area that Ives said "resembled the portals of the infernal regions." Fifteen years later Thomas Moran accompanied John Wesley Powell to the north rim to capture the dramatic coloring of a rainstorm drifting across the massive canyon (right).

Colorado Exploring Expedition, General Report, 1857–58

The Grand Canyon

The amazing spectacle of the Grand Canyon was first viewed by white men in 1540, when a band of Coronado's conquistadors under Lopez de Cardenas came upon its southern rim. For three days the Spaniards tried to descend to the river; but after getting only one third of the way down, they gave up and departed. During the next three centuries the canyon was a legend, unseen by white men. Then, in 1858 an expedition under Lieutenant Joseph Ives of the Topographical Engineers reached the floor of the chasm by descending to it through a maze of side ravines. Ives called the canyon, some ten miles from rim to rim, "unrivalled in grandeur," but he was wrong in believing that it would be "forever unvisited and undisturbed." Today, many of the national park's million and a half annual visitors zigzag down the canyon walls on muleback and reach the majestic inner gorge that eluded the conquistadors.

ABOVE AND BELOW: *Colorado Exploring Expedition, General Report, 1857–58*

The Lower Colorado

As it flows southward the Colorado River continues its role as one of the major forces giving form and character to the Southwest. Near present-day Blythe, California, H. B. Möllhausen sketched the river and the "turretted pinnacles" of Chimney Peak, as the exploring party of Lieutenant Joseph Ives steamed by in 1858 (above). In 1905 the Colorado added a new feature to the region when flood waters poured into the dried-up bed of an ancient sea, some 270 feet below sea level, and created California's huge, inland Salton Sea. The beachline of the prehistoric body of water is marked by ridges of fossil shell deposits (right).

A Möllhausen view shows Ives's steamboat in the "splendid corridor" of the lower Colorado's Mojave Canyon.

*"Sometimes the trail led us over large basins of deep sand, where the trampling of the mules'
feet gave forth no sound; this added to the almost terrible silence, which ever reigns in the
solitudes of the desert," wrote Kit Carson's companion, Lieutenant George D. Brewerton, who
painted this scene of a "Jornada del Muerto" (Journey of Death, a stretch between water holes)
on the Mojave Desert, which they crossed in 1848. Realtors are now selling home lots nearby.*

348

Spanish Trail

For twelve hundred miles it ran, arching across the Southwest from Santa Fe to Los Angeles, past juniper and piñon stands in northern New Mexico; over a spur of the Rockies into southwestern Colorado; across the twisting Colorado and Green rivers; down Utah's Sevier Valley; through the bleakness of Nevada's southern triangle; and past cactus and Joshua tree forests on California's Mojave Desert. The Old Spanish Trail, highway of the early Southwest, had many blazers—and many users.

Spanish missionary-explorers, trying to link settlements along the Rio Grande with those in California, pioneered the route. By 1830, mountain men were familiar with it, and thereafter mule caravans of American trappers and Mexican traders shuttled furs and goods along the hot, desolate road. Horse thieves and Mexican slave-catchers used stretches of it, and Mormons and California-bound emigrants knew its mirages and thirst. Today, highways parallel the trail, and cities like Las Vegas stand beside it.

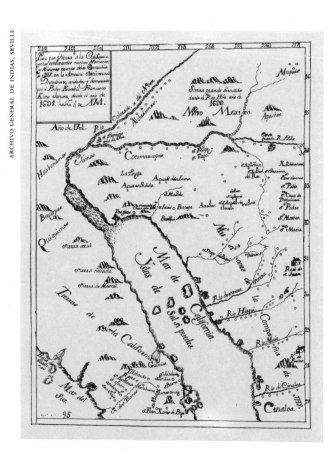

A 1701 map by Father Kino, a pioneer priest-explorer

The Western Hemisphere's lowest point: Badwater (282 feet below sea level)

Death Valley

In 1849 a party of California-bound gold-seekers wandered into Death Valley and almost starved before they found their way out. "Good-by, Death Valley!" they are supposed to have called as they finally made their exit—thus giving a name and a reputation to the 140-mile-long desert valley lying between two mountain ranges on the California-Nevada border. The reputation is overdrawn. Only one of the "49'ers" actually died there, and soon afterward prospectors were combing the valley and the peaks and canyons surrounding it. In the 1880's high-wheeled wagons drawn by twenty-mule teams took out cottonball borax (ulexite), and the workmen left behind piles of waste material (the dots in the aerial view of part of the valley floor at right).

Death Valley is now a national monument, a winter playground, and a place of unique natural history and geological interest. On an average, it experiences 283 days of clear skies a year. Winters are comfortable, but in the summer it can be the hottest place on earth, and visitors should not wander without water.

Northwest of Death Valley, in the White Mountains, are trees that may be the world's oldest living objects. Wracked and twisted by the winds at their 10,000-foot altitude, and polished smooth by the erosion of centuries, bristlecone pines (below) have survived in a dry, rocky environment. One of them, whose growth rings were studied by members of the University of Arizona's Laboratory of Tree-Ring Research, proved to be more than 4,600 years old, but many others are almost as aged. Although some of the pines are scarcely more than gnarled and battered stumps, they continue to maintain life (and even occasionally to produce cones), and owe their longevity to their ability to withstand periods of little rainfall.

PHILIP HYDE

351

VIII

THE

PACIFIC

By HAROLD GILLIAM

Here from this mountain shore, headland
beyond stormy headland plunging like
dolphins through the blue sea-smoke
Into pale sea . . .

Robinson Jeffers ("*The Eye*," 1948)

The Pacific shores of the United States, curving in an eight-thousand-mile parabola from the Aleutians to San Diego to the outpost atolls of Hawaii, encompass an opulent variety of lands and climates—foggy volcanic islands and glacier-sculptured peaks, rain forests and near-deserts, fertile coastal terraces, surf-carved escarpments, icy arctic capes, and smooth sandy beaches in the tropic sun. Despite their diversity, however, these regions are all dominated by a single overwhelming presence—the great ocean itself.

Here, unlike the Atlantic coast, wind and weather move generally from the sea to the land, and these Pacific shores respond in infinite ways to the ocean, its winds and storms, its moods and movements, its rhythmic rising and falling in cycles ranging from hours to aeons. On all these shores the flowing ocean currents of wind and water have given the land its shape and the climate its flavor, have nurtured and given form to the lives of plants, animals, and men.

For fifteen thousand miles around the rim of the North Pacific, the currents of air and water revolve in a clockwise direction. Along the northern perimeter of this circuit there takes place continually a momentous encounter of opposing currents. Warm Asiatic waters meet here the cold gray currents pouring down from the Bering Sea.

This is a place of beginnings. From this meeting of the waters, vapors of fog rise like cold steam. Here in the impact of cold and warm air masses are conceived the great storms that sweep eastward to North America with rain, wind, hail, and snow. In the midst of this region of winds and fogs and roiled waters, the fires of the earth have erupted into a chain of volcanoes a thousand miles long between the Asiatic and American continents.

There are some eighty volcanoes in the Aleutian Islands and the Alaska Peninsula, many of them spewing ash, steam, and fume at frequent intervals. A few, such as nine-thousand-foot Pavlof on the peninsula and Shishaldin, rising nearly ten thousand feet out of the sea, form cones as symmetrical as Fuji. Among the most active is Bogoslof, an island near Dutch Harbor. Here, during the past one hundred seventy years, cones, peaks, and pinnacles have risen from the water and emitted fire and steam, only to be worn away by erosion and subterranean collapse, followed in a few years by the appearance of new volcanic isles rising from the surface of the ocean.

For man, too, this is a land of beginnings. North of the Aleutians was the bridge from Asia over which the first human stepped onto the North American continent. Barren St. Lawrence Island is a remnant of that bridge, as are the two Diomede Islands, in the Bering Strait, where the

United States and the U.S.S.R. are about three miles apart.

In the summer the ice disappears from the Bering Sea, and the snow melts from all of Alaska's coastal regions. As if to compensate for the short growing season, life comes to these shores with fierce intensity. Fields of flowers bloom across meadows, mountains, and tundra. From the far reaches of the North Pacific, more than a million fur seals converge on the Pribilof Islands for the breeding season, and swarming shoals of salmon come to Bristol Bay and other coastal waters, heading for the rivers and lakes to spawn and die. And on the island of Kodiak the summer sun rouses from hibernation the Kodiak bear, largest carnivorous land mammal on earth, rearing to a fearsome nine feet in height.

Winds and storms born near the Aleutians in the conjunction of the two ocean rivers, gathering size and strength as they sweep on eastward with the circling currents, strike the southern and southeastern Alaska coasts and encounter there the Alaska Coast Ranges, their summits ranging up to eighteen thousand feet in elevation. Chilled as they move up the slopes of this barrier, the storms drop snow here in quantities so immense that the ice age glaciers have never entirely melted, although they continue to shrink over long periods of time.

John Muir, while first exploring the coastline of southeastern Alaska in 1879, was puzzled to find that the generally accurate charts made by Vancouver eighty-five years earlier failed to show such a conspicuous feature of the landscape as the deep fiord now known as Glacier Bay, extending inland for fifty miles between two ranges. The reason for the omission, Muir finally concluded, was that the bay had not existed in Vancouver's time. Its basin then had still been in the process of formation, buried by a glacier a thousand feet deep. In the intervening years the ice had melted, and it occurred to Muir that he was the first explorer ever to see Glacier Bay. He sailed up the magnificent fiord in a state of wonder, gazing on this freshly hewn landscape, like Adam on the morning of creation.

Although the main glacier had vanished, tributary ice fields dozens of miles long continued to flow into the bay. The pinnacled front wall of one of them, later named the Muir Glacier, was two miles across, rose more than three hundred feet out of the water, and extended some seven hundred feet below the surface. Every few minutes mountainous masses of ice toppled or slumped from the wall and hit the water with a great show of flying spray. Other masses broke loose from the submerged portion, springing far out of the water with a tremendous roar, plunging and

rising repeatedly before floating away placidly as icebergs.

"When sunshine is sifting through the midst of the multitude of icebergs that fill the fiord," Muir wrote, "and through the jets of radiant spray ever rising from the tremendous dashing and splashing of the falling and up-springing bergs, the effect is indescribably glorious."

The area explored by Muir is now part of Glacier Bay National Monument. The process of creation and revelation continues, leaving newly formed landscapes never before seen by man. In the years since Muir built a cabin on the shore near the foot of the Muir Glacier, the ice has continued to recede up the fiord and is now more than thirteen miles above the cabin site. Masses of ice still split off in the same spectacular display Muir witnessed.

Life advances in the wake of the receding ice in the same manner as it advanced following the retreat of the Pleistocene ice sheets from the continent. First, fungi, lichens, and mosses move over the newly uncovered rocks, decaying and helping to make soil for fireweed, dwarf willow thickets, cottonwoods, and alders—all of which prepare the way for the climax forest of arboreal giants: towering hemlock and Sitka spruce. At times in the prehistoric past, the process has been reversed: glaciers have advanced again, swallowing up whole forests, to be discharged centuries later as fossil timber when the ice again receded. Farther south, along the Alexander Archipelago and the

smooth blue waters of the Inside Passage, where the glaciers have long since disappeared, the ice-carved islands and peninsulas are blanketed with a mantle of the hemlock and spruce, most of which is embraced in Tongass National Forest. Conceivably the vanished ice could return, engulfing these landscapes and creating new ones to be revealed hundreds or thousands of years hence.

The North Pacific's circling rivers of air and water roll on southward down the coast of Washington, Oregon, and northern California. Here, as in Alaska, masses of marine air rise up the slopes of the coastal mountains and drop their moisture. The resulting persistent rains, averaging as much as one hundred forty inches a year in northern Washington, clothe the mountains at the sea's edge with an almost continuous stand of prime coniferous forests.

The last grand gesture of the cordilleran ice sheet that rumbled down out of Canada more than five thousand feet deep during the Pleistocene was the excavation of the long trough now filled with the waters of Puget Sound. The sound is a yachtsman's delight: hundreds of miles of thickly forested shoreline and channels winding through a maze of islands and peninsulas offering opportunity for leisurely exploration to last a lifetime. Nowhere is the boatman happier than in the San Juan Islands, along the international boundary. Not counting innumerable islets,

355

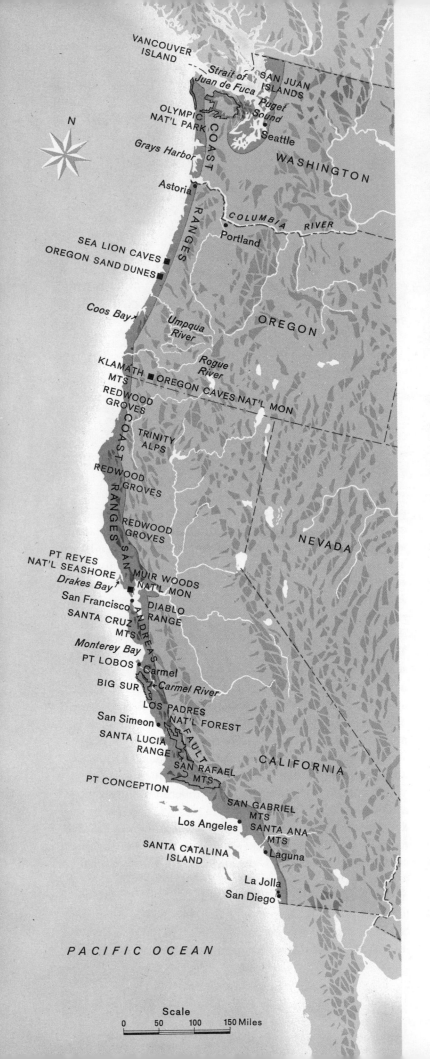

rocks, and reefs, there are about one hundred seventy-five of the San Juans, the peaks of a drowned mountain range.

On a bright summer morning long ago, a few weeks after I had graduated from high school, I stood at the rail of a ferry crossing through the San Juans as we passed island after island, many of them uninhabited, gliding over the lakelike waters of bays and inlets, following wide channels like rivers past wooded capes and promontories.

Above curving white beaches were green or tawny slopes rising to groves of red-barked madrones and walls of spiry Douglas firs and cedars. The islands were then—and are still—abundant with game: rabbits, wild goats, and deer. Woods and meadows were thick with wild berries, and the clear blue waters were full of leaping salmon. Inevitably, with the extravagant imagination of the very young, I pictured myself swimming ashore on one of these beaches to claim an island of my own and live in the wilderness, like Douglas Fairbanks in an old *Robinson Crusoe* movie.

I did not go overboard (the water looked pretty cold), but sometimes, in the decades since, these green isles of summer have come floating before my vision and the old secret yearning returned. The ambition remains unfulfilled, but simply contemplating the San Juans still has its effect. I always feel much better, just knowing that they are there.

Along most of the Pacific shoreline the young Coast Ranges stand high above the ocean in a vigorous upward thrust of the continent's edge. At their base the battering waves carve cliffs and plane away low-tide terraces. Where the rock is soft, the surf hews out bays and inlets. The harder rock remains as promontories, which are sometimes cut away from the rear and become sea stacks—small offshore islets and rocks that are sure signs of a young, rapidly retreating coastline.

But the retreat is only temporary. As if to compensate for the attacks of the surf, the mountains themselves rise at long intervals, rolling back the sea. As a sector of the range is slowly elevated over a period of thousands of years, the wave-cut cliff and the tidal beach-terrace below it are lifted high into the air. Coastal roads often follow these flat, elevated terraces, which in some places are as much as a mile wide. Sometimes several older uplifted cliffs and beaches of various eras are still visible as giant stairsteps on the hillsides above, partly worn away by erosion. Just south of Coos Bay, Oregon, there is a terrace that has risen fifteen hundred feet since it was carved by an ancient surf. Along the ocean's edge the waves are now creating a new terrace which may itself eventually be elevated and provide a convenient roadbed for whatever race of beings inhabits this coast tens of thousands of years from now.

As the mountains are lifted, the rivers draining them continue to cut their way down to the sea. At the end of the ice age the waters of the melting glaciers flowed to the ocean in such volume that sea level rose, flooding the mouths of the rivers, creating estuaries and drowned valleys. The mouth of the Columbia, second largest trunk stream in the United States, is an estuary ten miles wide. Upstream, low hills that were once along the riverbank are now islands, and for one hundred forty miles above its mouth the river rises and falls with the tides. Farther south, where the rivers draining the interior of California had sliced a gorge through the outer ridge of the Coast Range, the rising sea flooded through the break in the mountains and occupied the valley inside. The gorge became the Golden Gate, and the drowned valley inside it is San Francisco Bay.

Although the Coast Ranges along the Pacific shoreline have been elevated recently in geologic time and may still be rising, some stretches of the coast are low and seem to be subsiding. At such points, where the back shore slopes upward very gently, the sea winds carry the beach sand inland, creating dunes. San Francisco itself was once the largest dune area on the coast, but the sand has long since been built over. The finest remaining display of drifting sand along the coastline is at the Oregon Dunes, a proposed national seashore. Gleaming Sahara-like drifts as high as a twenty-story building, driven by the wind, continually migrate inland and have inundated part of a thick coniferous forest. By contrast, just north of the dunes is a high, cliffy shoreline in which the waves have hewn out huge chambers echoing with the thunder of the breakers and the barking and roaring of herds of sea lions. These are the Sea Lion Caves, believed to be the world's only mainland rookery of these aquatic animals, whose remote ancestors were not lions but possibly water-loving bears.

Another example of the dynamic nature of this coastline is visible at the Point Reyes Peninsula, just north of San Francisco. The peninsula itself, most of which is embraced in the Point Reyes National Seashore, is a one-hundred-square-mile region of white cliffs and beaches, high rocky headlands, meadows and wild flower fields, sprawling cattle ranches, waterfalls and small lakes, piny draws and coves, and a virgin forest of Douglas fir on a ridge rising a thousand feet and more above the ocean. The point curves around Drakes Bay, where the intrepid sea captain may have careened the *Golden Hind* in 1579 (although it is also argued that Drake did not land here, but some miles to the south and east in San Francisco Bay).

Between this peninsula and the mainland is a long, low valley—partly filled by arms of the ocean—created by grinding action along the San Andreas Fault. The San Andreas is perhaps the longest continental rift on earth, extending for more than five hundred miles north and south. The largest measured displacement along the fault during the San Francisco earthquake of 1906 was here on the Point Reyes Peninsula, where a road crossing the fault at the head of Tomales Bay was offset by twenty feet in a single instantaneous jolt. Throughout the peninsula are visible geologic freaks caused by quakes along the fault over a period of centuries—humped-up ridges, long, low escarpments, sag ponds, huge landslides, and in the Olema Valley parallel streams a quarter-mile apart flowing in opposite directions.

The peninsula is a geologic migrant; like the nearby Farallon Islands it was part of an offshore land mass that existed during Cretaceous times when most of the rest of California was still under the sea. Along with other lands west of the San Andreas Fault, it seems to be moving northward at an average rate of about two inches a year. At that rate, judging by carbon-dating of its rocks and of matching granitic formations to the south, the bedrock of this peninsula may have been moving northward for some eighty million years, traveling in that time, according to some estimates, an incredible three hundred miles.

The currents of the North Pacific move down the California coast with particular force in the spring and summer. Owing to an effect of the earth's rotation, the ocean river here tends to veer offshore, causing along the immediate coast an upwelling of cold water from the sunless depths. This streak of upwelled water is often frigid enough to condense the moisture in the winds that blow across its surface, creating the great fog bank that hangs along this coast intermittently from May to September.

The cool, foggy ocean air, drawn toward the warm interior valleys, flows massively through the only sea level break in the Coast Range, the Golden Gate. As a consequence, San Francisco Bay and the adjacent hills form a theatre for what may be the planet's most extraordinary display of atmospheric forms and movements.

Often on a sunny day in San Francisco I have heard the resonant chorus of foghorns and looked out to the Golden Gate to see a long sinuous arm of white vapor under the deck of the bridge, moving slowly inward across the blue waters of the bay. The advance salient of fog may strike Alcatraz and rise up over the island to form a translucent dome of vapor. Slowly the mass increases until it flows through the Gate hundreds of feet deep and overtops the adjacent hills, pouring down the leeward slopes like diaphanous waterfalls. San Francisco's Twin Peaks is clothed in a smooth cascade that rolls and rebounds like an immense slow-motion surf, sending up volatile plumes of spray a hundred feet high. Niagaras of dazzling white vapor pour over the hills in innumerable variations of form and motion. Flowing tides of light move through the passes and descend on the cities and towns of the inner valleys, bringing the cool, salty smell and feel and taste of the ocean rivers and sea winds.

The drifting summer fogs of the California coast are more than a spectacle; during the long, rainless summers they supply sustenance to the coastal redwood groves and the communities of trees and plants and animals that grow beneath them. The redwoods prefer the deep coastal canyons sheltered from the strongest blasts of the sea winds. But there is one tree that thrives in the fog and wind and salt spray along the granite margins of the ocean where no other tree can survive. It is the Monterey cypress, which grows naturally on two promontories near the mouth of the Carmel River—and nowhere else in the world.

On Point Lobos, a state reserve, the wind-sculptured cypresses grip the granite cliffs with gnarled roots to the windward, build big buttresses to the leeward, and seem part of the natural architecture of the wave-beaten headlands. A few yards inland they rise to greater heights in solemn congregations, where lace lichens hang from the branches like wisps of gray fog.

The venerable cypresses reflect in other ways as well the influence of the sea on this coast; they are the vestigial remnant of dense forests that covered the same ancient land mass of which Point Reyes was once a part. Now, like their relatives the Monterey pines, the bishop pines of Point Reyes, and the Torrey pines near San Diego, they grow only on isolated spots along the coast that were once part of that vanished land.

On sunny days at Point Lobos, the entire land-and sea-scape glows with a mosaic of color—deep blues and emerald greens in the coves, white in the breaking waves, darker greens in the cypresses and pines, vivid browns and glistening grays in the rocks and cliffs, brilliant reds and blues and purples when the spring poppies and lupine and paintbrush bloom in the meadows. At such times I have always become aware of a special quality of light distinctive to this headland. It is a classic light that seems oddly Hellenic—an impression heightened by the weathered granite walls, the bright sea like the Aegean, the contorted old cliff-top cypresses, the bearded inner groves that might be a wood near Athens, the ancient, timeless roar of the waves pervading the entire peninsula.

Behind Lobos and down the coast to the south, the young Santa Lucia Range rears abruptly out of the Pacific as if it were fresh-born, the water still streaming from its flanks, misty wreaths of vapor about its upper slopes. From Lobos south for ninety miles to San Simeon and beyond, State Highway 1 traverses long wave-terraces and at intervals climbs high along ridges where you can look down a thousand feet to the seething surf in deep granite coves. For mile after mile down the coastline high green ridges fall to the sea in headlong promontories where the wave-bursts rise and fall against the dark cliffs with hypnotic rhythm. White cascades roar down out of redwood canyons and plunge over cliffs to the ocean.

This is the Big Sur, Robinson Jeffers country ("Gray granite ridges over swinging pits of sea . . ."). Like this coast itself Jeffers' poems combine the violence of the sea's assault on the land with the serenity of the granite and cypress, symbols of endurance.

This wild coast, Jeffers wrote, cries out for tragedy. Part of its tragic aspect is that its wildness evidently is doomed. The subdivisions are spreading south from Carmel, and highway builders are anxious to slash a major freeway across the seaward slopes. What will happen if they are successful is evident at the southern end of this incomparable stretch of coast. Near the popular Hearst castle at San Simeon, now a state historical monument, sectors of the widened highway along the ancient wave-terrace are lined with new motels, billboards, drive-ins, and hot dog stands, bringing the inevitable litter and clutter, neon-lighted "slurbs," clawing their way across the landscape. This climactic coastline at the continent's end should be a national preserve, off limits to the spoilers.

From a Big Sur cliff top one day my wife and I, peering into a cove below, saw another symbol of man's plundering of his environment. The four-foot-long creature floating there on its back was a sea otter, one of the rarest mammals on earth—and one of the most intelligent.

The family life of the sea otters is uncannily human. They mate for life and give birth to one offspring at a time. Their forefeet are used as hands for many purposes—to cradle the young or to toss them playfully in the air and catch them, to play ball with pieces of seaweed, to shade their eyes from the sun, to pry succulent abalones from rocks, even to pick up a stone and pound open a particularly tough crustacean. They dine floating on their backs, manipulating the food with their forepaws like a man eating corn on the cob. After eating they carefully wash, then take a nap in the same face-up floating position, often tying themselves to a piece of kelp anchored to the bottom to keep from drifting away.

In the early nineteenth century fur hunters slaughtered these engaging creatures by the thousands, using rifles, nets, spears, and even clubbing the friendly mammals from small boats, until there were no more to be found. It appeared as if human greed had eliminated the species from the face of the earth. Then in 1938 someone spotted a few of the animals playing in an offshore kelp bed on the Big Sur coast near Bixby Creek. Somehow, among the cliffs and caves of this remote coastline (inaccessible by highway until 1937) a few of the sea otters had managed to elude the voracious hunters, raise their families, and carry on the species.

Now, protected by law, they have increased to possibly several hundred in number and are seen along this coast as far north as Point Lobos. Perhaps the survival of the sea otter is a happy augury that some portion of the natural beauty of this coastline may also survive the depredations of the plunderers.

At Point Conception the California coast swings sharply eastward. The main wind and sea currents continue south, however, seaward of the protecting Channel Islands. Consequently the ocean and the air in southern California are far warmer than they are to the north, changing the entire aspect of the land. Redwoods and pines give way to palms, and the lonely, wild northern coastline is here supplanted by a sunny, genial shore as populated as the Mediterranean coast it resembles.

There is one stretch of this coast, however, that has not been seriously affected by the population explosion—the submarine gardens along the margins of the land just under the shallow offshore waters. To don a face plate and fins and dive into this undersea realm—among the coves and channels at Laguna or La Jolla or Catalina Island—is to enter a fourth dimension. Here you abandon the fight against gravity and float effortlessly in "mid-air." Sea plants of brilliant colors rise up around you from the bottom, undulating rhythmically as each wave passes overhead. There are green grassy meadows, deep pools with floors of white sand or of pebbles like gems, dimly lighted caverns and chambers, rock surfaces coated with purple urchins and pink algae, schools of iridescent fish—all transmuted and shimmering in the emerald atmosphere.

Offshore kelp beds, which seem from above to be an uninviting morass of tangled seaweed, appear from below as a parklike forest of well-spaced trees growing up from the bottom and spreading at the surface into a leafy canopy. Shafts of sunlight illuminate the rich brown textures of the kelp and make patterns on the white sandy floor of the cove. Passing fish swim in and out of the shadows. Occasional jellyfish, shapeless blobs when cast up on the beach, float here in panoplied splendor, big umbrella shapes trailing long delicate filaments that seem continually to change color in the filtered sunlight.

Another aspect of the Pacific shoreline that can be enjoyed most fully on this warm southern coast is the spectacle of the breaking waves. On some occasions these splendid beaches offer the best surf show on the continent. Protected from the strong northwest winds that hit the coastline farther north, the ocean surface here tends to be smoother, affording unimpeded passage for the huge ground swells that originate in storms far at sea, occasionally as far away as the Southern Hemisphere.

These giants appear first far offshore and rise slowly to majestic heights, sometimes fifteen feet or more, until they are intolerably top-heavy. Then at the critical point the upper masses of water plunge forward to form for one instant the most fantastically beautiful concave curve in all nature, emerald in the sun, as transcendentally perfect in form as a phrase in one of Beethoven's last quartets.

Then the curve is completed, and tons of water hit the flat surface ahead with a reverberating thunderclap that volleys along the entire front as other sectors of the wave, variously affected by differences in the ocean floor, plunge forward a second or two apart. After the impact comes the rebound: raging masses of white rise again and leap forward to charge to the shore in an exuberant turbulence of watery chaos. Sometimes a breeze rips banners of spindrift from the breaking crest and from jets of water that may shoot up behind the wave in a delayed rebound like a battery of geysers.

From the coast of California the North Pacific winds and currents circle south and west and some two thousand miles offshore strike the biggest mountains on earth. The peaks are on the island of Hawaii, the easternmost of the fifty islands and islets of the Hawaiian chain, which extend for another two thousand miles across the central Pacific.

Step off a plane in Honolulu and the first thing you notice is the warm, silky smoothness of the trade wind on your cheek and its exhilarating tingle on your nerve ends. The sensation is appropriate, for here on these islands even more than on the other Pacific coasts of the United States, the circling oceanic currents of air and water have strongly influenced the shape of the land and the quality of life that has developed upon it.

The trade winds blow almost continually from the northeast, dividing each of the major islands into two very different sectors—windward and leeward. Rising up the wind-

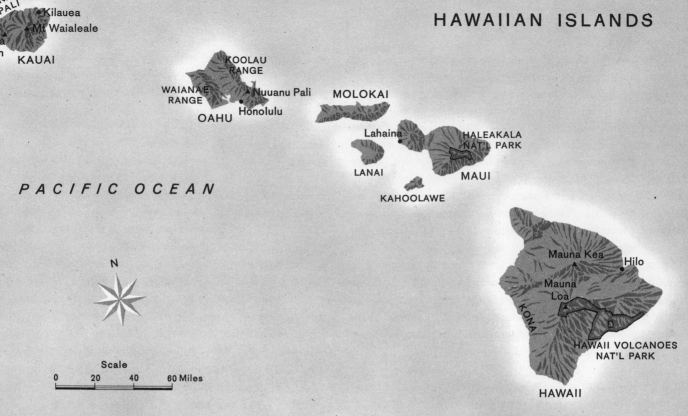

ward slopes of the mountains, the trades cool into clouds that drop prodigious quantities of rain, two hundred inches a year and more in some places, as compared to twenty to thirty inches on the drier leeward sides.

To feel the full impact of the winds, drive a few miles up in the mountains behind leeward Honolulu to Nuuanu Pali, where the trades funnel from the windward through a gap in the mountains with enough force to rock your parked car like a small boat in a high sea. Below are the green coastal terraces and white beaches of windward Oahu. Flanking the pass are two-thousand-foot cliffs and knife-edge ridges plunging down toward the ocean in zig-zags as jagged as a Wall Street graph in a bear market.

The striking terrain is characteristic of eroded lava. The islands are all the tops of volcanoes, which were built a few feet at a time as molten lava flowed intermittently from a long rift in the ocean floor. The oldest of the Hawaiian volcanoes, beginning with Kure and Midway at the far northwest end of the chain, have been planed down almost to sea level by storms, the trade winds, and their rains and waves.

At the southeast end of the chain are the younger major islands. Of these the oldest and most eroded is Kauai, known as the Garden Isle because the soils washed down from the mountains have created wide forested valleys, often dominated by the red-blossomed ohia tree; fertile coastal plains covered with bright-green cane fields; and curving beaches of white sand where you can sit under a palm and dream you are in Bali Ha'i.

The most spectacular example of erosion in all the islands is Kauai's Waimea Canyon, where the Waimea River has cut deep into the horizontal layers of old lava flows. Standing on the verge of this abyss, you are inevitably reminded of the Grand Canyon of the Colorado. But here, instead of the barren flat-topped buttes and mesas of the desert, are razor-back volcanic ridges covered with dense vegetation, dropping off into bright-red escarpments. Long, pendulous waterfalls, like those on Chinese scrolls, plummet down into tributary gorges so deep and narrow that they are never penetrated by the direct rays of the sun.

The origin of this vast system of gorges is not hard to find. Back in the mists that perpetually hover over the island's summit is five-thousand-foot Mount Waialeale, where the clouds of the trade wind deposit an average four hundred sixty inches of rain a year, the greatest recorded precipitation on earth.

For a different example of this violent volcanic topography go to Haleakala National Park on the younger island of Maui. The volcano Haleakala rises ten thousand feet into the tropic sky from a sea level base thirty-three miles in diameter. This is a superb example of a "shield" volcano—the gently sloping, flattened-dome type, contrasting with the steep cone volcanoes of Alaska, which are built by thicker lavas and more explosive eruptions.

Looking into Haleakala's nineteen-square-mile summit "crater" is like standing on the surface of the moon. Rising from this apparently lifeless lunar landscape are volcanic cones of many hues—pinks, lavenders, grays, browns, blacks, each representing eruptions of various eras. Contrary to legend, the crater, which is not a crater at all, was not the result of a single cataclysmic explosion that blew the top off; like Waimea Canyon it was created by the persistent action of the trade winds and their rains, which over thousands of years sliced deep canyons in Haleakala's flanks. The heads of two drainage systems converged from opposite directions and gouged out this valley in the top of the mountain. Further eruptions filled in parts of the eroded canyons and left the series of lunar cones and craters across the valley.

Hawaii, the "Big Island," youngest of the chain and larger than all the others combined, was created by five volcanoes, culminating in the colossal twins Mauna Kea and Mauna Loa, each nearly fourteen thousand feet above sea level. The latter is the world's biggest active volcano and probably the largest single mountain on earth. Rising more than thirty-two thousand feet above its base on the ocean floor, it dwarfs Mount Everest, which is only a nine-thousand-foot peak on the twenty-thousand-foot Himalayan Plateau. Mauna Loa rises so slowly and gradually from sea level that it looks not so much like a single mountain as a great smooth swelling of the earth.

The road that skirts the lower slopes of Mauna Loa for more than one hundred miles from Hilo to the Kona coast crosses one after another of lava flows which have spilled down the mountain in the past century or two, all labeled with the year of occurrence. The more recent flows are black and barren; the older ones are gray-brown or dark red and support in places a thin layer of soil on which plants and small trees can find a foothold. Between these are oases of far older flows which have been converted to soil—"kipukas," where luxuriant forests grow.

Even more active than Mauna Loa is Kilauea, youngest of Hawaiian volcanoes and like a sector of its larger neighbor part of Hawaii Volcanoes National Park. Kilauea is only four thousand feet above sea level but is still growing. It has averaged in recent decades an eruption every two years. Like Mauna Loa, Kilauea erupts not only at the summit but along rifts in its flanks as well. In 1960 on a rift twenty-eight miles east of the summit there rose a battery of flaming lava fountains half a mile long, two of them higher than the Empire State Building.

To climb down into the summit *caldera* is to walk backward into time. I made the hike one morning in spring, strolling down through the tropical forest immediately below the rim, where hundreds of birds sang in the tree ferns. At the *caldera* floor the forest ended, and I walked out into a silent desert of lava. Clambering over smooth, rolling lava contours, I felt absurdly like an ant walking across a plate of fudge. I crossed flattened domes, fans, and bubblelike bulges and felt beneath my feet the fine ballooning and swelling of various-textured lava surfaces from several eruptions.

Far below the surface the latent fires were still burning. Steam rose around me from hundreds of vents across the *caldera* floor, and as I walked across the old inferno I was increasingly possessed by the illusion that the earth was young and that its crust beneath my feet had just cooled, ready for the advent of life. It occurred to me that from this kind of lava flow on the floor of the Pacific, multiplied a billion times, these islands first rose as barren rock from the sea. Somehow from such desolation there came in time the islands' lush, green jungles, their dazzling floral color, their palm groves and fern forests. All the abundant native plants originated as seeds or spores or shoots brought from some far island or continent by storms or birds or the warm breath of the trade winds and the flowing currents of the ocean—the rivers of air and water that sweep around the North Pacific and down the shores of America from the icy rocks of the Aleutians to the verdant isles of this tropic archipelago.

Even down in the volcano I could feel the pervasive presence of the great circling winds of the Pacific, diminished here to errant zephyrs, but still bearing the seeds of life. Near my foot, in a lava crevice kept moist by a nearby steam vent, I saw the first vague green of a primitive moss and beside it a single small-leaved plant.

Sir Francis Drake, by an unknown artist

New Albion Headland

In 1579 Francis Drake, sailing along the California coast in his ship, the *Golden Hind*, came ashore probably beneath the cliffs of Point Reyes Peninsula (right) and, receiving the homage of Miwok Indians, who thought he was a god, named the land New Albion. Later, Spanish ships found haven from storms in the harbor—which was named Drakes Bay—and fur hunters, traders, and whalers of many nations frequented the area. In the nineteenth century, Russians came down from Alaska and built short-lived posts on the coast. Mexican ranchers loosed their stock across the rolling hills, and in time herds of American dairy cattle succeeded the long-horned Spanish steers.

Through all this activity, Point Reyes Peninsula remained relatively unchanged. Its tall cliffs, rising abruptly from the sea, are unscarred by man, and its beach is beautiful and undefiled. Waterfowl continue to visit its marshes, and deer and beaver still abound in its woods and grasslands. But with the suburbs of San Francisco crowding dangerously close, Congress in 1962 established the Point Reyes National Seashore to save the area from destruction in the future.

362

An almost-ever-present fog, drifting in from the Pacific, sends groping fingers through the valleys and canyons of the Coast Ranges.

Unexpected Wilderness

Surprisingly close to California's most heavily populated centers are mountainous wilds, scarcely known to most of the city dwellers. Not far from Los Angeles, among granite cliffs and chasms in the Los Padres National Forest, the huge California condor (left), with a wingspread of up to ten feet, is making its last stand against extinction. In 1845 frontiersman James Clyman saw immense numbers of them, hovering over the mountains, "cutting the wind with their wings and creating a Buzzing sound which may [be] heard at a miles distance." Today, only about sixty of the orange-headed birds survive. Farther north, in the Big Sur country, where the coastal ranges meet the sea below Monterey, an artists' and writers' colony perches on the edge of another rugged area of crags and canyons of lonely and haunting beauty.

365

Glories of the Coast

Each man who has come to know the Pacific coast, from the quiet of its misty mornings to the flaming spectacle of its western skies at sunset, possesses his own hoard of special treasures. In the south, they may be warm coves and tidal pools, surfboards on rolling breakers, or grunion runs and whales and tuna. They may be gleaming, mother-of-pearl abalone shells, banks of wind-swept cypress trees at Monterey, long beaches from which to dig clams, rocky points and capes, or a starfish several feet in diameter with suction cups that help it to cling to rocks and withstand the surge of the surf. Farther north, where the coastal ranges are wetter, they may be the delightful San Juan Islands in Puget Sound, steelhead in the Umpqua and Rogue rivers, the towering sand dunes in Oregon, or the tall redwoods in northern California.

The Oregon Dunes (below), a proposed national seashore of almost forty-five thousand acres from the Siuslaw River to Coos Bay, stretch inland from the ocean in shifting mounds as high as two hundred feet. In some places the older and higher dunes are covered with lakes and forests. The redwoods (right), related to the giant sequoia trees of the Sierra Nevada, grow in groves in twenty-mile-wide strips along the coast, reaching straight and tall up to three hundred sixty feet above dense and luxurious carpets of fern and trillium, like columns in a hushed cathedral.

ANSEL ADAMS

The coastal redwoods, taller but not as old or wide in girth as the sequoias in the Sierra, provided generations of Californians with wood for homes, cradles, railroad ties, wine barrels, and coffins. As groves disappeared, a Save-the-Redwoods League was formed, and John Muir wrote, "No doubt these trees would make good lumber after passing through a sawmill, just as George Washington after passing through the hands of a French cook would have made good food." Many groves are now protected, and one, Muir Woods, is a national monument.

A bellowing bull on the seal rookery at St. Paul Island

The Fur Seal

Sea otters and fur seals first lured white men in numbers to the northern Pacific coast—and both species in time came close to extinction.

The seals fared better than the otters. In 1872, when the latter were almost gone, Henry Wood Elliott, an American naturalist, visited the Pribilof Islands in the Bering Sea and was still able to witness the annual arrival of the seal herd from warmer wintering waters. In May the six-hundred-pound bulls came ashore, followed a month later by the females, whom the bulls herded into harems. Pups were whelped, and in July the males departed, leaving the cows to care for the new-born. By December the females and young had also left the islands.

Elliott estimated that there were six million seals. As he studied and painted them, the Alaska Commercial Company harvested one hundred thousand pelts. Three-year-old bachelor seals were herded together, bludgeoned with clubs, and skinned. There was, however, no danger to the survival of the species until the late 1870's, when pelagic sealing—the indiscriminate killing of seals from schooner-based canoes at sea—increased rapidly. As pregnant cows continued to be slaughtered, the United States in 1892 sent warships to the area and seized a Canadian vessel. But the situation was not alleviated, and soon men on the Pribilofs also began to kill seals, regardless of age or sex. By 1910, only some one hundred thirty thousand fur seals remained alive.

For years, William T. Hornaday and others had tried to end the destruction. But not until 1911, when Japan, Russia, England, and the United States agreed to co-operate, was pelagic sealing halted; and not until 1913 did the American government step in to save the seals on the islands. Today the herd is up to a million and a half and each year makes a wondrous sight on the rocky breeding grounds of the Pribilofs.

Henry Wood Elliott's water colors of 1872 show Aleuts herding a procession of fur seals to the slaughtering grounds and, below, clubbing them to death near a group of others that have already been skinned.

The 190-foot-high cliff of South Crillon Glacier on Crillon Lake

Avenues of Ice

Although there are glaciers on every continent except Australia, probably nowhere are they more spectacular than along the great arc of the Gulf of Alaska. Lying beneath the many snowy peaks of the St. Elias, Fairweather, and Chugach ranges, they reach tremendous proportions: Hubbard Glacier, perhaps the longest on earth, extends for seventy-five miles, and the Malaspina piedmont glacier, forty miles in width, is two thousand feet thick at its center. Many of the glaciers are stable or retreating, but some are still advancing, including the famed Muir Glacier in Glacier Bay National Monument, which on occasion has moved twenty to thirty feet in one day.

The high forward edges of the glaciers may be viewed from bays, though craft must beware of tall waves and bergs created by falling ice chunks. Close-up inspections can be made on foot, as John Muir did in 1880, when he crossed deep crevasses on slivers of ice. But most rewarding of all are views from the air, revealing scenes like the one at left of the medial moraine of Barnard Glacier and its tributaries, looking like paved highways.

371

David Douglas

Volcanoes and
a Botanist

Seven years after Douglas's death, Titian Peale painted this view of the smokes of Kilauea.

The loveliest fleet of islands that lies anchored in any ocean," Mark Twain once said about Hawaii. Of all its enchantments, the fiftieth state's volcanoes—Mauna Loa, Mauna Kea, and Kilauea on the Big Island (Hawaii) and the dormant Haleakala on Maui—have proved most intriguing. In 1834 the great botanist David Douglas visited the islands to study their flora, and tragically lost his life examining Mauna Loa. "Fine groves of *Bread-fruit*" and "grassy undulating plains," aflame with exotic blooms, interested Douglas; but he also climbed the broad slope of the volcano to view a "fiery lake, roaring and boiling in fearful majesty. . . ." Shortly afterward, still exploring Mauna Loa's flank, he fell into a pit used to trap wild bullocks and was trampled to death. Visitors are still enthralled by dramatic eruptions on the Big Island, like that of Kilauea (right), seen hurling lava some nineteen hundred feet high in November, 1959.

NIIHAU

Mt
Waialeale

Waimea
Canyon

KAUAI

Lihue   Kapaa

Mt
Kaala

OAHU

Pearl Harbor

HONOLULU

Diamond
Head

Kailua

PACIFIC OCEAN

Hualalai

Kailua

Mauna Loa
13,680

Great Lava
Fissure

Mokuaweoweo
Crater

The
Great Crack

RT 11

Waiohinu

Naalehu   Honuapo

HAWAII

Ka Lae

Kaalualu

HAWAIIAN ISLANDS

Kamakou
4,970

Lanai
City

Puu Kukui

Haleakala
Crater

M O L O K A I

L A N A I

Lahaina

Wailuku

HALEAKALA
NATIONAL PARK

K A H O O L A W E

M A U I

Kaupo

Hana

ALENUIHAHA CHANNEL

Hawi

Mahukona

Kohala
Mts

Waipio
Valley

Kawaihae

Mauna Kea
13,796

RT 19

Honokaa

Akaka
Falls

Hakalau

RT 20

Papaikou

HILO

VOLCANO
HOUSE

PARK
HEADQUARTERS

RT 11

Keaau

KAU
DESERT

Kilauea
Crater

HAWAII VOLCANOES
NATIONAL PARK

Makaopuhi
Crater

Pahoa

RT 13

Kalapana

Land's End

Beyond Diamond Head, Waikiki, and the Pali of Oahu is the island of Kauai, to many persons the image of a modern Garden of Eden. Its beaches, fragrant with ginger and frangipani, are like those of the South Seas. Waimea Canyon, its verdant cliffs often lit by a rainbow, drops spectacularly beneath the mists around the peak of Mount Waiale-ale, the world's wettest place. Near-by, flanking Kalalau Valley, 4,000-foot-high walls are lush with "fantastic draperies of tropic vegetation," described by Jack London in his volume of Hawaiian stories, The House of Pride. *And on the north-west coast, past the lovely beach at Hanalei, where* hukilaus *(group fishing in shallow water with nets) bring in a mess of radiantly colored fish, the rugged rampart of the Na Pali (left) faces the far frontier of the western Pacific—and another continent.*

377

U.S.A.—2000 A.D.

The awesome scene at the right, the sprawling megalopolis of Los Angeles, is possibly not the look of the United States that Americans enjoy the most, but it is the one that the overwhelming majority of them now know the best. It is also one of the most familiar images of America to foreigners, as well as the disquieting sign of a crisis that is silently spreading across the face of the nation. For, in every photograph in this book—whether of the plains, the mountains, or the remote deserts—one thing has been just beyond the range of the camera: a recent work of man. It need not happen; but, without enough persons who care, the rapid increase in population and the accelerating demands of an expanding civilization may have man living elbow to elbow clear across the United States by 2000 A.D., and a mother by that time may be hard put to instill in her children a love for the natural wonders and beauty of their country.

378

ACKNOWLEDGMENTS

Ansel Adams, Carmel, California

Horace M. Albright, Los Angeles

American Forestry Association, Washington, D. C.: James B. Craig, John Prokop

American Museum of Natural History, New York: George H. Goodwin

American Philosophical Society, Philadelphia: Richard H. Shyrock

Amon Carter Museum, Fort Worth: Mitchell A. Wilder

Appalachian Mountain Club, Boston: C. Francis Belcher

The University of Arizona, Laboratory of Tree-Ring Research, Tucson: C. W. Ferguson, Dr. W. G. McGinnies

Bostwick Studio, Omaha: Homer O. Frohardt

University of California, Berkeley: Bancroft Library, Mrs. Helen Bretnor; Robert H. Lowie Museum, William Bascom

City Art Museum of St. Louis: Agnes Gray

The State Historical Society of Colorado, Denver: Mrs. Laura Ekstrom

Jim Conway, Miami

Denver Public Library: Mrs. Alys Freeze

Charles and Lindley Eberstadt, New York

Everglades Natural History Association, Homestead, Florida: Ernst Christensen

Museum of Fine Arts, Boston: Virginia Gunter

Free Library of Philadelphia: Dorothy H. Litchfield

Ralph Friedman, Portland, Oregon

The University of Georgia Library, Athens: Mrs. William Tate

Gilcrease Institute of American History and Art, Tulsa: Dean Krakel

Harvard University: Fogg Art Museum, Agnes Mongan; Harvard University Library, Robert Haynes, Natalie Doyle; Peabody Museum, Mrs. Katherine B. Edsall

Hawaii Visitors Bureau: Richard F. MacMillan

Warren Howell, San Francisco

Idaho Department of Commerce and Development: Louise Shadduck

Idaho Power Company, Boise: Robert J. Brown, Jr.

Joslyn Art Museum, Omaha: Eugene Kingman

Gary Koeppel, State University of Iowa

Richard L. Kohnstamm, Timberline Lodge, Mount Hood, Oregon

The Library of Congress: Milton Kaplan

Mike and Elaine Loening, Salmon, Idaho

Frank E. Masland, Jr., Carlisle, Pennsylvania

Fred and Jo Mazzula, Denver

State of Michigan Tourist Council: George J. Kooistra

H. Donald Miller, Joseph, Oregon

Museum of Modern Art, New York: John Szarkowski

Historical Society of Montana, Helena: Michael Kennedy

National Archives, Herman R. Friis

National Audubon Society, Inc., New York: Robert J. Woodward

Museum of New Mexico, Santa Fe: Albert G. Ely

The New York Botanical Garden: Frank C. MacKeever

Sigurd Olson, Ely, Minnesota

Oregon Historical Society, Portland: Thomas Vaughan, Mrs. Barbara Elkins, Robert Fessenden

Malcolm D. Perkins, Boston

Dick Rivers, Lewiston, Idaho

Sierra Club, San Francisco: David Brower

State of South Dakota, Department of Highways: Glenn E. Kietzmann

Ada Stoflet, State University of Iowa

Union Pacific Railroad: Richard V. Herre, Edwin C. Schafer

U.S. Department of Agriculture, Washington, D. C.: Office of Information, Russell Forte, Mary Cowell; Forest Service, William

Bergoffen, Leland J. Prater

U.S. Air Force: 363rd Tactical Reconnaissance Wing, Shaw Air Force Base, South Carolina

U.S. Department of the Interior, Washington, D. C.: Bureau of Reclamation, Ottis Peterson, W. J. Garrity, Freda Ocheltree; Fish and Wildlife Service, B. L. Flanagan, Robert W. Hines, Charles Most; Geological Survey Library, Denver: Mrs. Ruth Alley; National Park Service, Carlos Whiting, Joseph F. Carithers, John T. Houbolt, Jack E. Boucher, M. W. Williams

National Parks and Monuments:

Acadia, Harold A. Hubler; Arches, Bates E. Wilson; Big Bend, Stanley C. Joseph; Death Valley, William C. Bullard; Everglades, Warren F. Hamilton, Jack B. Dodd; Glacier, Fred W. Binnewies; Grand Canyon, John S. McLaughlin, Andrew C. Wolfe; Grand Tetons, Fred C. Fagergren, H. L. Bill; Great Smoky Mountains, Fred J. Overly; Hawaii Volcanoes, Fred T. Johnston; Lassen Volcanic, Frank E. Sylvester, Raymond L. Nelson; Mount Rainier, John A. Rutter; Sequoia–Kings Canyon, Richard C. Burns; Wind Cave, Jesse H. Lombard; Yellowstone, Lemuel A. Garrison, Luis A. Gastellum, Aubrey L. Haines; Yosemite, Douglass H. Hubbard

Mrs. Burnette Vanstory, St. Simons Island, Georgia

Cull White, Coulee Dam, Washington

The State Historical Society of Wisconsin, Madison: Paul Vanderbilt

Worcester Art Museum: Daniel Catton Rich

Yale University Library: Archibald Hanna, Mrs. Lorelle Christie

PHOTOGRAPHY: Ansel Adams, Ray Atkeson, William A. Bardsley, A. Aubrey Bodine, Lee Boltin, Jack E. Boucher, Sonja Bullaty, J. Gordon Edwards, Richard Erdoes, William A. Garnett, Joern Gerdts, Jerry Greenberg, Weldon F. Heald, Grant Heilman, Robert P. Holland, George Hunter, Philip Hyde, Frank Jensen, Carl Koford, Herbert Lanks, Angelo Lomeo, Laurence Lowry, Dick McGraw, Frank E. Masland, Jr., Shaw Mudge, John C. Nugent, Ernst Peterson, Winston Pote, Hal Rumel, Kosti Ruohomaa, Eric M. Sanford, A. Schmitz, James R. Simon, Spence Air Photos, Bob and Ira Spring, Werner Stoy, John Szarkowski, Dade W. Thornton, A. E. Turner, Paul Vanderbilt, Nelson Wadsworth, Bradford Washburn, Marlin Spike Werner, Edward Weston, Jack R. Williams, M. W. Williams, James Yarnell

Grateful acknowledgment is made for permission to quote from the following works:

"American Letter" by Archibald MacLeish. Reprinted from *New Found Land* by Archibald MacLeish by permission of Houghton Mifflin Company, Boston

Autobiography by Theodore Roosevelt. Reprinted by permission of Charles Scribner's Sons, New York

The Grapes of Wrath by John Steinbeck. Reprinted by permission of The Viking Press, Inc., New York

Great Surveys of the American West by Richard A. Bartlett. © 1962 by the University of Oklahoma Press, Norman. The quotation from William H. Jackson on page 228 reprinted by permission of the University of Oklahoma Press

The Sierra by W. Storrs Lee. © 1962 by G. P. Putnam's Sons, New York. The quotation from John Muir on pages 292–93 reprinted by permission of G. P. Putnam's Sons

"The Eye" by Robinson Jeffers. © 1948 by Robinson Jeffers. Reprinted from *The Double Axe and Other Poems* by Robinson Jeffers by permission of Random House, Inc., New York

INDEX